NEWCOMERS

NEWCOMERS

Gentrification and
Its Discontents

MATTHEW L. SCHUERMAN

THE UNIVERSITY OF CHICAGO PRESS | CHICAGO AND LONDON

The University of Chicago Press, Chicago 60637

The University of Chicago Press, Ltd., London

© 2019 by Matthew L. Schuerman

Published 2019

Printed in the United States of America

28 27 26 25 24 23 22 21 20 19   1 2 3 4 5

ISBN-13: 978-0-226-47626-1(cloth)

ISBN-13: 978-0-226-47643-8(e-book)

DOI: https://doi.org/10.7208/chicago/9780226476438.001.0001

Furthermore:
a program of the J.M.Kaplan Fund

Publication of this book has been supported by Furthermore:
a program of the J. M. Kaplan Fund.

Library of Congress Cataloging-in-Publication Data

Names: Schuerman, Matthew L., author.
Title: Newcomers : gentrification and its discontents / Matthew L.
    Schuerman.
Description: Chicago ; London : The University of Chicago Press, 2019. |
    Includes bibliographical references and index.
Identifiers: LCCN 2019016538 | ISBN 9780226476261 (cloth : alk. paper) |
    ISBN 9780226476438 (e-book)
Subjects: LCSH: Cities and towns—United States. | Gentrification—
    New York (State)—New York. | Gentrification—Illinois—Chicago. |
    Gentrification—California—San Francisco.
Classification: LCC HT175 .S265 2019 | DDC 306.760973—dc23
LC record available at https://lccn.loc.gov/2019016538

♾ This paper meets the requirements of ANSI/NISO Z39.48-1992
(Permanence of Paper).

For Meredith

In succession
Houses rise and fall, crumble, are extended,
Are removed, destroyed, restored, or in their place
Is an open field, or a factory, or a by-pass.

T. S. ELIOT, *Four Quartets*

CONTENTS

INTRODUCTION

Gentrification is all around us. It's in the neighborhoods we walk through, the conversations we have, the blogs we read. It's in the clothes we wear (boutique or chain) and in the food we eat (organic or conventional). It's reflected in the walls of our homes—sheetrock indicates new construction, while unpainted brick expresses authenticity—and in the gardens we plant on vacant lots (an example of "reclaiming" the inner city from abandonment). It's in the decision to bike, take the subway, or drive to work. Gentrification is arguably in every breath we take: Is it a dirty breath of air polluted by a dying manufacturing base? Or is it a clean one because you live in a city with a postindustrial office economy?

Most of the thoughts and conversations we have on the topic, however, reflect a simplistic understanding of the phenomenon. It's easy to think of gentrification as something that happened when people who are richer than *we* are move into *our* neighborhood and destroy its charm. Except, five or ten or even twenty years earlier, when we moved into this neighborhood, someone *else* may well have thought *we* were the ones destroying its charm. *We* were the ones who didn't patronize the bodega because it didn't stock organic milk. *We* were the ones who didn't go to the laundromat because we had our own washing machines. If you go far enough back, you will arrive at some point in the 1950s, as white middle-class flight to the suburbs was reaching its peak. While those with means were moving *out* of the city, a few prescient beings decided to move back *in*. They renovated brownstones, passed historic preservation legislation, and fought off urban renewal schemes. In contrast to suburbanites, they were looking not just for a home, or a good school for their kids, or a shopping strip where they could get their groceries. They liked what cities had to offer in terms of proximity, vibrancy, and diversity. They wanted, like Goldilocks, a "just right" neighborhood: one that was not too expensive, not too dangerous, not too far from their jobs.

As time has passed, these "just right" neighborhoods have become increasingly wrong due to their own popularity. Now, more than 50 percent of households in New York City pay what's officially considered "unaffordable" housing costs. In San Francisco, the percentage is even higher. And the rate of gentrification is accelerating. *Governing* magazine determined that between 1990 and 2000, fewer than one out of every ten poor neighborhoods gentrified; the following decade, that number grew to two out of every five. And that's nationwide: in celebrity cities like New York City; Portland, Oregon; Minneapolis; Seattle; Washington, DC; and Austin more than two out of every five poor neighborhoods, and sometimes three out of every five, gentrified.[1] Along the way, central cities have lost thousands of African Americans and Latinos, numerous mom-and-pop stores, and many rooming houses that served as housing of last resort for poor, single, unemployable men, especially those with mental health problems. In some ways, the back-to-the-city movement, as it was called in the 1950s, brought *too* many people back to the city. It has ended up destroying many of the traits that attracted middle-income professionals to urban centers in the first place: diversity, affordability, and authenticity. In the 1920s and '30s, sociologists developed what might be called the *donut theory* of urban development. University of Chicago Professor Ernest Burgess placed the central business district in the center, surrounded by a ring he called the *purgatory of "lost souls,"* filled with vice and squalor, surrounded by successively better-off rings.[2] Now, our cities are becoming like Boston Creams, the centers rich and pampered while the exteriors are plain and hard to get through.

Meanwhile, gentrification has become a tremendously polarizing issue. In East Austin, bandana-wearing protestors gather regularly outside a café located where a piñata store once stood, at least once resulting in bloodshed; in Seattle, the city council attempted to impose a "head tax" on major employers to raise money for affordable housing, but backed down after Amazon and other corporations poured hundreds of thousands of dollars into an opposition campaign; in Los Angeles, a group has taken aggressive measures, such as online trolling, to tell an art gallery and a real estate bike tour that they are not welcome. And in numerous places, rent-controlled tenants have been harassed, threatened, discouraged, and evicted if their units could fetch more on the open market. There is no sign that the pace of gentrification, nor the vigor of the backlash, will subside soon.[3]

GENTRIFICATION, DEFINED

One tongue-in-cheek definition of gentrification is that it's something that happens when people richer than you move into your neighborhood. In other words, people tend to see themselves as victims of gentrification more frequently than perpetrators of it, and only protest when it threatens their ability to remain. It is a very subjective term, which is one reason I have adopted a very simple definition: *gentrification* is the process by which a low-income neighborhood becomes a wealthy neighborhood. (To qualify, the neighborhood's median income has to move from less than the median of the surrounding metropolitan statistical area, to more than the area median). Some other definitions of gentrification also consider whether housing prices increase, or the ethnic and racial make-up of a neighborhood shifts, or the education level among residents changes. I do not see a need to complicate the definition, since higher rents, more education, fewer people of color are all ancillary effects.

(Another term worth quibbling about is "middle class," which I tend to avoid. I prefer *middle income* to designate people in the third quintile of the income range of a particular Census-defined metropolitan area; *upper middle income*, and *upper income* refer to the fourth and fifth quintiles, while *low income* and *very low income* refer to the second and first quintiles, respectively.[4])

I use the term *gentrification* widely in this book. Some people think it has become pejorative; I think it's the *process* of gentrification that has gained so much negative press such that the word cannot be seen in anything but an unfavorable light. British sociologist Ruth Glass, who is credited with coining the term in 1964, recognized that the process has positive and negative effects, and yet approached the topic with equanimity. "The social status of many residential areas is being 'uplifted' as the middle class—or the 'gentry'—moved into working-class space, taking up residence, opening businesses, and lobbying for infrastructure improvements," she wrote. Glass at once ascribed gentrification to a "switch from suburban to urban aspirations," but also warned, tongue in cheek, that "London may soon be faced with an *embarras de richesse* in her central area—and this will prove to be a problem, too."[5]

Alternative terms sound euphemistic. "Recycling" an old poor neighborhood into a new wealthier one popped up in the mid-1970s; the word has a certain charm, but it never really caught on. "Renovation" was in vogue in the 1980s, but it applies more aptly to first-generation gentrifiers who remodeled their homes themselves. "Revitalization," meanwhile, has a positive spin to what is clearly an ambiguous phenomenon. Many government officials and policy professionals prefer "reinvestment." However, I have never been sure who was supposed to be doing the reinvesting. Was it banks? Perhaps. But banks were reinvesting in these neighborhoods only because professionals wanted to move into them—professionals who at first had to fight tooth and nail to get a mortgage from those same financial institutions. (See chapter 2.) Once they realized how much money was to be made, banks certainly *enabled* the renewed affluence of selected neighborhoods in the past sixty years. But to suggest they were the primary drivers misses the mark. Is it the home-buyers themselves who are doing the "reinvestment"? Sure, a home is an investment, but for the upper-middle income professionals who moved to brownstone neighborhoods in the 1950s and 1960s, it was primarily a home that just happened to appreciate in value. "Reinvestment" describes inputs—the money being spent within a neighborhood—while "gentrification" describes outputs—the changing demographics.

The term *displacement* is related to *gentrification*, but it's different, and it *does* have unavoidable negative connotations. *Displacement* describes the forced relocation of a household because its home can command a higher price than it can afford. Neighborhoods may change because low-income residents are forced out by rising rents, or perhaps, the low-income families were about to move out anyway and higher-income households took their place. (This latter process is sometimes called *succession*.) I discuss the complicated question of whether gentrification causes displacement throughout the book. It is my conclusion that gentrification does not cause as much displacement as might be expected, but it causes enough disruption to individuals that we should try to mitigate its impact.

This brings me to three main arguments.

GENTRIFICATION IS NEITHER GOOD NOR BAD

It is not a cause, but a symptom of a macroeconomic transformation much larger than any of us, the transformation from an industrial economy to a professional and then a "creative" one. The corporate managers who proliferated in America's post–World War II economic expansion valued loyalty and teamwork, and even spoke of being a "cog in the wheel" with a certain pride. Journalist William H. Whyte observed that preplanned suburbs were perfect for the Organization

Man of this era, for they were "communities [built] in his image."[6] By contrast, the "creative" economy that has emerged more recently ostensibly values independence, adaptability, and imagination; creative workers seek neighborhoods that express those traits—or at least purport to. Other demographic trends, such as the proliferation of two-earner families and the choice by women to have children later in their lives, have also contributed to the appeal of living in a city.

Among academics, such an explanation of gentrification's origins is known as a *consumption-side* theory: *consumers* drove the migration of middle- and upper-middle-income individuals back to the city. Chapter 6 explains the "production-side" model, which holds that real estate developers, investors, and marketers were instead responsible.

THE HISTORY OF GENTRIFICATION IS MORE COMPLICATED THAN YOU MIGHT REALIZE

While I have chosen a deliberately simple definition of the term, gentrification is an amorphous process that frequently changes its guise. Its starting point is unclear, but earlier than most people would assume; its end point is, right now, unforeseen. The line between "good" gentrification (the kind that makes cities thrive) and "bad" gentrification (the kind that pushes people out of their homes) has never been clear and is largely a subjective distinction—meaning, different people will draw the line in different places. I have interviewed many people who began our conversation by vociferously criticizing gentrification, but by the end realized they have contributed to it—sometimes in the most well-meaning ways.

PUBLIC POLICY MAKERS HAVE DONE A POOR JOB OF CONTROLLING GENTRIFICATION

Just as gentrification began much earlier than many realize, so too did the backlash. By the mid-1970s, editorial writers, activists, and a few academics were warning that the trend was causing displacement. Mayors and other local leaders were quick to pooh-pooh such concerns, and the federal government acted too slowly. Nor did the nonprofit sector effectively intervene; instead it chose to battle redlining. The answer these apologists gave again and again was that gentrification was a fringe phenomenon—until, suddenly it wasn't. At that point, the solutions that would have been cheap to impose in the 1970s and '80s were several times as expensive.

There has been plenty written about gentrification recently, though it tends to come in two flavors: academic literature that provides very little sense of what it is like to live in a city undergoing change; and more general works that give that view from the street but do so snidely, with little appreciation for the complexities and paradoxes of urban development. This latter set of writings often idealizes a moment in the neighborhood's development—sometimes the moment when the author started living there. It is that moment, the author argues, when the neighborhood was its "true" self—and in the years since, it has become less so, glammed up by newcomers, city government, and developers.

This book recognizes that cities are dynamic places; our conception of them today as places of commerce and culture contrasts sharply with their functions thousands of years ago as tools of civil defense or centers of religious worship. It is hard to argue that a neighborhood *belongs* to one people or another. Many of today's gentrified neighborhoods were once built for the gentry of the nineteenth century, fell from fashion in the mid-twentieth century, and have become desirable again in the past few decades. Other gentrified neighborhoods descend from working-class roots but have gone through considerable ethnic changes: Williamsburg was German before it became Puerto Rican; the Mission District was Irish before it became Chicano. Nor do I find arguments that gentrification ruins a neighborhood's *cultural identity* to be terribly compelling, or at least I see them as far less important than material changes in an individual's circumstances—whether someone must move miles away from a job or social network or family. Likewise, I don't presume tenants have a moral "right to the city" as some activists have suggested they do; but I do agree society is better off minimizing the disruption to the lives of large numbers of people.

I also try to avoid any nostalgia of pre-gentrified urban places. Those supposedly noble industrial jobs of the 1940s and '50s where people (or at least white men) could earn an honest living often involved back-breaking labor and were unsafe; the quaint neighborhoods we miss today gained their sense of community from segregation and ethnic tribalism. The breakdown of those communities came in part due to antidiscrimination laws, intermarriage, and assimilation. Many writers lament the fact that cities have become less "interesting" because of the disappearance of ethnic enclaves. But think about this: If you come upon a place and declare it "interesting" or "uninteresting," aren't you seeing a neighborhood as something that exists for your enjoyment, rather than viewing it from the perspective of the people who are living there? Let's judge neighborhoods first on how they serve their inhabitants rather than on whether they please visitors.

I provide some historical context to gentrification in order to challenge these preconceptions from the Left and Right. Readers must recognize the sorry state in which most American cities found themselves in the 1950s and '60s in order to consider fairly whether gentrification has done more harm than good. A historical account also shows just how difficult it is to distinguish between the idealism that sparked gentrification, and the exploitation of that ideal. Most of all, history tells us what it was like for mayors, homeowners, and landlords to be there, at any number of critical junctures over the past sixty years, uncertain whether cities would flourish or perish.

THREE CITIES, SIX DECADES

Admittedly, this book could have started in many places. I chose 1956 in Brooklyn Heights, when "young marrieds"—affluent, college-educated couples—chose to stay in New York City and raise families instead of moving to the suburbs. They were self-conscious about that choice. They began to organize themselves, and to talk about the joys of urban life, and how wonderful it was that people with families were taking over rooming houses and renovating them into single-family homes. They were proudly rebelling against suburbanization in a way that earlier gentrifiers had not.

Chapter 1 also reveals two other hallmarks of early gentrification. One is early gentrifiers' uneasy relationship with urban renewal, the post–World War II strategy of reviving cities by bulldozing large tracts of so-called slums and replacing them with large modern buildings for residential or institutional use. Young marrieds were opposed to urban renewal on principle, but found it could bring them certain pragmatic advantages, such as increasing the critical mass of young professional families like themselves. The second hallmark is early gentrifiers created an alliance with the remaining old-money families in their neighborhood, and became that much more politically powerful as a result. It is important to realize that gentrification was not born with the paradigm it's now known for—an unrelenting belief in historic preservation, opposition to large-scale renewal, and a preference for small, independently owned shops—but was trying to find its way.

The young marrieds' fever caught on, moving further south and east into Brooklyn, first to Cobble Hill, and then to Park Slope, which is where I go in chapter 2. Evelyn and Everett Ortner moved there when, in effect, Brooklyn Heights had become too gentrified and too expensive for them. They were an effective pair: Everett was a World War II veteran whose military training served him well while fighting for his neighborhood; Evelyn, an interior designer, helped to secure Park Slope's historic designation. The Ortners first made alliances with real estate brokers, banks, and city officials, and then with organizations in gentrifying neighborhoods across the country through their annual "Back-to-the-City" conferences.

Chapter 3 takes place in San Francisco, a city that shares many of the attributes of gentrifying cities around the globe, but which also has unique features that have exacerbated its housing shortage. The city's geographic area—a mere 46 square miles, some of which is undevelopable due to its topography—was prematurely circumscribed in the nineteenth century. The economic development of the Bay Area would further complicate San Francisco's future, because job centers grew both downtown and in the farmland 30 miles to the south, which came to be known as Silicon Valley. Those two factors would lead to housing and transportation problems that found their locus in the Mission District, a working-class area with a strong sense of community.

In chapter 4, the action moves to the Near North Side of Chicago, a notable area where great wealth and deep poverty have existed nearly adjacent to one another since the early 1900s. In the 1950s and 1960s, the same back-to-the-city impulse that affected Brooklyn Heights took root in Chicago's Old Town. Affluent residents both embraced urban renewal and advocated historic preservation, not realizing that they would price out the idiosyncrasy and diversity that had made their neighborhood special. As Old Town's wealth spread, it butted up against one of the city's most violent public housing complexes, Cabrini-Green, right at a time when the Chicago Housing Authority had come to a standstill, unable to build new complexes because of politics, or to repair the old ones because of finances. Those two factors—the growing affluence of the city, and the collapse of public housing—would together set the stage for the unthinkable: the gentrification of Cabrini-Green.

The second part of this book describes the era from the mid-1970s to 2000. Gentrification was fully underway and had in fact engendered a backlash that we have largely forgotten about today. I devote chapter 5 largely to the activities of a university professor from Philadelphia, Conrad Weiler, who tried to make the public, and government, aware of the potential downsides of gentrification. He proposed many of the solutions that are still circulated today—such as buying up buildings and converting them to permanently affordable housing. Those ideas would have been a lot cheaper had they been implemented at 1975 prices than at today's.

I revisit New York and San Francisco in chapters 6 and 7, respectively tracing how the rise of the so-called creative class was partly, though not wholly, responsible for those cities' fiscal health in the 1980s and 1990s—as well as their gentrification. Brooklyn's Dumbo neighborhood provides a fascinating case study of artist-led gentrification, as well as of a developer's ability to take advantage of it. The developer in question, David Walentas, cleverly crafted a myth that the neighborhood was dead when he found it, and encouraged artists to lend the area some cachet before kicking them out. But Walentas also deserves more admiration than he typically receives; he meticulously re-created the development patterns he witnessed in SoHo and applied many of the principles outlined by Jane Jacobs in her 1961 treatise, *The Death and Life of Great American Cities*, which has emerged as the bible of contemporary planning.

San Francisco made its housing shortage worse for itself—though sometimes in ways that no one could have predicted. Housing and community preservation activists were so burned by the excesses of urban renewal in the city that it took a strict no-displacement approach. As a result, they pushed for zoning changes that permitted very little new residential building, and limited the amount of new office space that could be created in any single year. The idea was that by curbing the growth of jobs, the legislation would also reduce the price pressure on housing. Unfortunately, real estate developers and employers found ways around the law.

I also devote a chapter to rent regulations, which have recently gained popularity as an antidote to gentrification. While it is tempting, as many conservative commentators believe, to argue that rent restrictions exacerbate high housing prices, the evidence suggests their impact has been minimal. In large part, that's because contemporary rent laws already accommodate some degree of free-market economics. At the same time, poorly written rent control laws can exacerbate income inequality, or, alternatively, provide loopholes that encourage tenant harassment. Rent regulation is an extremely tricky, but at times essential, solution to the affordable housing shortage: it is important that policy makers rescue it from ideologues on the Left and the Right and apply it carefully.

Part III describes gentrification as we know it today: a highly contested process that has taken on the dimension of a culture war. Real estate developers, construction workers, economic development interest groups, and political conservatives have joined together (sometimes with young, affluent would-be residents) to advocate for increasing the supply of housing as a way out of the current crisis. On the other side lie community organizations, historic preservationists, tenant groups, people of color—and their political patrons—who fear that new development will not sate the hunger for housing but only increase the appetite for city living. Of course, there are exceptions to these groupings, as well as some geographic variation, but they generally prove the rule. Increasing supply, I find, is a clumsy and insufficient way of reducing displacement pressure, if also one that we cannot ignore.

The Chicago Housing Authority's demolition of its high-rises, as detailed in chapter 9, raises the question of whether cities can use gentrification to rectify past injustices. Here, the Daley administration leveraged the "back-to-the-city" Zeitgeist to replace vertical ghettoes with mixed-income, low-rise communities—which in many ways was exactly what the young marrieds of Brooklyn Heights had been aiming to create half a century earlier. Among the many consequences of Daley's plan, the most startling may be how out of place former public housing residents have felt in their new/old neighborhoods, and how deep class tensions run among the new inhabitants as well.

In the conclusion, I discuss what my account can teach us about addressing gentrification today—though I think what we learn best by examining the past is not what to do in the future, but what NOT to do. Some of what we should learn NOT to do are ways of thinking.

Chief among them is the stance, adopted too often over these past six decades by people in power, that gentrification is a fringe phenomenon that is not likely to grow, and whose benefits outweigh its costs. We had solutions to displacement all along; what we failed to do was to implement them.

Despite the current crisis, I hope readers find something to laugh at in this book. The history of gentrification is full of inspiration and humor, of unintended consequences and delightful surprises, of very committed individuals working—at times at cross purposes or with bitterness toward one another—but nonetheless with the common conviction that humans living in close proximity to one another, sacrificing private space in favor of communal space, encountering strangers and acquaintances on the street, is the best civilization has to offer.

PART ONE

BEGINNINGS, 1956–1978

ONE

THE DEMISE OF URBAN RENEWAL

One evening in December 1956, a 27-year-old television producer named Martin L. Schneider left his office on West 57th Street, picked up his fiancée from her publishing job, and traveled with her by subway to Brooklyn. They got off at the first stop on the other side of the East River. The station, at Clark Street, was so deep underground they had to take an elevator up eight stories to reach street level.[1]

When the couple emerged in the cool night air, it had just begun to snow lightly. Behind them stood the Hotel St. George, a giant Italianate tower made of thousands of white bricks, the very intricacy of which added to its splendor. Down the street was a line of neat row houses. The light from streetlamps bounced gently off of the wrought iron gates and railings. Martin and his fiancée, Rona Kass, instantly fell in love with the neighborhood. It was quieter than Manhattan but had many of the same attributes. The houses were, with a few exceptions, about three to five stories high, and dated from the mid-1800s. Many had the well-proportioned windows and high stoops characteristic of Federalist architecture. In fact, the neighborhood was in many ways *nicer* than Perry Street in Greenwich Village, where Martin then lived. The buildings there were shorter and wider, built for a simpler and even earlier age.

The apartment that Martin and Rona came to see was in the attic of a row house on Willow Street. The living room was in the front, with two dormer windows looking out onto the street. There was no separate kitchen: the burners and sink lined one wall in the bedroom. The bedroom had a skylight, but otherwise it was dark. The place looked to Schneider like the Parisian garret in *La Bohème*. The couple, who were two months away from getting married, agreed to rent it right away.

"Why would you ever want to move to dirty Brooklyn?" snorted Charles Kass, Martin's father-in-law, when he learned the young couple was moving to the Heights. Martin struggled to explain that they would be living in a *nice* part of the borough. At the time, in the public's imagination, there was no nice part of Brooklyn. The Heights was a long narrow triangle, bordered on two sides by slums and the other side by water, and plenty of its once-elegant brownstones had long since been cut up into crowded rooming houses. Gangs roamed in the section to the south; heroin was taking hold. "Everywhere in the city, factories were closing," writer Pete Hamill recalled in his memoir of growing up in Brooklyn, *A Drinking Life*. "In the daytime, there were more men in bars, drinking in silence and defeat."[2] Giant gang rumbles took place in Prospect Park, with two hundred or three hundred teenagers, fighting with knives, zip guns, and revolvers.[3] Martin had been born in Williamsburg, about three miles north of the Heights, where bulky industrial buildings stood cheek-by-jowl with short brick tenements. Schneider's father, also named Martin, emigrated from Russia in 1906 at the age of 17. He worked hard, at any and all jobs, and ended up owning a hardware store. A few years after Martin Jr. was born, the Schneiders moved out of Brooklyn and onto Long Island. If you had asked the younger Martin when he was growing up where he would end up, he would not have imagined Brooklyn. He certainly wouldn't have fantasized about it. For college, Schneider went to Rensselaer Polytechnic Institute in upstate New York, then to

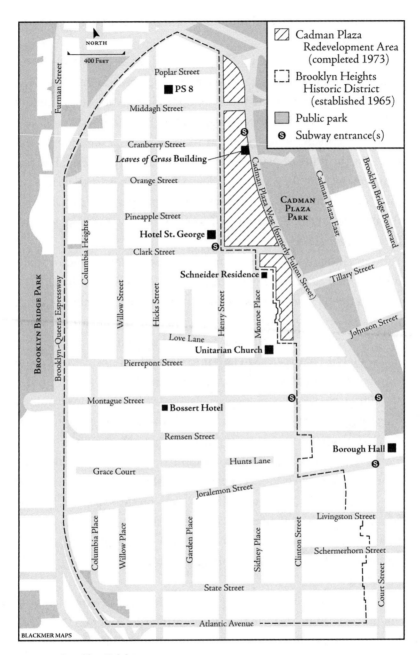

FIG. 1.1. Brooklyn Heights.

Iowa State for graduate school. When he returned East, he moved to Manhattan.

But the Heights in the mid-1950s offered many advantages. Situated on a bluff overlooking the East River, the northern reaches of the neighborhood lay just one subway stop from Wall Street: a 5-minute ride, waiting time included. Plus, the neighborhood was relatively cheap: Martin and Rona could not afford a house in the suburbs—at least not the types of places where their peers were moving. Besides, they weren't sure they wanted to leave the city. In Brooklyn Heights, they found a burgeoning crowd of other "young marrieds" who, like them, were college-educated professionals looking for an adventure. Brooklyn gave them one.

Their landlady was a woman named Diane Foster who had a knack for fixing up rundown houses in the simplest of ways. With a little paint in the hallway and a side table in the corner, she could change the character of the place while accentuating the old architectural details. Brooklyn Heights had good bones—most of the housing had been built between 1820 and 1910 for well-off businessmen who worked in Manhattan. It was near four subway lines. Foster understood that attracting young marrieds like Martin and Rona wouldn't only bring her rent money; it would lift the value of the neighborhood as a whole. They would tell some friends, and their friends would tell some friends, and pretty soon, the Heights would be as desirable as Greenwich Village. Foster cultivated the Schneiders: when she bought a new house, on Sidney Place—on the southern, less desirable end of the neighborhood—she let them move to the ground floor apartment on the condition that they fix the place up. It was a bit larger and had a small yard in back, which was a luxury, even in Brooklyn.

It was easy for the Schneiders to meet friends. Like expatriates living in Paris, young marrieds could identify each other on the street. More than that, the Heights felt like a small town within a great city. Family-owned businesses lined Montague Street, the main commercial drag, many of which offered delivery to your door. (The ads in the

Brooklyn Heights Press for Sal's Meat Market read, "YOU RING—WE BRING.") New mothers brought their children to the playground and met other young mothers there as well. Writer Norton Juster and cartoonist Jules Feiffer met one evening while taking out the trash, then ended up collaborating on the children's classic, *The Phantom Tollbooth*.[4] Another Heights writer, Frank O'Connor, once said, "I like it here because it is folksy. People are readily identifiable. The newsstand dealer, for instance, tells me what Truman Capote is doing and gives Truman the news of me."[5]

The influx of artists and writers can be traced back to at least 1940, when W. H. Auden, Carson McCullers, Benjamin Britten, and Paul Bowles roomed together in a dilapidated house at the north end of the neighborhood.[6] As the grand Heights families died off and Greenwich Village became too expensive, bohemians moved across the East River. Norman Mailer's semi-autobiographical *Barbary Shore* describes an aspiring novelist who, in the late 1940s, takes a room on the top floor of a Heights brownstone with but one tiny window "opening upon laundry lines and back yards to the fire escape of an apartment house upon the next street."[7] By the late 1950s, the neighborhood was putting on contemporary plays by Christopher Fry and Jean Anouilh. A single block at the northern end of Hicks Street housed three art galleries.[8] At a coffee house nearby, Lawrence Ferlinghetti and Kenneth Rexroth once read their poetry while a jazz quintet provided accompaniment.[9] The *Press* would regularly introduce new residents of the Heights in its columns; they were often actors and theater directors, their credentials scattered like stardust. ("Mr. Astin is an assistant director of 'Ulysses in Nighttown,' in the Downtown National Theatre," read one. "Mrs. Astin's professional name is Suzanne Hahn.")

The editor of the *Press*, Dick Margolis, and his wife, Diane, were important figures, both in furthering the character of the Heights and in articulating it. The son of a Minnesota rabbi, Margolis came east to seek his fortune in journalism; he ended up in the promotions department of *Ladies Homes Journal*. After they moved to Brooklyn Heights in 1955 and learned the neighborhood's weekly was for sale, the Margolises decided to buy it on a whim. They had gotten into a car accident near Ithaca and received a large insurance settlement that they used for the purchase. Diane stayed at home, took care of their newborn, *and* acted as reporter and managing editor; Dick commuted to his other job in Manhattan every day and came by the newspaper's office in the evenings. On press days, they would sometimes stay up all night proofreading. Then he'd shave, change his shirt, and ride the subway into Manhattan for another day at the magazine.[10]

Margolis was a master at allowing Brooklyn Heights to gaze at itself, sometimes lovingly, sometimes critically. In addition to the usual notices about toy drives and Cub Scout inductions, Margolis published profiles of local writers such as Capote and O'Connor, and instigated a regular feature, "Walk on the Heights." It consisted of a single photograph that evoked a thousand words about the neighborhood: a wrought-iron newel post from the nineteenth century, or a window box with a tiny American flag stuck into the soil with a toothpick. Margolis invested care and wit in even the smallest headlines: "Fortnightly Club to Meet Weekly"; and above a story describing a cave-in along the bluff on the East River, he wrote, "(W)hole Thing Is a Mystery to Experts."[11]

Margolis, like many Heights residents at the time, thought urban living was superior to suburban, and he played up the rivalry whenever he could. Once he recounted a speech given by the state commerce commissioner about the lack of planning in the suburbs. "The people who wanted to escape the city have ended by building their own [cities], and the improvement has not been striking," Margolis noted.[12] Another time, when a *New York Times* journalist and his wife moved with their children from the far-off suburbs to the Heights, he made a front-page story out of it. "The thing that discouraged me," the Timesman's wife explained, "was being a slave to an automobile."[13] At another point, Margolis described what had become a Sunday ritual: entire families—tot with hula-hoop, baby in carriage—strolling through the neighborhood, looking for a "multiple dwelling" or "reconverted rooming house" to buy. In a 1950s version of a humblebrag, Margolis asked: "Who but an urban-phile would live in confines so narrow as 20 feet wide? Yet each week dozens of young families go out in search of these tough old structures with the history of generations built right inside."[14] Calling these newcomers "urban-philes" may have been an exaggeration. The historian Suleiman Osman aptly notes that the Heights in the 1950s wasn't urban in the same way that Manhattan was, but rather a "middle cityscape" that had some of the attributes of the city along with the greenery and spaciousness normally associated with suburbia.[15] Still, for these young upwardly mobile professionals, the Heights represented the road less traveled. "Garden City was a beautiful place," said Wall Street lawyer Otis Pratt Pearsall, referring to a tony Long Island enclave where his parents lived. "But what passes for life in Garden City was certainly nothing that appealed to me. I had a natural born proclivity to be a provocateur, and there was nothing there for me."[16] Instead, Pearsall moved to the Heights in the mid 1950s, became friendly with the Schneiders, and spearheaded the effort to make part of the neighborhood the first historic district in New York City.

"A BEDLAM OF NOISE AND DISTURBANCE"

While once the province of New York's gentry, the Heights' aristocratic air had begun to fade as early as 1883 when the Brooklyn Bridge opened. The bridge, at the northern end of the neighborhood, connected trolleys in Manhattan to their counterparts in Brooklyn, allowing the upper class to move deeper into the borough (then its own city) or Long Island. In subsequent years, heirs were unable or unwilling to maintain the elegant homes; they sold their properties to real estate investors, who in turn carved them into rooming houses. Blue collar workers and immigrants, many of whom worked on the shipping piers along the waterfront and in the nearby Navy Yard, moved in. By 1925, literary critic Edmund Wilson, a Heights resident at the time, lamented: "The empty quiet is broken only by the shouts of shrill Italian children and by incessant mechanical pianos in dingy apartment houses." (At the time, southern Europeans were frequently not considered white; as a result, they were accorded the same scorn Puerto Ricans and blacks received later.) "At night," Wilson continued, "one gives a berth to abandoned drunkards sprawling out across the pavement from the shadow of darkened doors."[17]

In the 1930s, the city launched the redevelopment of the area between the Brooklyn Bridge and Brooklyn Borough Hall, the "gateway" to the borough's civic center.[18] Buildings and elevated train tracks were torn down to make way for a giant, lifeless plaza bordered by a boulevard. On the plaza the city built a new courthouse but stopped its work before crossing the street into Brooklyn Heights, where crowded tenements and commercial buildings were located.[19]

Schneider later described the Brooklyn Heights of that era as being "down at the heels, dingy at the edges, and plain worn through in spots," but not entirely dilapidated. Before catalytic converters, refined heating oil, and the flight of heavy industry, city living was far grayer than it is today. "The ubiquitous dirt and grime had turned the once handsome-looking pre-Civil War houses into dark-stained and seemingly worn out old-timers," Schneider explained.[20] By the late 1950s, the Brooklyn *Blue Book*—a list of households "accepted into society" and modeled after *The New York Social Register*—included 214 families that lived on the Heights.[21] But the recent in-migration of Puerto Ricans had created vast inequalities in wealth. Passenger ships from San Juan docked at piers at the bottom of the bluff, turning the waterfront area to the south of the Heights into the most heavily Latino district in the city.[22] Some members of the old guard reacted with derision. One resident advised the Brooklyn Heights Association to be "more concerned about the influx of Puerto Ricans into the Heights and investigating the unscrupulous rooming housekeepers [sic] who willingly overcrowd their houses away. They are a disgrace to the community, which should live up to the charm it is famous for."[23] Another association member alleged the brownstone next door to hers was illegally divided and housed twenty-one children on four floors. In one apartment, a family of eight shared a

16-by-16-foot room, with a small kitchenette and bath off to the side. "This house is strictly a bedlam of noise and disturbance both day and night, especially during the warm weather season," she wrote.[24] The Brooklyn Heights Association formed a "Housing Violations Committee," which one year brought nineteen overcrowded or derelict rooming houses to the attention of the city's buildings department.[25]

Nor was the old guard amenable to the influx of artists and writers. To many middle- and upper-income Americans at the time, the idea of "bohemians" still connoted lazy ne'er-do-wells. (Indeed, the term's transition to mean "creative" and "iconoclastic" has much to do with gentrification, as will be discussed in chapters 6 and 7.) When a Manhattan transplant named Sylvia Taylor wrote a letter to the *Brooklyn Heights Press* and expressed hope that a café and art house cinema would open, many longtime residents objected. "Let the Heights stay exactly the way it is," one reader, Fitzhugh White, responded; another, who identified herself as Mrs. William R. Willets, added: "We who have lived on Brooklyn Heights for many years have always appreciated the quiet, home-like neighborliness and decent surroundings."[26]

A "SAUL ALINSKY MOMENT"

In May 1958, the Schneiders felt ready to make a bet on which way the neighborhood was going. With the help of some family money, they made a down payment on a row house on Monroe Place, not far from where they had first exited the subway that December evening. It was handsome, but not exorbitant, made of orange-red brick, square on top and with white trim. They paid $57,000. In addition to the Schneiders' living space it had not one, but two apartments, each rented by likable single tenants; with their rent, the Schneiders could pay off the mortgage and make repairs. Like any investment, the purchase carried some risks. *If* the neighborhood fell into decline, their tenants might move out and they might have to lower the rent to attract new ones. They would be left not just with an overvalued house, but with a lower income stream. And if *that* happened, their mortgage would be in jeopardy. Their financial future, they recognized, was tied up with the future well-being of Brooklyn Heights as a whole.

Martin was convinced that their bet would pay off. Like their previous landlord Diane Foster and the newspaper publisher Dick Margolis, Schneider understood the revival of Brooklyn Heights hinged on attracting more young professionals like himself, and he worked hard to make that happen. In his view, the principal neighborhood organization, the Brooklyn Heights Association, was headed down the wrong path. He believed the group, founded in 1910, represented the neighborhood's old guard: the blue-blood families that had remained in their mansions through both world wars, and in spite of white flight. Many of them worked right across the river in Wall Street firms, or they were heirs, too house-poor—or too stubborn—to move out to the suburbs. In their eyes, the neighborhood was hanging on by a thread, threatened by street gangs, heroin, and crime. Brooklyn Heights had once been one of the city's most opulent destinations; by 1950, its median household income had fallen to equal to or below that of the metropolitan area's—some sections of the neighborhood were as much as 30 percent poorer than the regional median.[27] One of the association's more prominent members talked about building a wall around the neighborhood to keep what he considered to be a less desirable demographic (i.e., blacks and Puerto Ricans) from encroaching from the east and north.[28]

At one point, the Schneiders' copper downspout was ripped right off their house, stolen presumably by a heroin addict to be sold as scrap metal. Yet to Martin's liberal sensibilities, the idea of building a wall seemed offensive. In Arkansas in the fall of 1957, the government sent in federal marshals to protect black students entering Little Rock High School from the hostility of whites. "Isn't Brooklyn better than that?" he wondered. Martin, Rona, and a number of other young marrieds wanted to send their children to a public school, but they also wanted to make sure that school was a good one. Public education, Schneider later wrote, "was a democratic inheritance that deserved support and encouragement."[29] At the time, old guard Brooklyn Heights households were aging, their children few. Blacks and Puerto Ricans were being bused in from the nearest public housing complex to fill classroom seats. The young (white) marrieds did not want their children to be a small minority in the classroom. Their plan wasn't to keep out blacks and Puerto Ricans, as whites had tried in Arkansas, but rather to inundate the school with enough of *their* children to maintain its "quality." Yet Public School 8, Schneider felt, would never attract enough middle-class families unless there was more middle-class housing.[30] Most of the housing stock at the time was made up of brownstones: narrow, tall houses with just a couple of rooms per floor. They were too large for one family to afford, but each floor was too small for a whole family to fit in.

At about that time, Robert Moses, the head of the New York City Slum Clearance Committee (as well as at least eight other authorities and commissions[31]), was toying with the idea of bulldozing four blocks of row houses on the northern end of the Heights to make way for a large housing complex. He would use urban renewal funds authorized by Title I of the Housing Act of 1949, which gave cities hundreds of millions of dollars to acquire deteriorating property and redevelop it. The preliminary design looked a lot like the "wall" that the Brooklyn Heights Association member had desired: a tall flat building would stretch for two blocks across the northeastern corner of the neighborhood, with apartments priced on the upper end of the rent spectrum, and consisting mainly of studios and one-bedrooms.[32] A low-slung shopping area would cover the southern end.[33] Some 184 families and 79 single people would be displaced; Moses assumed most of them would somehow find spaces in already crowded public housing.[34] The new project was, as far as anyone could tell, meant to appeal to unmarried Wall Street employees. The streets between these blocks would be "de-mapped" to create more buildable space, and also to isolate the enclave from the surrounding minority neighborhoods.

Moses was a legendary figure, a ceaselessly driving, scheming administrator whose intelligence and cunning made him arguably

more powerful than any elected official in New York City. His handi-
work can still be seen in virtually every part of New York, knitting
together the disparate islands that comprise the city, and carving the
arterial roadways along which we still drive today. By the time the
young marrieds arrived in Brooklyn Heights, Moses had constructed
eight parkways, eleven bridges, sixteen oversized swimming pools,
and hundreds of playgrounds. The United Nations was meeting in
a building made possible by Moses' planning, and he had turned
the heavily polluted Jamaica Bay into a protected natural resource
ringed by parkland.[35] But as federal funding priorities shifted, Moses
began to take on more controversial projects: expressways that cut
through viable neighborhoods in the Bronx and Brooklyn, and numerous urban renewal projects for which "slums" were bulldozed to
make way for concrete high-rises, university campuses, and cultural
institutions. Moses's first objective, the late architectural historian
Hilary Ballon argued, was "to recapture the middle class, which had
chosen the suburbs over the city, by building modern, affordable
housing."[36] But Ballon held a minority view; history's perception of
Moses has been largely shaped by Robert A. Caro's savagely critical
1974 biography, *The Power Broker*. Caro calculated that Moses threw
250,000 people out of their homes for highways, and tens of thousands of others for urban renewal.[37] "He tore out the hearts of a score
of neighborhoods," Caro wrote, "the vital parts of the city that made
New York a home to its people."[38] By the late 1950s, Moses was still
held in high esteem, a man who unveiled breathtaking feats of engineering several times a year. But his luster was beginning to fade.
In July 1956, he lost the "Battle of Central Park," a fight over his plan
to build a parking lot where a popular play area stood. Protesting
mothers pushing baby carriages won the support of the public, a sign
of the priority the city was beginning to place on quality of life over
"progress."[39]

The old-guard members of the Brooklyn Heights Association embraced Moses' plan for high-rises. But the Heights had a strong iconoclastic tradition—it had once been the home of poet Walt Whitman

FIG. 1.2. Robert Moses' initial plan to redevelop Cadman Plaza called for a wall of high rises (center right of image) that would separate Brooklyn Heights, in the background, from Cadman Plaza Park, in the foreground. To the left is Borough Hall. In the rear and to the right lies Manhattan. (From *Cadman Plaza: Report to Mayor Wagner and the Board of Estimate by the Committee on Slum Clearance*, 1959)

and abolitionist Henry Ward Beecher—which was reawakened by Moses' proposal. In 1957, a Unitarian minister in the neighborhood, the Rev. Donald W. McKinney, appealed to Moses to turn the Cadman Plaza redevelopment into a cooperative middle-income settlement. "We are," McKinney wrote, "anxious to continue owner occupancy in this area which has been strengthened traditionally by such occupancy with the resulting increased interest in community responsibility." Moses, a prodigious correspondent, replied a few days later: "I am sorry to advise you that your proposal for building cooperative housing in this area is impractical." Moses noted that the city had supported subsidized cooperative housing elsewhere, but "in this case, the proposed location, with its proximity to the financial community and other centrally located transportation and shopping facilities, makes this highly desirable for the redevelopment of private, fully tax-paying housing."[40]

McKinney looked for another way to influence the proposal. He reached out to about a dozen neighbors and invited them to a meeting in his church study one evening in November 1958. Martin Schneider came—he lived just down the block—as did Otis Pratt Pearsall, the Wall Street lawyer and preservationist, and a number of other young marrieds. Dick and Diane Margolis, the husband-and-wife newspaper team, attended as well. To get to the minister's study, they all passed through a doorway above which McKinney had attached a sign saying "Thought Shop," the same name Socrates had given his study.

Schneider saw the meeting in the minister's study as a "Saul Alinsky moment"—meaning that it was then that all the participants found common cause in their divergent perspectives. In the late 1950s, Alinsky was becoming a household name as a founder of a new concept called "community organizing." He had formed a formidable coalition among unions, white ethnic groups, and the Catholic church in Chicago's Back of the Yards neighborhood, and wrested power and money from the city's Democratic machine. Schneider was significantly more bourgeois than Alinsky (who had spent his early 20s on Chicago's streets doing research on gangs), but they both shared a knack for coalition-building.

That evening in the minister's study, Schneider sympathized with each of the concerns brought forward: home ownership, historic preservation, a stronger public school. He didn't believe it would be possible to block Moses from demolishing homes along the edge of the Heights, and he even saw some benefits to redevelopment. Young marrieds, Schneider believed, lacked the critical mass to transform Brooklyn Heights and save P.S. 8 unless they got some help. The neighborhood needed more housing, he thought, apartments rather than row homes, affordable to middle-income professionals, and large enough to accommodate parents with children. Schneider set about to amend, but not end, Moses' plan. By allowing the construction of hundreds of new family-sized cooperatives, the community would attract the population needed to ensure a bright future for the neighborhood and P.S. 8. Otis Pratt Pearsall made perhaps the biggest compromise of all the participants by going along with Schneider's agenda: the lawyer wanted the city to designate Brooklyn Heights as a historic district, meaning that there would be an extra layer of review any time a developer wanted to tear down a building or change its exterior. Allowing the destruction of dozens of nineteenth-century buildings in the Cadman Plaza footprint contradicted his principles, but Pearsall figured he would never attain his aim in the long run by fighting Robert Moses in the short term. Ultimately, Pearsall made what he later called a "cold-blooded" decision, and supported his friend Schneider, sacrificing a handful of buildings on the hunch that many more would be preserved later on.[41]

The group of young marrieds named itself the Community Conservation and Improvement Council, the acronym for which was "CCIC"—pronounced "Kick." Schneider appreciated the aggressive, if silly, overtones of the acronym. He wanted to kick two things: the stuffy Brooklyn Heights Association, and the old way of "saving" cities by destroying them. CCIC believed that instead of shutting the city out, the Heights should invite it in. They argued against the "wall" of buildings proposed by Moses, and against wholesale demolition in general, favoring rehabilitation and "spot clearance" (the removal of just one or two of the most dilapidated buildings here and there). In its manifesto, the group declared: "Our housing, historic structures, and the architectural character of the Heights must be vigilantly preserved." They called for a plan that would address schools and social services as well as improvements in the neighborhood's physical appearance. Far from seeing a city as a diseased corpus requiring surgery—as Robert Moses and other urban renewal adherents did— CCIC treated cities as living organisms that could heal themselves.

A little while later, CCIC arranged an in-person meeting with one of Robert Moses's top aides, William S. Lebwohl, the director of the Committee on Slum Clearance. The meeting went nowhere. Lebwohl insisted that the new development pay full taxes; Schneider contended that if CCIC itself built the complex it could both keep the apartments affordable and succeed without subsidies. A few days later, when briefed on the meeting, Moses predicted, "Apparently there will be a row over Cadman Plaza housing," and quickly moved to shore up support from John Cashmore, the Brooklyn borough president. At the time, land-use decisions in New York City were made by the Board of Estimate, which consisted of the borough presidents as well as the mayor and other officials. "You will recall the long history of our negotiations," Moses wrote the borough president. "This was to be a full tax paying project, which is what the neighborhood really calls for."[42]

This back-channel discussion between Moses and Cashmore was unknown to Schneider when, in June, he and another CCIC leader, Malcolm Chesney, paid Cashmore a visit at his ornate office on the second-floor of Borough Hall. Yet far from offering sympathy to the needs of middle-income families, the borough president told them fully tax-paying luxury housing was "what I think the city really needs." Furthermore, he said the Heights was no place for families, and urged Schneider and Chesney to move instead to Coney Island, where they could have bigger homes and larger yards.[43] The comment stunned the two men and reinforced their suspicion that the New York establishment lacked the vision needed to revitalize the city.[44]

Shortly afterwards, Schneider traveled with four of his allies to Randall's Island in the middle of the East River, where Moses' office was located. During a meeting of the Slum Clearance Committee, they made a presentation about their proposal. Otis Pratt Pearsall, the Brooklyn Heights preservationist, happened to mention Radburn, New Jersey, a planned town with community-oriented zoning practices. It was, Pearsall argued, a model which New York might imitate. Moses shot back, "New York does not take lessons from New Jersey!"[45]

Unable to convince Moses or Cashmore, Schneider had better luck with the Brooklyn Heights Association. At first, the 49-year-old organization had given the middle-income co-op plan a chilly reception. Its newsletter said the low rents proposed by CCIC "would not be realistic," while a leading Republican called Schneider's plan "the best way to run down the Heights."[46] That attitude changed in April 1959, when CCIC held an open meeting at the Bossert Hotel,

FIG. 1.3. A portion of Old Fulton Street in 1958, showing the storefronts and small apartment buildings that were cleared to make way for the Cadman Plaza redevelopment. (Photo by John Morrell; courtesy of the Brooklyn Historical Society)

an elegant high-rise on Montague Street; an astounding 350 people came.[47] Rather than urging outright defeat of Moses' Cadman Plan, CCIC suggested modifying it to make it more family friendly. CCIC wanted cooperatives instead of rentals; subsidies that would bring the monthly costs down by a quarter to a third; and more family-friendly 2- and 3-bedroom units. And, with Otis Pratt Pearsall now on board, the organization did not quibble with the underlying premise of mass clearance.

The high turnout surprised even CCIC members and forced the

Brooklyn Heights Association to acknowledge that young marrieds were a potent political force that needed to be harnessed. In the following months, the association agreed to bring four members of CCIC onto its board, including Schneider, and to support cooperatives and larger units in Cadman Plaza. In other words, the association essentially co-opted the upstarts rather than risk losing face; CCIC, meanwhile, allowed itself to be taken over. Schneider believed that the merger was well worth it: the association had much more influence in city government than CCIC ever would. He was put in charge of making sure the revised Cadman Plaza plan went through.

Soon, Schneider won over the local Democratic city councilman, the Brooklyn arm of the Liberal party, *and* the Republican organization.[48] Meanwhile, Robert Moses' clout was waning. After he was accused of flagrant conflicts of interest at other urban renewal sites, his Slum Clearance Committee was disbanded, replaced by a new agency called the Housing Redevelopment Board, which was instructed to take a much more conciliatory approach toward community objections, of which there were many.

At that point, a new element entered the fray: the North Brooklyn Heights Community Group. One of its founders, Elias Wilentz, owned the Eighth Street Bookshop in Greenwich Village, a Beat hangout; he lived on Middagh Street on the northern end of the Heights. Two other founders were Eric and Lorna Salzman, classical music composers and critics, who lived a few doors down in a house they had bought from Eric's parents. The houses at the northern end of the Heights were older, and cheaper, many of them wood frame instead of the ruddy brownstone or brick common throughout the rest of the neighborhood. The members were generally new to community activism; they tended to be musicians, writers, or professors, instead of the lawyers or other professionals who lived in the central Heights. Few of them were even aware of the protracted battle between CCIC and the Heights Association that had occurred just two years earlier.[49]

But their naivety gave them an advantage. Unlike Schneider, the

North Heights group was unrestrained by concerns over pragmatism or politics. It shared urban planning ideals similar to those of CCIC but took them to their logical extremes. The North Heights group issued its own manifesto, written by Martin James, a Brooklyn College art professor, that called the idea of demolishing tenements "largely archaic and obsolete." He catalogued the historic value of seventy-five buildings that would have to be torn down under the city's plan. One of them was the building where Walt Whitman's *Leaves of Grass* was first printed.[50]

Even more so than CCIC, the North Heights group did a tremendous job with public relations. They enlisted Jane Jacobs, a well-known Greenwich Village activist who was about to publish her masterpiece, *The Death and Life of Great American Cities*. "There is nothing to prevent the city from stopping badly conceived and destructive plans like Cadman Plaza right now," Jacobs said.[51] Soon, the group built a formidable advisory committee that included two New York City congressmen, sociologists Paul Goodman and Nathan Glazer, and urban historian Lewis Mumford.[52] The *Brooklyn Heights Press* was too small a stage for them; their activities gained coverage in the *New York Times*. An ancillary effort to save the *Leaves of Grass* building drew support from the poets Carl Sandburg, Robert Frost, and e. e. cummings, as well as the playwright Arthur Miller. Even Rev. McKinney—the Unitarian minister who had hosted the young marrieds in his study three years earlier—ended up moving away from the CCIC plan and endorsed the North Heights plan instead. "The real moral question," he said in a sermon explaining his decision, "is whether the city, whether we as citizens, have any right to endorse and appropriate money for it which will primarily provide another haven of refuge for the well-to-do."[53]

An architect, Percival Goodman (brother of sociologist Paul), came up with an alternative site plan to match the North Brooklyn group's precepts. It included 600 apartments to be rented out to middle-income families, two high-rise apartment towers, the rehabilitation of some of the row houses, and the conversion of the Walt Whitman

building into a museum. "The Goodman proposal is a sound, rational plan that combines modern thinking with the needs and desires
of the whole Heights," its supporters declared.[54] Despite the rhetori-
cal distinction from the CCIC/Brooklyn Heights Association plan,
the two schemes were quite similar. The Goodman Plan had more affordable housing and one fewer high-rise tower, but it still would require some demolition. The leaders of the Brooklyn Heights Association seemed to understand the threat the new proposal made to their
own plan, however, and feared city officials would withdraw funds
if the community was not united.[55] With the Housing and Redevelopment Board likely to make a decision at any moment, the Heights
association became heavy-handed. In a press release, the organization's leadership warned that the city might end up doing nothing
out of frustration with the neighborhood's internecine warfare: "To
support the Goodman Plan, in effect, is to throw that whole northeast
corner of the Heights to the real estate wolves."[56] Robert T. H. Davidson, a prominent lawyer, lamented that the association was losing the
public relations battle, and urged the group's president to find some
reinforcements to help Martin Schneider bolster his defenses.[57] The
association bought an ad in the *Brooklyn Heights Press*, warning that
the Goodman Plan proposed by the North Heights group "is no more
than an attractive, hopelessly impractical fantasy."[58]

The association's gambit backfired: its leaders had underestimated the community's support for Jane Jacobs–style principles and
its antipathy toward urban renewal. Even members of the Brooklyn
Heights Association rebelled against Moses' worldview. One of them,
after being asked to submit his annual dues to the organization, wrote
a terse note to headquarters: "I consider your attack on the Goodman
Plan so pernicious, unfair, and short-sighted that I cannot in good
conscience renew my membership."[59] On another renewal notice, a
member scrawled, "Please do not use my dues to pay for a small part
of any advertisement telling me how stupid and hysterical I am to
disagree with the officers who represent me."[60]

The Cadman Plaza fight shows just how much, in three short years, prevailing opinion about the urban ideal had swung. In 1958, the leadership of the Brooklyn Heights Association still believed in making the neighborhood into a fortress to ward off blight; next came an upstart group—CCIC—that contended the city could heal itself if enough moderate-income families moved in; finally, by the fall of 1961, rank-and-file association members felt that even that compromise approach was overly destructive. It's no coincidence that this remarkable shift in the Zeitgeist came amid the neighborhood's gentrification—the young marrieds were presumably confident that New York City could prosper by continuing to do what it had been doing. Nonetheless, urban renewal did not end all at once and let the private market take over. That transition was a messy one, involving hybrid plans for demolition and rehabilitation, public subsidies, and the free market. It would take years before the now-familiar pattern of gentrification emerged, in which private developers renovate existing structures to make them appeal to higher-income inhabitants.

In March 1962, when the city's Housing and Redevelopment Board finally announced it would move forward on the Cadman Plaza redevelopment, each of the three community factions won a piece of what they wanted—but only a piece. Old-line association members were heartened to see the essence of Robert Moses' plan survive: the city would tear down five blocks' worth of scruffy brownstones. But in a bow to CCIC, *all* of the new apartments would be co-op, many of them large enough for families. The North Heights group also fared well: even though the site would be completely cleared, the design itself wasn't too different from what architect Percival Goodman had outlined: a combination of tall towers (he had proposed just two high-rises, the city approved three) and modern row houses. In addition, more than half of the units would be priced for middle-income families. The Walt Whitman building and other historic structures would be destroyed, however, with some vague suggestion that the community should erect a plaque to commemorate it. While the chairman of the Housing and Redevelopment Board, Milton Mollen, recognized the need for more low-income housing in the neighbor-

hood, he didn't want to subject the Cadman footprint to any more debate. Instead, he called on the city to build 175 units of public housing
in the Heights at some unspecified time in the future.[61] A few weeks
later, the New York Times editorial board said Mollen's balancing act
had "exceptional promise" and hailed it as "the best plan put forward
by the Housing and Redevelopment Board."[62]

SPOILS OF VICTORY

The Cadman Plaza plan was an early example of an urban community
coming together to determine its fate. The young marrieds thought
they were building an ideal neighborhood, one that was both safe and
affordable, family-friendly and lively, diverse and close-knit. Yet as
the critical mass of well-educated, affluent residents grew, the definitions of those words proved problematic: Affordable for whom?
Diverse in whose eyes? (Both questions are still being asked today.)
In 1963, the city Housing and Redevelopment Board returned to the
Heights with a proposal for a smaller low-income building, this one
to hold a mere 173 apartments—one for almost each family directly
displaced by Cadman Plaza. Some of the same actors in the North
Heights Community Group who had favored subsidized apartments
at Cadman Plaza now argued that the proposed building would be
an "isolated, festering barracks" made up of "rabbit warrens" that
would be cruel for the individuals who ended up living there.[63] This
time, instead of fighting against the establishment Brooklyn Heights
Association, the North Heights group joined forces with its erst-
while adversary. Together, they distributed five thousand flyers in
just one weekend, asserting that the public housing proposal was
"a dreary repetition of the large-scale project approach which has
failed throughout the city."[64] The comparison was disingenuous—
the "large-scale" projects under construction at the time in New York,
such as the Taft Houses in East Harlem, consisted of more than 1,000
units each, not 173—but opposition in the Heights was fierce and the
proposal died.[65]

CCIC produced one other indelible victory. In 1965, Brooklyn Heights became the first historic district in New York City, which ensured that hardly any of the structures within the 45-block area could be torn down for taller buildings. The designation was largely a result of campaigning by Otis Pratt Pearsall, one of the original participants in the 1958 meeting in the church basement. At the time, he believed historic preservation would *combat* what, at the time, seemed something like gentrification—the demolition of nineteenth-century row houses to make way for modernist, six- to eight-story elevator buildings and dormitories for Jehovah Witnesses, whose world headquarters was nearby. But in the long run, the historic designation has enhanced the cachet of the Heights—and the 130 other neighborhoods in New York City that have also been named historic districts since then—by keeping the architecture intact.[66] In addition, in the late 1960s, the city imposed height limits on new buildings in the Heights, restraining the growth of the supply of housing—a factor that would presumably increase prices across the city years later as demand increased.

Cadman Plaza, which was not completed until 1973, was by no means the last gasp of urban renewal.[67] But wholesale slum-clearance was becoming less and less popular. Congress began to require rigorous plans for resettling residents displaced by urban renewal, which made Title I projects much costlier and less common. In 1974, Congress replaced the program with the Community Development Block Grant system, which gave cities a set amount of money to use for a variety of improvements, from community centers to streetscapes to housing—though local governments rarely chose to spend the money on housing. Urban planning scholar Alexander Garvin notes, "America had lost faith in government-subsidized redevelopment."[68] Instead, government administrators turned toward gentrification as a strategy to revive their tax base and make their cities attractive again.

Since the late 1950s, the Heights has risen from a place of fading elegance to a destination for New York's elite, its median household income climbing from less than the metropolitan median (88 percent) to well above it (158 percent). Martin Schneider still lives on Monroe Place; he still remembers when many of his neighbors were Puerto Rican and played bongo drums and guitars late into the night, and he does not miss that. "I felt that this neighborhood, this housing stock, had a better future," he said recently. In 2012, the house where Truman Capote once lived sold for $12.5 million. In 2018, the apartments at 54 Garden Place, once described as "a bedlam of noise and disturbance," were renting for between $3,000 and $5,500 per month.[69] Another of the rooming houses that neighbors complained about, a four-story home at 88 Joralemon Street, recently sold for nearly $6 million.[70] Brooklyn Heights is no longer a middle-income utopia, but an upper-income one.

TWO

BACK TO THE CITY:
NEW YORK CITY, 1963–1978

One of the people priced out of Brooklyn Heights in the early 1960s was Everett Ortner, a mustachioed magazine editor who had been renting, with his wife, Evelyn, a floor of a brownstone on Remsen Street for the previous decade. They loved the elegance of the place but were ready to become home owners. Everett was then in his early 40s. He was the chief copy editor at *Popular Science*, where he had been working for sixteen years. Evelyn was a partner at an interior design firm. But house prices in the Heights—a minimum of $40,000—were more than they could afford.

The neighborhood that most resembled Brooklyn Heights at the time was Park Slope, a long rectangle alongside Prospect Park. It was not adjacent to the Heights, but almost three miles to the south and east. Park Slope—so named because the streets are laid out on a grid that slopes downhill from the park—is further from Manhattan than the Heights, and it had seen far less of an influx of "young marrieds." But its housing stock was similar: grand houses of three to five stories dating from the decades following the construction of the park, which was designed by Frederick Law Olmsted and Calvert Vaux in the late 1800s.

Park Slope's row houses were built out of large blocks of brownstone quarried in Connecticut and barged across Long Island Sound. Brownstone was far cheaper than marble or limestone, and easier to work with, making it possible for developers to erect row upon row of homes that were at once relatively affordable and unusually elegant. Inside these homes, walnut or mahogany lined the walls and staircases, with intricate curlicues carved by immigrant craftsmen. The fancier brownstones, located closer to Prospect Park, often sported panes of stained glass in their front parlor windows.

In the mid-twentieth century, after the children and grandchildren of these merchants and industrialists moved out of the city, many of these brownstones were divided up into rooming houses. Sometimes this was done by widows desperate for income, or by landlords who believed they could profit off of a declining neighborhood. They put locks on the bedroom doors so each one could be rented out separately and added walls to divide the large parlors. But, as in Brooklyn Heights in the late 1940s and early '50s, there were just enough of the old families to keep Park Slope from slipping into oblivion and provide a bridge to the next phase of affluence.

One member of one of those old families, Robert Makla, believed in preservation long before it became fashionable. In the late 1950s, he revived the Park Slope Civic Council and began giving annual tours of the neighborhood's most striking houses. The Ortners attended in 1962. A year later, they were contacted about a house for sale on Berkeley Place, just a few doors down from the park. It was four stories tall. The parlor measured 15 feet by 38 feet; its 12-foot-high ceilings were decorated with ornate plasterwork. The carved mahogany, glasswork, and "lincrusta"—embossed Victorian wall covering— were all intact. A brass chandelier and a handful of sconces still ran on gas.[1] The Ortners bought the house for $32,000, which was high for the Slope. But it was in move-in condition, and even had a wooden stair chair installed by the penultimate owner, an elderly widow. She had passed the house down to her housekeeper, who wanted to cash in and leave.[2]

PRETENSIONS OF GRANDEUR

Both Evelyn and Everett had grown up in humble surroundings, but somewhere along the way they developed a playful taste for extravagance, as if what they did for fun was pretend to be rich. They held their wedding on New Year's Day, 1953, on the roof of the Beekman Towers Hotel in Midtown. Later, Evelyn would dress up in Victorian dresses for photos that would portray life during the neighborhood's first gilded age. Yet Evelyn had grown up in Yorkville, a working-class German neighborhood on the Upper East Side. She attended public schools, and then Hunter College at the City University of New York, doing her homework on the subway. In the late 1950s, she took courses in interior design at the Pratt Institute.[3]

Everett was born in the mill town of Lowell, Massachusetts. At age four, he and his family moved to New York. In 1933, during the Great Depression, his father was laid off from his job at an insurance company. When Everett graduated from Jamaica High School, in the far eastern end of Queens, he wanted a college that was cheap and far away. He ended up at the University of Arkansas.[4] Everett flourished; with encouragement from his professors, he majored in literature, and once even qualified for a graduate-level course. On the side, he wrote short stories and plays that satirized hypocrisy and avarice.[5] After college, Ortner struggled to get a job—anti-Semitism was rampant. He ended up in ghost writing, even drafting college theses for students.[6]

One of the most formative events of his life came a few years later, when Everett was in Europe, commanding a machine gun platoon in Patton's Third Army. He was grateful for having a respectable mission to pursue, and he proved himself far more capable of staring down danger than one might expect from a bookish intellectual. "You begin to hear this deep rumbling every few seconds," he said later, explaining the sensation of approaching the front lines in France. "You realize that it's coming from the canons. As you get closer, it continues to grow in intensity until it sounds like the end of the world is coming."

Some of his fellow soldiers cried when they came under machine gun fire, but Ortner remained calm. He said later, "You were cautious, and had a sense of fate. You had no choice. Everyone has to be brave."[7]

One night as his platoon advanced on Metz, near the German border, Ortner and two other men mistakenly walked right into a large German camp and were promptly captured. He was taken to Potsdam, outside of Berlin. Conditions for prisoners of the collapsing Reich were, needless to say, deplorable. Everett lost 30 to 40 pounds and became extremely ill. "Most men in the war dream about home and their families, and their wives," he once said. "But when I was captured, I dreamed about food. It was all I could think about." When the Eastern Front was overrun, the Red Army took custody of all German prisoners, including Everett. He quickly realized that the Soviet soldiers got drunk at a certain hour every night; a few days later, during one particularly Dionysian ritual, Ortner escaped and walked 30 miles back to US lines. On his return voyage to the States, Everett purchased an entire carton of Milky Way candy bars and ate them, one by one, in his cabin.[8]

Ortner approached the restoration of Park Slope with the same methodical coolness he had shown during World War II. One acquaintance said of him, "Pressures do not seem to bother him."[9] When Everett arrived on Berkeley Street, he found the neighborhood dismal but not dispiriting. He estimated that one-third of the storefronts along its main shopping strip, Seventh Avenue, were vacant. The A&P had rotting fruit. There were no children playing in the streets. It would be an exaggeration to call the area a slum: the median income in the Ortners' census tract was just 15 percent below that of the metro region as a whole. But there were other trends suggesting that it was succumbing to white flight. During the 1950s, the nine-block area around the Ortners' house had lost 683 whites—nearly 10 percent of the population—and gained 661 blacks and other minorities, who, on average, earned substantially less than white households.[10] Everett applied to twelve banks before one—the Williamsburgh Savings Bank—finally gave him a mortgage.[11] The Ortners' monthly home payments were $283.12, including principal, interest, city tax, water charges, and fire insurance.[12]

While Everett's attitudes on race are unclear, he traced the neighborhood's troubles to what he once referred to as "the invasion of black people." (Historians know it as "The Great Migration," the movement of six million African Americans from the South to the North, largely during and after World War II.) Ortner also faulted attempts to desegregate the city's public schools in the 1960s and '70s, explaining that "in that case where the schools were halfway tolerable, it turned them all black."[13] However, Everett more frequently ascribed Park Slope's decline to "vulture buyers" who were "picking up bargains, turning them into [rooming houses], breaking up the old houses, destroying their beautiful interiors, scaring off old people."[14] To him, preserving the original architecture was a moral issue, and the landlords who had cut up these Victorian masterpieces were scoundrels.

The widow who had owned the Ortners' house had also rented it out by the room, but the interior had been hardly touched. Evelyn and Everett treasured the little bits of history they found in its nooks and crannies. In winter, they continued to use the original 7-foot high furnace that pumped hot air through ducts and vents—a primitive form of forced-air heating—and they preserved the coal chute at the front of the house. By contrast, Everett villainized wealthy Upper East Side brownstone owners because they had enough money to rip out rooms, expand windows and add balconies. "People who are rich don't preserve [brownstones]," he once said. "They destroy them."[15] The Ortners occupied what they saw as the perfect middle-ground: neither so poor as to chop up their house for income, nor so rich as to alter it for their own vanity. Everett saw himself as an Everyman who, because of his vision and courage, was able to live in a much fancier abode than he otherwise would have been able to afford. "A schoolteacher can live in a house in Park Slope, the same house like a millionaire lives [in] on 63rd Street," he said.[16]

The Ortners were not the first white professionals to move back to the Slope, but they would become the most prominent of their era. In 1966, Everett gathered more than forty of the newcomers on one of the neighborhood's iconic front stoops for a photograph. They called themselves "pioneers," apparently without any irony, for they believed they were civilizing the urban frontier.[17] One of them, Joe Ferris, was an Irish schoolteacher born and raised in the Slope who returned in adulthood, determined to revive the area.[18] Ferris, Ortner, and a handful of others formed the Park Slope Betterment Committee, intending to recruit their middle-class peers to buy brownstones at risk of being turned into rooming houses. The first property they targeted was a mansion on Sixth Avenue once owned by a doctor; its walls were lined with walnut paneling.[19]

The Betterment Committee played an active role in promoting the neighborhood. Its handful of members would scan newspapers and survey real estate agents to identify inventory, then set up free weekend tours around the neighborhood of "Houses you can buy for $20,000." At the end of the afternoon, the visitors would gather in the undercroft of a church, where they could talk with the "pioneers" and eat cookies and drink lemonade. Real estate lawyers, mortgage brokers, and representatives from (private) schools set up booths to facilitate easy transitions to the neighborhood. Everett would collect the names and addresses of everyone who came and, weeks and months later, send them cards. On one side, the cards would have lists of homes for sale; on the reverse was a schedule of neighborhood events. Soon, the Betterment Committee was sending the cards to hundreds of potential neighbors.[20]

The Ortners and their neighbors took other approaches as well. They formed a neighborhood watch, walking their large dogs (the Ortners had a German shepherd) up and down Berkeley Place at night while carrying flashlights.[21] Another member of the Betterment Committee, Charles Monaghan, worked at the *New York Times* and placed favorable articles about the neighborhood's renaissance in the paper's real estate section.[22] Because of the difficulty buyers had obtaining mortgages, Everett wrote a letter to David Rockefeller, then

FIG. 2.1. In 1966, Everett Ortner gathered more than forty "pioneers" of Park Slope onto a front stoop for this photo. On the back of the print is written: "Early Birds." (Courtesy of the Brooklyn Historical Society)

the head of Chase Manhattan Bank, imploring him to extend credit to middle-class households willing to buy property in the city. Ortner included a list of all the upstanding professionals who had recently moved to Park Slope, how much they earned, and how much they had paid for their homes. Rockefeller passed along the letter to the bank's vice president in charge of lending, who committed Chase to making $100 million in inner-city loans—an enormous amount, enough to finance 4,167 more brownstones at the price the Ortners paid.[23]

CINDERELLA HOUSES

Everett also formed an early alliance with Brooklyn Union Gas (BUG), a utility that faced a precarious future. Its executives understood that as cities fell from favor, so would company revenues—and Brooklyn had lost 110,000 people in the 1950s. "We can't just pick up our pipes and run," Fred Rider, BUG's public relations chief, would say. Another factor was urban renewal, which had torn down numerous small gas-heated apartment buildings in favor of modern high-rise towers that ran on oil. That's why Rider and his associate Al Jennings embarked on a plan to buy and renovate a brownstone, then use it as an example of how middle-class families could live affordably and comfortably in a gas-powered home.[24] The company's interest in historical architecture didn't come out of nowhere; it emanated from Malcolm Chesney, the utility's director of economics who was decades ahead in predicting the popularity of urban living. "The city," Chesney declared as far back as 1957, "is the new frontier."[25] Chesney lived in Brooklyn Heights and had been one of the members of the Community Conservation and Improvement Council that challenged Robert Moses' urban renewal plan for Cadman Plaza (chapter 1).

In 1966, BUG's public relations officials thought they should create their showcase home in Prospect Heights, a neighborhood adjoining Park Slope. But residents there, who were largely Caribbean, protested, fearing crowds and traffic.[26] To Ortner, however, crowds meant progress; he was consciously trying to build up a critical mass of upper-middle-income professionals to stem the neighborhood's decline, and the more publicity, the better. The Ortners heard about BUG's predicament and invited Rider, Jennings, and a few other executives from the utility over for dinner. Everett and Evelyn pointed out a house just down the block from them. "The windows were broken, and pigeons were living there, and the roof leaked," Everett remembered. The gas company purchased it, fixed it up to create two separate units, and opened it up for tours. Evelyn, being a professional interior designer, furnished the inside: She turned a bathroom into a modern kitchen with natural-gas-powered appliances (double oven, fridge, dishwasher), placed period antiques and a grand piano in the main parlor, and decorated one of the master bedrooms in the maraschino red that was in style at the time. Some 4,000 people came to tour the building over the following six months, including Mayor John Lindsay. BUG sold the building for $65,000, a 300-percent mark-up.[27] It was the first of some twenty "Cinderella Houses" that BUG would renovate in the borough.

The gas company took other steps to promote gentrification as well, holding yearly "brownstone fairs" in their Brooklyn Heights headquarters up through the 1970s, each one attracting as many as 25,000 visitors, and producing four films to publicize the restoration of old Brooklyn neighborhoods.[28] In 1979, BUG used a photo of Everett and Evelyn in front of their Berkeley Street home—Everett with a bowtie, Evelyn in a fashionable hat—as the centerpiece of a full-page ad in the *New York Times*. "Today Brooklyn is probably the best place to buy a brownstone," read the headline. Nothing so clearly indicated that Everett's life had itself become a fairy tale than that ad: He grew up poor and ended up famous, by being brave and having a sense of fate.

The Ortners loved entertaining and used their spacious Victorian dining room to great effect as they wooed the gas company, banks, and city officials to share their love of Park Slope. "We are anxious to hear about the work of the Brownstoners in which you and your friends have taken such an active part," wrote the president of the city's Economic Development Council, George Champion, in accepting an invitation for dinner and cocktails in 1972. "I think it one of the finest things that is happening in New York City."[29] Kenneth Patton, a neighbor who also served in Mayor Lindsay's cabinet, helped make sure government officials supported revitalization efforts. The Ortners hosted New York State's first lady, Katherine Wilson, as well as the deputy majority leader of the State Senate, William T. Conklin. Once the couple rented a double-decker bus to take guests from Park Slope to the Brooklyn Academy of Music about a mile way.[30] (BAM is itself a gentrification story—a boarded-up neoclassical opera house that became a celebrated venue for avant-garde performances—with the Ortners supporting it all the way.)

What the Ortners asked of government was limited, but it was necessary to broaden their influence. When Everett and his neighbors decided to found a citywide organization to promote historic restoration, the Brownstone Revival Committee, the cost of a staff member and office space was paid for by the city Economic Development Council.[31] Eventually, the state kicked in $20,000 a year to pay for a patrol car to roam the streets of Park Slope every night so that Everett could retire his German Shepherd.[32]

Since the young marrieds in Brooklyn Heights had prompted the city to enact historic district legislation, Park Slopers could strive to attain the designation for their neighborhood. In the late 1960s, Evelyn researched the provenances of 1,800 houses and wrote capsule summaries of them with a neighbor and friend, William Younger. They presented the documentation, along with photos, to the Landmarks Preservation Commission in 1970 as part of an application to receive the same historic district designation that Brooklyn Heights had received five years earlier. No other neighborhood in Brooklyn had been landmarked since the Heights, and in order not to appear racially biased, city leaders wanted to certify a largely black neighborhood first. "We're going to get your designation for Park Slope," Borough President Sebastian Leone promised Evelyn, "but we have to designate Bedford-Stuyvesant first."[33] To work through the backlog of applications, the city changed the law: instead of voting on historic districts only once every three years, the Landmarks Preservation Commission could do so as often as it pleased. Park Slope became a historic district in 1973, which, while not preventing new construction outright, put enough obstacles in developers' paths that the neighborhood's housing density remained pretty much as it had been in the 1920s.

The Ortners spun their web of influence wider and wider. In 1974, he took his mission to the national stage. The coalition rented out the Starlight Room at the Waldorf Astoria in Manhattan—an appropriately historic venue—to throw a weekend conference called "Back to the City." Everett wanted to expose New York City officials and preservationists to the progress made in other cities, and vice versa. "The New York 'brownstone' experience," an advertisement for the conference read, "shows that the turnabout from blight to bloom can begin simply with promotion—first by the communities, which sell themselves the same way advertising men sell soap, then by word of mouth, as satisfied customers sell friends and relatives on their communities." Speakers came from Philadelphia; Pittsburgh; Cincinnati; New Orleans; Norfolk, Virginia; Portland, Maine; Kansas City, Missouri; and Pasadena, California—an indication of just how widely gentrification had spread. The keynote address was given by Boston Mayor Kevin White.[34] Some 11,000 invitations went out to people all over the United States, and a few even in Europe. The organizers promised each registrant an intimate dinner party on Saturday night in a historic house, though no one, including Everett, had quite thought that part through. When 250 guests RSVP'd—from places as diverse as Pittsburgh and Peoria; Savannah and Sacramento; Birmingham, Alabama, and Boise, Idaho—the Ortners strained to find places for them all.[35] Evelyn valiantly worked the phones. "We got a lot of people we knew together," Everett recalled. "They would say, 'Well, I'll take ten or twelve people.' 'I'll take thirteen.' 'I'll take six.'" Somehow it all worked out, and the friendships made that night remained decades later.[36]

The success of that weekend propelled Everett to incorporate Back to the City as an organization with annual conferences: first in St. Paul; then San Antonio; next Washington, DC; Hartford; and so on, well into the 1980s. The conferences gave early gentrifiers from across the country a place where they could share strategies and swap sto-

FIG. 2.2. Everett and Evelyn Ortner preserved the historic details of their Victorian brownstone, such as mahogany woodwork and lincrusta wall covering. Everett took their German shepherd on safety patrols in Park Slope after dark. (Photo by Dinanda H. Nooney; Photography Collection, New York Public Library)

ries. The Ortners also made friends in Washington. Everett convinced the National Trust, an influential nonprofit organization made up, in his view, of "little old ladies who were preserving Jefferson's home," to focus on inner cities—and contribute $1,500 to the first Back to the City conference.[37] He later worked with Nellie Longsworth, whose firm, Preservation Action, lobbied Congress to give tax benefits to owners who renovated historic structures, and served on her board.[38] Their bill eventually passed in 1976.

The impact of historic preservation tax credits on gentrification is controversial. Longsworth argued tax credits for preserving old buildings were populist by nature: otherwise, only the wealthy could afford to take part in the conservation movement.[39] But homeowners could not receive historic preservation tax credit for restoring their own homes. Rather, the program applied to commercial properties, and was well used by developers to convert abandoned train stations or old school buildings, for instance, into condominiums or offices. Over the following forty years, these developers claimed $23.1 billion in credits.

Even as early as the mid-1970s, the media began to question the impact of "recycling" or "revitalizing" brownstone neighborhoods. The *New York Times* editorialized: "When brownstone revivals take place, the price for neighborhood improvement is high: those streets then turn into upper-middle-class enclaves, displacing the less privileged residents."[40] The pioneers were quick to object. "The truth is," Ortner wrote in response, "that the brownstone movement has benefitted poor and middle class alike in reintroducing a vigorous and young population in deteriorated areas, stabilizing them, preserving some of New York's finest residential architecture, and paying taxes for the privilege."[41] Having lived through urban renewal, the War on Poverty, and Model Cities, one of Ortner's close friends, Clem Labine, was jaded. "Historic preservation in urban neighborhoods has attracted critics merely because it is one of the few things that have WORKED in reviving older cities," he once wrote. "Countless millions of dollars of taxable real estate have been saved—without a penny of public money being spent."[42]

Ortner once noted cavalierly that when he and his wife bought the house on Berkeley Street, six tenants were living there. "Now, we got rid of the tenants, or they went very rapidly, on the first and second floors, so we had a duplex in our house and we had four tenants upstairs," Everett remembered. "Now, over the years we've gotten rid of two of the tenants who occupied the rear apartments on the third and fourth floors." In a house where eight people once lived, now just four did. That too was an attribute of gentrification: in some cases population density actually decreased as wealthier households, able to afford more space, moved in.

The downsides of gentrification were never far from view.

POLAR OPPOSITES

The Ortners lived on what was considered the "Gold Coast" of Park Slope. Though it was not on any body of water, it bordered the 585-acre Prospect Park. Up the street lay Grand Army Plaza, which was Brooklyn's version of the Place de l'Étoile, complete with a traffic circle, giant memorial arch, and heroic bas reliefs. As one moved west, down the slope of Park Slope toward the Gowanus Canal, the neighborhood was less elegant, its architecture and inhabitants more modest. Even the size of the brownstones changed: they were five stories tall near Prospect Park, but only three stories between Fourth and Seventh Avenues. Urban anthropologist Susan Draper called the first phase of in-movers in the 1960s and early '70s "nesters" who fixed up their homes only to the extent needed for them to be comfortable.[43] The next stage were restorers, who bought homes and returned them to the historically correct condition of the era in which they were built. Finally came the group that bought already rehabbed homes. The Ortners were unusual in that they bought a home that was in excellent shape and had never been renovated.

At the time, Park Slope was full of nesters, which is to say hippies and former hippies and others with a distinct countercultural orientation. (It was to become home to one of the largest, if not *the* largest, concentrations of lesbians in the country.[44]) One of the neighborhood's most distinctive institutions to this day—the Park Slope Food Co-op—was founded in 1973 in the back room of a community center on Union Street, about four blocks from the Ortners' home, in part as a reaction to the corporatization of the food industry. At the time, there were other health food stores in the city, but they were expensive. The idea was, if enough like-minded people came together and pooled their resources, they could buy produce cheaply from the city's wholesale market in the Bronx, transport it to Brooklyn, and sell it to one another. The early years were rough. While everyone who shopped at the co-op had to work for three hours a month (for no pay), the bulk of the work ended up on the shoulders of a handful of core members. The store was open only one day a week, and only for a few hours in the evening; long lines would form outside, and the store would run out of food in a matter of hours.[45] Within a couple of months after its grand opening, the co-op had to shut down, in part because 10 to 20 percent of its food was being "consciously or unconsciously" stolen.[46] The co-op board instituted a $3 membership fee to raise capital and instill a sense of responsibility, and the store reopened a month later. The co-op's newsletter related: "After a few weeks of shopping at the supermarket and health food stores, we were all convinced of the importance of the co-op and were glad it opened again."[47] Yet the co-op continued to have chronic problems, particularly in the summer, when members were likely to travel out of town and the store over-ordered for the number of customers it had. After losing hundreds of dollars to rotting vegetables, the co-op forced members to pre-order what they wanted to buy, so that no food would go to waste. When they first tried this system, on a Thursday in July 1974, volunteers packed up everybody's order and then called out names. But that process was also terribly time-consuming, and volunteers did not start calling out people's names until 9:15 p.m., more than two hours later than scheduled. Before the night was over, the co-op had run out of plastic bags and masking tape, and lost $50 when mice got into the almonds. The newsletter editor wrote: "As you can see, with our co-op, when you solve one problem, you seem to wind up with three new ones."[48]

The experience of the co-op demonstrates—along with the higgledy-piggledy progress of the fight against Robert Moses at Cadman Plaza—how Brooklyn's "pioneers" were indeed venturing into new territory. Some of their endeavors succeeded, others failed. To suggest, as some critics of gentrification do, that imposing an upper-middle class lifestyle on a formerly marginal area was effortless is to underappreciate what these early pioneers went through. The Park Slope Food Co-op ended up outlasting the community center in which it was based, taking over the entire building, and then expanding into the one next door. It has flourished even as the neighborhood around it has changed, growing from 124 working members in the mid-1970s to 17,000 members today. It is now open seven days a week, from morning until night, and it still requires its member to work about three hours a month.[49] And despite its scruffy beginnings, some of its members are well-off enough to have nannies . . . some of whom even work their employers' shifts.[50]

The crossover appeal of the Park Slope Food Co-op also exemplifies one of the paradoxes of gentrification that arises again and again. The institution made the neighborhood attractive to many people with unconventional ideologies—a class of people who turned out to earn quite a bit of money after they put their liberal arts degrees to work in marketing, project management, or the burgeoning non-profit and education sectors (more on that in chapter 6). In the 1970s, one longtime Park Slope couple remarked that the neighborhood *must* be going downhill because newcomers were walking around in jeans and sloppy shirts; another elderly resident remarked spitefully, "They use shutters; they don't use blinds."[51] To the contrary! Jeans and shutters signaled the neighborhood's ascendency. Gentrifiers have their own semiotic hierarchy: casual dress indicate they have the luxury not to conform to sartorial norms; shutters demonstrate their affinity for the authentic and original. As the basis of the nation's economy moved from industry to information, a countercultural appearance became an indicator of wealth instead of poverty. Between 1960 and 1985, the price of a Park Slope brownstone rose nearly twice as fast as inflation, soon giving the neighborhood, as one observer noted, "a slick urban image."[52] Even as early as 1981, a local bartender and PhD student named Timothy O'Hanlon complained to the *Times*, "The whole area is turning into a vast commodities market."[53] Just six years after the New York City fiscal crisis, it was already proving impossible to stop the juggernaut of gentrification, to suspend the neighborhood at a moment exactly in between decay and rejuvenation. Even Clem Labine would tease Everett Ortner that what he had really done was make Park Slope safe for a $4 ice cream cone.[54]

GENTRIFICATION AMID DECAY

The class and racial aspect of "renovation" or "recycling" was undeniable: in the mid-1970s, one survey found that 60 percent of the Harvard College class of 1968 was engaged in restoring old homes.[55] A later survey of Park Slope renovators found that only 1.4 percent were black, and their average household income was between $65,000 and $100,000, well above the median.[56] By contrast, in New York City's low-income neighborhoods, arson was rampant, police officers corrupt. Over seven years, New York lost 660,000 jobs, about one-fifth of the total. Manufacturing companies, which had for years given unskilled workers a decent living, headed to southern states and overseas; or they laid off human beings in favor of machines. The RAND Corporation estimated in 1970 that 38,000 apartments were "abandoned" each year—meaning their owners were no longer paying taxes or collecting rents.[57] Parts of the city had become so lawless that landlords were afraid to walk up and down their own stairwells to collect rent from tenants. But the living was cheap. Later that decade, the writer Luc Sante moved to the Lower East Side, where he could get an apartment for $150 a month. "Avenue C was a lunar landscape of vacant blocks and hollow tenement shells," he remembered. "Over there, commerce—in food or clothing, say—was often conducted out of car trunks, but the most thriving industry was junk, and it alone made use of marginally viable specimens of the building stock. The charred stairwells, the gaping floorboards, the lack of lighting, the entryways consisting of holes torn in ground-floor walls—all served the psychological imperatives of the heroin trade."[58]

The juxtaposition of gentrification and decay was a curious one, and it defied the logic of supply and demand. In the late 1970s, 15,000 units were built each year on average—yet about 45,000 apartments were lost, either abandoned by their owners or outright demolished, resulting in a net loss of 30,000 units a year. At the same time, New York was losing population—about 5 percent in a mere three years, falling under 7 million inhabitants in the middle of the decade. Yet, nonetheless, the city had a housing shortage: less than 3 percent of the city's habitable apartments were vacant.[59]

As a result, New York City grew increasingly unaffordable. In 1978, 57 percent of households were paying more than a quarter of their gross incomes in rent, the highest percentage recorded up to that point.[60] And it wasn't just that New Yorkers were getting poorer, though they were. (About a third of the city lived on incomes at or below 125 percent of the federal poverty rate.) Housing prices were growing faster than inflation and maintenance costs combined.[61] The high demand for housing should have stimulated new construction and prevented abandonment. But it didn't. Production slumped; Nixon's moratorium on federal aid had gutted affordable housing production, and in 1970s New York, there was not much of a market for market-rate housing. More importantly, real estate is a confidence game; if investors didn't think the city had much of the future, they wouldn't place long-term bets on it.

Brownstoners like the Ortners were about the only people willing to risk their money in the city, and they alone were able to take advantage of the favorable economics. A few years later, Columbia University Professor Peter Marcuse noted that abandonment and gentrification often occurred "around the corner from each other." Marcuse believed this paradox was a result of the transition from an industrial to an information economy, writing that "demand for blue-collar workers and potential blue-collar workers [decreases] in or near the downtown area, while professional and technical workers are in increasing demand there." One neighborhood can be on the upswing while another can be in decline simply because of its location. Marcuse, like his father, Frankfurt School philosopher Herbert Marcuse, was a sharp critic of capitalism. He argued the poor were squeezed on both sides: they left abandoned neighborhoods only to cram into more stable low-income areas; then prices in those low-income areas rose because of higher demand. And then *those* stable low-income areas also became destinations for middle-income pioneers—not because they were abandoned, but rather because they were functional neighborhoods that were far cheaper than other functional neighborhoods. Hence, the popular belief that gentrification was "reviving" cities was not quite true; gentrification was reviving just certain urban neighborhoods. "For the gentrifiers, all roads lead to downtown," Marcuse wrote. "For the poor, all roads lead to abandonment."[62]

Around this time, the city embarked on two competing real estate strategies that would have divergent lessons many decades later. One approach—enlisting the help of tenants to renovate abandoned buildings—was crafted by lawyer Robert Schur, a jocular bear of a man known for holding court slumped in his chair, chain-smoking cigarettes, at the reform Democratic club on Manhattan's West Side. When Mayor Lindsay, a moderate Republican, was running for reelection in 1969, he tapped Schur to write a white paper on low-income cooperative apartments, in which each household would own a certain number of shares in the building, much as stockholders own shares in a company. Together, the co-op shareholders would elect a board to represent them and oversee the building's management. New York City had a rich history dating to the 1930s of co-ops built by and for labor unions. Those buildings were new from the ground up, sometimes on land cleared by Robert Moses and the Slum Clearance Board's eminent domain powers. But urban renewal–style redevelopment, as discussed in chapter 1, had fallen out of favor. There had been only a few attempts to convert existing, dilapidated rental housing to ownership units, and they were fabulously labor-intensive exercises.[63]

Once Lindsay won a second term, Schur became director of the newly created Office of Special Improvements, which was to run a low-income co-op program. When one of his interns, Philip St. Georges, came to him with a list of prospective properties to convert, Schur asked him what he planned to call the program.

"What's wrong with 'Multi-Family Self-Help Housing'?" St. Georges offered.

"What kind of cockamamie WASP name is that?" Schur shot back with a snicker. "If there is one thing I'll teach you about New York City housing, it's that you have to be bold, daring, innovative. This is a sexy program. It needs a sexy, catchy name."

The young intern, fresh out of college, with a pony tail and Mao cap, asked him what he had in mind.

"How about 'Sweat Equity'?" Schur answered.[64]

The name stuck, and the concept caught on. One evaluator later observed that "a growing succession of often eye-catching groups—welfare mothers, a street gang, women ex-offenders—were engaged in dramatic sweat equity projects."[65] Schur knit together financing packages from federal programs, a city loan program, and the state's Mitchell-Lama funds. He also had access to an impressive inventory of buildings: not only all the properties abandoned by their owners, but also others seized from slumlords for neglect.[66] During his time in office, Schur inspired fifty-four buildings, housing hundreds of individuals altogether, to seek co-op status.[67]

Not all of them fared well. The co-op boards that ran these buildings were reluctant to raise monthly maintenance fees enough to keep pace with rising expenses. One evaluation in the mid-1980s determined that about 85 percent of the properties that had sought co-op status during the Schur era were still operating, but many were financially troubled. More than half were in arrears on their debt service, and 17 percent were in court over unpaid property taxes.[68]

However, after falling from favor during Mayor Abe Beame's term (1974–77), sweat equity experienced a renaissance under the Koch administration, when the city came into possession of so many tax-delinquent properties that it couldn't handle them all. It turned to nonprofit groups, which helped organize tenants to buy the buildings and renovate them. (One of the nonprofits, the Urban Homesteading Assistance Board, was cofounded by Schur's acolyte Philip St. Georges.) Now there are approximately 30,000 low-income apartments in New York City owned by their former tenants. This model, while far from perfect, had wide-ranging influence as city administrations across the country sought ways to rehabilitate their physical environments, provide affordable housing, and avoid resorting to cumbersome and costly urban renewal techniques. A national program, funded through HUD, had brought homesteading to thirty-nine cities by 1981.[69] What was not understood at the time is the extent to which sweat equity would also serve as an anti-gentrification strategy decades later. Many of the units rehabbed in those early years are located in gentrified areas such as Williamsburg, the Lower East Side, Harlem, and Bushwick, and have allowed their low- and moderate-income occupants to become homeowners, all but impervious to displacement, no matter how high their property values rise.[70]

PLANNED SHRINKAGE

The other approach to addressing New York City's housing crisis relied on the private sector and was exemplified by Roger Starr. A tall dapper man in his 50s, Starr would be considered a neoconservative today—but he was far more complicated than that label implies. He was educated at Yale and, perhaps because he felt himself a victim of anti-Semitic discrimination there, developed a keen nose for injustice of any sort. During World War II, he offered to enlist in an all-black regiment, then tried his hand at journalism before being called back to head his father's barge company. In middle age, Starr plunged into the public sphere as head of the centrist Citizens' Housing and Planning Council, and later joined Mayor Beame's cabinet as chief of the city's housing administration. As such, he was Bob Schur's boss. (Schur stayed on after Lindsay left and Beame became mayor in 1974.) Starr loved to argue with people, and for the most part did so amiably. The one exception was with Jane Jacobs, whom he hated with a passion. Starr, like Robert Moses, believed in reinventing the city rather than just patching it up, and favored new construction over rehabilitation.[71] He burdened Schur's co-op conversions with additional

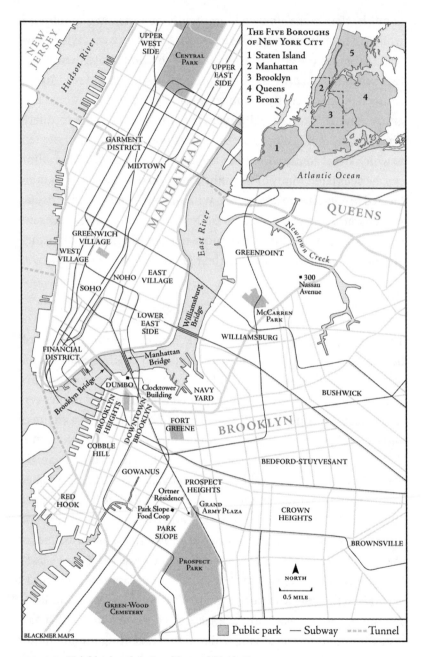

FIG. 2.3. Neighborhoods in Brooklyn and Manhattan.

requirements that delayed their completion and killed at least one project.[72] Later, when the city put thirteen brownstones on the Upper West Side up for sale, Starr excluded a bid from a group of tenants that wanted to convert them to low-income cooperatives.[73] Finally, Starr fired Schur.[74]

In many ways, Starr was a brilliant thinker. He once astutely observed that gentrification resulted from a sea change in white middle-class attitudes toward lower economic classes and minorities. "The people who are moving in are professionals, young lawyers, architects, doctors, people in the investment community," Starr told the *New York Times Magazine*. "Blue collar workers are moving out because they have less social distance from the poor, whereas the professional person has eminent social distance. He's willing to put up with a reduced physical distance."[75] This idea of "social distance" explains a great deal of gentrifiers' willingness to live cheek by jowl alongside minorities. The professional person, in this view, did not feel a need to prove himself by living in a prestigious suburb; the professional person defined his self-worth through his work. Nor did professionals fear the social stigma of living in low-income neighborhoods: their breeding, speech, and education would set them apart. First- and second-generation immigrants might own shoe repair stores or barber shops; their capital was locked up inside small businesses that would be threatened by a neighborhood's deterioration. Gentrifiers' capital instead lay in their talent, education, and creativity—and they could bring those things to any neighborhood they chose.

Yet Starr did not imagine gentrification would ever be powerful enough to turn around the city. He and other New York City officials struggled to find a means to encourage housing production. One of them, Alexander Garvin, a young planner who worked under Starr, had a eureka moment one day in his office in the mid-1970s. There was a program dating to 1956 called J-51 that gave landlords breaks on their property taxes when they undertook certain renovations. Garvin was signing a stack of applications for this incentive one day when he realized it was not costing the city anything, and yet was improving, and to some degree increasing, the city's housing stock. He suggested to Starr that the city promote and expand the J-51 program—which it did, chiefly by applying the incentives to industrial properties that were converted to residential uses.[76] The impact of the J-51 on housing production was significant: about 30 percent of new homes built by the private sector in this era came under the J-51 program; another 13 percent were new buildings that received the 421-a tax exemption, a program set up a few years earlier under Mayor Lindsay.[77]

Developers who took advantage of the J-51 incentive also promised some degree of affordability. If the building was a rental, the developer could increase the rent, either to market-rate (if the unit had been vacant) or by a percentage of the amount the owner spent on the renovations (if the tenant had remained in place). After that, the apartment was supposed to be covered by the city's rent regulation laws as long as the property tax abatement stayed in force (which was between fourteen and thirty years)—meaning that the monthly rent could rise by only a few percentage points a year. Some critics held that the J-51 encouraged evictions of low-income tenants by providing an added enticement to raise the rent (a charge substantiated in a city-commissioned report).[78] The program also failed to provide any regulatory structure to police the affordability requirements. Garvin—who would go on to write extensively about urban planning, teach at Yale, and advise Deputy Mayor Daniel L. Doctoroff in the early 2000s—thought New York City tenants were savvy enough to keep tabs on their landlords and know whether they were charging them too much rent—a theory that was to be sorely tested over the following decades.[79]

Despite his adept deployment of tax incentives, there was little joy for Roger Starr at the city's housing agency. He lived at a time, he recalled, "when the future was hidden behind the doomsday of the next payroll date, or the next call from City Hall setting a quota of new firings."[80] Starr became desperate; he had taken the job expecting that the housing administration superagency would be split into two, and that he would be put in charge of housing development. Instead, he was forced to do triage. In a series of newspaper interviews in early 1976, he began to float the idea of "planned shrinkage." Starr predicted the city would continue to lose population, and with it, he argued, "The same miles of streets cannot be patrolled, cleaned, repaired, and served with public transportation." Selectively de-servicing certain neighborhoods, he explained, was the only option to prevent the city from slowly turning off the spigot to a bigger geographic area that would die a long, drawn-out death. "The poor, who need the greatest services from the city government, would be worse hurt by the failure of the city to use its resources economically," he said.[81]

Unsurprisingly, Starr's idea was not very popular. He was denounced by a colleague, picketed at speaking events, and derided as "genocidal, racist, inhuman, and irresponsible." The city council's black and Puerto Rican caucus called for him to be fired.[82] Mayor Abe Beame refrained from criticizing Starr publicly— "I do not gag my commissioners," the mayor said—though the mayor did disavow "planned shrinkage."[83] It's unclear what Starr meant by "shrinkage," so it is difficult to evaluate the idea dispassionately. Would schools close? Subway lines stop short? Could sewers be taken offline? He never gave specifics, though he noted people still living in underpopulated areas would not be forced, but "induced," to move elsewhere. (The examples he gave were the South Bronx and Brownsville.)[84]

A few months later, Starr left city government, ostensibly *not* because of the brouhaha over his comments, but by his own volition, and ended up joining the *Times* editorial board. In some ways he was proven right: by not planning for shrinkage, New York City experienced *un*planned shrinkage. In the latter half of the Beame administration, the city closed firehouses and underfunded schools, chiefly in low-income neighborhoods, while letting residents continue to live there. Starr was perhaps too honest to be a government official: he refused to mislead the public into thinking that the city's economy would improve, except that he also underestimated how much the economy *would* improve. As a private citizen, Starr continued his pessimistic predictions—warning as late as the mid-1980s that New York would lose its preeminent status in the nation.[85]

There is a third important person in this story about New York's critical moment, a man who had the same interest in rehabilitation as Bob Schur, but also the same allegiance to the private market as Roger Starr. This man—Ed Koch—struck the public as a typical loud-mouthed New Yorker through and through. But he came from the place where gentrification was born—Greenwich Village—and launched his political career by defeating a member of the old Democratic machine, Carmine DeSapio. Koch had about him a keen understanding of the importance of the rising professional class and knew that he desperately needed its energy to pull the city out of its morass.[86] On New Year's Day, 1978, the 53-year-old congressman stood before a crowd outside City Hall and took the mayoral oath of office. "A better city requires the one ingredient that money cannot buy: people who are willing to give of themselves," he bellowed. Koch even adopted the language of gentrifiers, lauding "the urban pioneers of this generation" who were rehabilitating houses and reclaiming schools. Koch's vision was a third way, a solution to the problem of revitalizing dying Northeastern cities without undertaking the public investment that sweat equity required, nor the desperate amputations called for under planned shrinkage. To rely on "pioneers"—the term that at once hides and belies the imperialistic aspect of gentrification—Koch would stuff private investment, idealism, and history into one giant golden bullet. It seemed at the time to be a perfect way out of the urban crisis of the late 1970s.

With echoes of President John F. Kennedy's own inaugural seventeen years earlier, Koch concluded his address that afternoon with an appeal to the nation's young: "I ask those who are not with us now, those who are seeking a challenge: Come east and join us. Come east and grow up with the new pioneers. Grow up with the City of New York."[87]

The applause was tepid.

THREE

GEOGRAPHY IS DESTINY: SAN FRANCISCO, 1966-1980

To begin to understand why San Francisco has become the most expensive city in the country, place your right hand face-down on a table. Imagine your thumb to be the San Francisco peninsula; your thumbnail is the city itself; the space between your thumb and your forefinger is the San Francisco Bay. Oakland and Berkeley are across the bay, at about the bottom knuckle of your forefinger. The thumbnail—the City (and County) of San Francisco—is just about 46 square miles, a good portion of which is covered by streets, sidewalks, hospitals, parks, universities, office towers—and steep hills that no one can build on. Chicago covers nearly five times the amount of land and is nearly entirely flat; New York City is close to seven times that size. San Francisco is smaller geographically than Madison, Wisconsin, and Boise, Idaho; it is one-sixteenth the size of Jacksonville, Florida, the largest city in the continental United States in terms of area. Yet San Francisco is the thirteenth largest city in terms of population.

Size is important for two reasons: it allows a city to expand its tax base, and also to produce more housing and bring down prices without having to build vertically. In the late nineteenth and early twentieth centuries, American cities frequently expanded their boundaries and annexed adjacent areas, but San Francisco's size was prematurely restricted—first due to concerns about municipal corruption, then later because of the city's reputation for arrogance. In 1856, San Francisco County reached down to today's Santa Clara County, while the city of San Francisco's boundaries are where they are today. Pushed by reformers, the California legislature agreed to consolidate San Francisco county and city governments into one administration and to make their borders contiguous—it was thought that by reducing the number of governments, they would reduce the likelihood of graft and corruption. Instead of making the city larger, the legislature shrank the county to the same size as the city; San Mateo County, just to the south, was formed from the leftovers. Then, after the 1906 earthquake and fire scattered San Francisco's population, the city's business interests launched a drive to annex its neighbors to the north, south, and east. But they were done in by their own hubris. "San Francisco has pursued for many years a policy of belittling Oakland yet wonders now why the big city across the bay should object to the submergence of its identity by consolidation," one newspaper observed. In the 1920s, business leaders again attempted to expand to the south; eventually, they settled for ad hoc regional ties—Bay Area Rapid Transit (BART), the Association of Bay Area Governments, and the Bay Area Council, a business group.[1]

These regional organizations should not be underestimated. Recently, urban planning professor Michael Storper considered the relationship among Northern California municipalities to be a paragon of cooperation compared to the Los Angeles area, which he called backwards-looking and fragmented. Storper argued the Bay Area's synergies helped propel its per capita income far above that of L.A.[2] Yet synergy is not the same as planning; as we shall see, the Bay Area has had no problem creating jobs, but it has shown less willingness to shelter its workers, resulting in the nation's highest housing prices.

San Francisco has long been buffeted between two competing

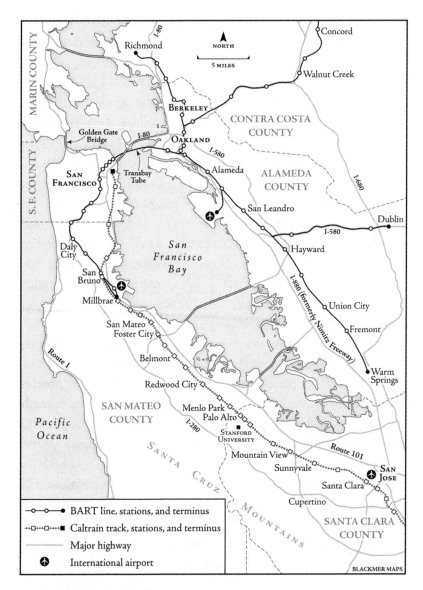

FIG. 3.1. San Francisco Bay Area.

forces, one eager for growth, and the other quite hostile toward it. Both strains perhaps stem from the same source, the Gold Rush, which helped establish the city both as a center of avarice as well as a place for sexual tolerance.[3] Beginning in the early 1900s, business boosters began to craft the city into the commercial capital of the Pacific Rim. In the 1950s, the federal urban renewal program steered money into stratagems to clear the shabby Embarcadero and South-of-Market areas (on the right upper edge of your fingernail) and make way for office construction and a convention center. Between 1961 and 1980, some 30 million square feet of office space was constructed downtown, including what was at the time the eighth tallest building in the world, the Transamerica Pyramid.[4] At that point, more jobs in banking, international commerce, and insurance were located in the financial district than anywhere else in the country aside from Manhattan—though San Francisco had fewer people than even Baltimore or Indianapolis.

Outside of the business and political elite, however, San Franciscans shared little of the hubris or ambition of New Yorkers: they were content to live in a pleasant place, rather than in the world's greatest city. In the 1920s, the city restricted the heights of buildings in northern (read: wealthy) neighborhoods; in 1972, a 40-foot height limit was imposed on nearly all residential areas.[5] On a peninsula plagued by cool weather and frequent fog (not to mention earthquakes), low buildings were seen as necessary. Former San Francisco Planning Director James McCarthy once referred to the city as a "tight little medieval Italian hill town."[6] Toward the end of the century, as the buildings grew higher than what you might find in Piedmont, architecture critic Allan Temko argued against skyscrapers and the shadows they cast. "Access to the sun should be a civic birthright," he wrote in the *San Francisco Chronicle*. "The sun is the key to the half-Mediterranean mood of *dolce far niente*."[7]

After World War II, San Francisco lost population—about 32,000 inhabitants between 1950 and 1960—and manufacturing jobs. But the city was never reduced to begging the way New York City was.

For one thing, San Francisco had not depended on heavy industry as much as its East Coast counterparts had, and growth in the finance and commerce sectors more than made up for the bleeding. The Bay Area's ability to generate jobs is one of its remarkable unsung attributes—though it would come back to haunt it. In the short term, at least, the area basked in an ideal equilibrium: short commutes, reasonable housing prices, and a reputation for the unconventional.

That reputation was what lured René Yañez to the East Bay in 1966; a friend, Harry Israel, told him that was where things were happening. Yañez had just been released from the Army, where he had avoided serving in Vietnam by teaching art at a military psych ward in North Carolina. Most of his students were conscientious objectors or privates who had just returned from the front and were suffering from shell shock. Harry was Jewish and Yañez was Mexican American, but they were best buddies. They had met each other at art school in San Diego, before they were drafted. Once out of the army, Harry enrolled in the School for the Arts, in Berkeley, and urged Yañez to move back to California. The crazy thing called the '60s was just emerging: The previous May saw 35,000 people turn out for a Jerry Rubin–inspired anti-war rally on the University of California's flagship campus; across the bay, Jefferson Airplane had just released its first single; the *Berkeley Barb* was publishing some of the first underground comics; and tie-dyed T-shirts had gone viral. Thousands of long-haired young people in jeans milled about on Cal's lawns, strumming guitars and smoking weed. A plethora of tables with literature promoting causes on both political extremes dotted Sproul Plaza.

Yañez was particularly captivated by the emerging Chicano cultural scene in the Bay Area. He quickly found work with La Causa, an organization that was trying to bring more Chicanos into the University of California system. In the evenings and on weekends, he'd work on his art. La Causa was based in a Victorian house, and it let him use the lobby for exhibits, first for a solo show and later an exhibit called "New Symbols for *La Nueva Raza*." In it, about a dozen artists, including Yañez, rendered portraits of Manuel Delgado, a leader of the Third World Liberation Front that had just organized a four-month student strike to force the creation of an ethnic studies department at Cal. The artists had decided that Delgado should be *the* symbol of "the New People": dashing, proud, and uniting the disparate hyphenated nationalities south of the Rio Grande that were seeking a common identity.[8]

Yañez became a visual and performance artist working in multiple media, but he would distinguish himself most as a curator. Soft-spoken and unassuming, Yañez was able to mingle with people from different backgrounds and bring them together. Yañez began looking for a better venue to display Chicano art. He wanted a space that was more civic in nature—and less like a stranger's living room—in which to announce Latino artists and show off their talents.

That desire steered him across the bay to the Mission District, a heavily Latino neighborhood in San Francisco then enjoying cultural ferment. If San Francisco is your right thumbnail, the Mission District is situated about midway down, a little off-center to the right. The neighborhood, in real life, is about a mile wide, a mile and a half long; its topography, unlike the rest of the city, is almost entirely flat. Its low elevation makes the Mission warmer than the rest of the city by several degrees, and it is sunnier and less windy. The names of its streets evoke the sun and the Spanish heritage of the city's founders: Valencia, Florida, Balmy Alley. The streets are laid out in a grid, like Manhattan's, only the north-south blocks are much longer than in New York.

Yañez found a large apartment in the Mission for just $80 a month. (On a scale of 1 to 7, with 1 being the highest rent district, the Mission rated a 5 at the time.[9]) Soon, Yañez and other Latino artists rented a storefront on 14th Street. They called it La Galería de la Raza. The term *la raza*—literally "the race" or "the people"—went back to 1920s Mexico, when the writer and philosopher José Vasconcelos used the word to describe what we now call Hispanics or Latinos; but *la raza* had special significance for him. Vasconcelos argued the Ibero-

American people were poised to lead civilization into a new era because they had already proven themselves tolerant of racial mixing.[10] On the West Coast in the 1960s, *la raza* signified an ethnic identity distinct from Spanish Americans, one in which country of origin was not as important as a common *mestizo* heritage.

The term was particularly apt in the 1960s Mission, which at the time was turning from Irish to Latino. By the 1970s, the Mission was bursting with immigrants from all parts of Mexico and Central America. The artists at La Galería wanted to bring those immigrants together and build a sense of common identity. They held classes in printmaking and filmmaking and held opening bashes for each show they curated. The poet Alejandro Murguía wrote of one reception, "The energy was electric that night, the place was packed. I'm not sure anyone needed wine, but the wine did flow, as did the conversation. . . . I was sure there wasn't a place in the world I'd rather be, not Paris or New York. At that moment, it seemed to me that I was standing in the artistic center of the universe."[11]

After a couple of run-ins with rowdy guests, the owner of the building—a prominent sculptor named Fred Hobbs—asked the gallery to leave. It was perhaps just as well: 14th Street was on the north side of the Mission, far away from the critical mass of Latino activity. For several months, Yañez and a few other artists pounded the pavement almost every day, trying to find the right space to call their own.

Yañez had gotten a job as the Mission's liaison to the city's Arts Commission, a position that put him in charge of a fair amount of cultural funding and made him a man for other artists to get to know. In that capacity, he began to commission murals for the neighborhood. Yañez figured City Hall would like murals because they were a highly visible way for the city to show off its multiculturalism, and the community would like them because they would make their neighborhood more colorful. But while the art form had a long history in Mexico, it was not prominent in the Bay Area, and Yañez had a hard time convincing his artist-friends to take on an assignment. The exception was Spain Rodriguez, an underground comic book artist

FIG. 3.2. Spain Rodriguez, "An Average Day on Mission Street" (1975). Rodriguez, an underground comic book artist, was the first artist employed to paint a mural in the Mission. This line drawing appeared in *Arcade: The Comics Revue No. 2*. (Courtesy of Susan Stern)

who had a reputation for doing anything for money. Yañez gave him $300 to paint a wall of a youth center, Horizons Unlimited, at Folsom and 22nd streets. Rodriguez divided the wall into four panels, each one expertly rendered with black-and-white lines, the spaces between them filled in with deep blues and reds. One panel showed typical faces from around the neighborhood. Another, a view straight down Mission Street, with glittering store marquees on either side. The lower left panel featured a cameo of the roguish Rodriguez himself, dressed in black leather and sitting astride a blood-orange motorcycle. Behind him sat a *chica* with high-heeled boots. When the other Mission artists saw Rodriguez's piece, suddenly they realized how cool painting on walls could be, and they too wanted in.

It was a mark of the medium's youth that Yañez supplied his artists not with mural paint, but latex house paint mixed with gesso. As a result, the early murals eroded quickly from exposure to the elements. No matter. Murals were by their nature transitory, subject to the whims of nature, graffiti artists, and property owners. (Muralists were supposed to seek permission of the property owner before painting, but that didn't always happen.) To spend three or four or five days painting a wall in the middle of a city was an act of faith. Yet during the 1970s, pretty much any Latino artist of note in the city at the time—and a number of non-Latinos as well, including underground comic book artist R. Crumb—expressed their devotion.

Within a few years, the streets in the Mission had become open-air art galleries. Styles, subject matter, and quality varied greatly. Struggle was a constant theme, as were family, health, nature, and community. Portraits of Latin American figures appear again and again. Over the years, more than 500 murals have been painted in the Mission. Perhaps the most famous one was done in 1994, when seven artists erected ten-stories' worth of scaffolds and decorated the exterior of the massive Women's Center, a collection of nonprofit offices and service centers on 18th Street. A swirling chain of rainbows and braids connect 20-foot-high faces that seem to pop-out in three dimensions. One pediment featured a Latin American Venus; the other Rigoberta Menchú, a heroine of the Guatemalan Civil War.

One muralist, Ray Patlan, enlisted teenagers to help paint his pieces. If a young person could transform his walk to school into a meaningful, artistic corridor of colors, Patlan thought, he could be inspired to take on greater things as well. His subjects were not Latin American folklore or history, but everyday characters who resided in the Mission at the time, like twin sisters who lived across the street from each other, or the owner of the vintage clothing store. He later explained: "Just the idea of being able to change one's own visual environment for people who have never had any power whatsoever in their lives is pretty heavy influence towards the whole concept of making change, voting, getting your garbage picked up, calling the city, and telling them you need things."[12]

The murals would become one of the primary ways through which Anglos interacted with the Mission, ending up in guide books, attracting sightseers, and eventually lending the area a warm, creative, vibrant patina that fostered gentrification. And yet at the beginning, they served as the opposite, as a means to empower the low-income people crammed into the neighborhood because there weren't many alternatives.

WAITING FOR THE BART

Another development in the late 1960s and early 1970s that would shape the fate of the Mission was the BART train line. Around the time of Yañez's arrival, a boring machine—it looked like a rocket on its side—was drilling horizontally under Mission Street, the north-south spine of the neighborhood. BART—a hybrid subway-commuter rail—had been conceived shortly after World War II as a means to relieve traffic congestion. By 1959, the region's highway system in general was declared beyond "free flow capacity"; the Nimitz Freeway between San José and Oakland (now Interstate 880) had bumper-to-bumper traffic during rush hour—and that was well before the tech industry took root.[13] Part of the problem was geography: Water takes up much of the greater San Francisco Bay region, and while such an arrangement was conducive to ships hauling cargo, it spreads out population thinly. As people began to live on one side and commute to the other, a regional authority proposed to create a high-speed rail system that could move 30,000 people an hour, up and down the peninsula, to and from San Francisco, and across the bay to Oakland and Berkeley and beyond.

BART's planners promised that rapid transit—70 miles an hour on straightaways, and an average of 50 miles an hour including station stops—would "serve effectively to reduce the size of the Bay Area, shrinking distances along all the major routes." For employers, the system would expand the labor pool from which to recruit workers; for workers, it would increase the number of jobs and homes within easy commuting distance of each other.[14] For San Francisco, BART made sure that white residents who had fled to the suburbs could still commute easily to their jobs downtown, ensuring that property tax revenue from office buildings did not suffer even though collections from residential areas may have decreased.

The BART system would have significant effects on the Mission District decades later, though many of the decisions on its route were made by happenstance. To get up and down the peninsula, BART's engineers thought it made the most sense to burrow a tunnel straight through the heart of the neighborhood. While BART's planners didn't expect to pick up many passengers in the Mission itself—in October 1961, only *one* station was projected for the neighborhood, at 22nd Street—it was the quickest way to get from downtown San Francisco to the southern suburbs.[15] At the time, BART was proposing a much larger network than ever got built: it would extend trains from downtown west along Geary Street and then north over the Golden Gate Bridge into Marin County. That spur would have added seven stops in San Francisco, which agency officials thought would entice the city to adopt the plan.[16]

But the Golden Gate Bridge Authority, another quasi-independent entity, blocked the BART line from crossing into Marin for fear it would siphon toll revenue from the bridge. That in turn gave the BART much less incentive to build the Geary Street spur. (The ridership from the seven stations alone wasn't seen as enough of a justification for the expense.[17]) If San Francisco wasn't going to get BART stations in Pacific Heights (along the upper left of your fingernail on your thumb-map), the city's leaders wanted more stations elsewhere in the city; BART planners complied. Instead of just one station in the Mission at 22nd Street, as indicated on an October 1961 map, the final version called for two: one at 16th Street and the other at 24th Street.[18]

An extra train station might not seem neighborhood-changing. But it was. The Mission District had something no other residential neighborhood had: two BART stations. It essentially doubled the area that was within an easy, half-mile walk of an admirably fast commuting tool (see Figure 3.3). Residents of the Mission could reach the Civic Center in five minutes, the financial district in seven, the

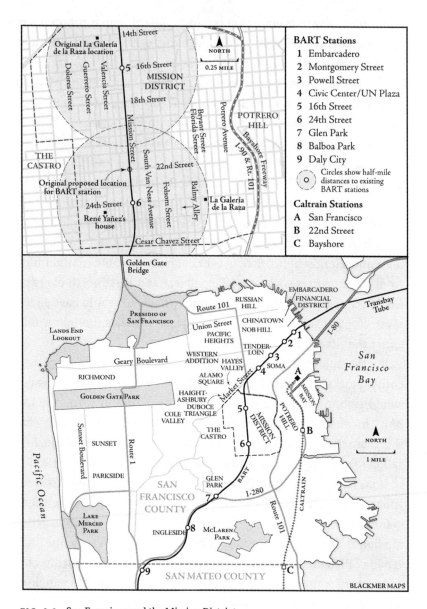

BART Stations
1 Embarcadero
2 Montgomery Street
3 Powell Street
4 Civic Center/UN Plaza
5 16th Street
6 24th Street
7 Glen Park
8 Balboa Park
9 Daly City

⊙ Circles show half-mile distances to existing BART stations

Caltrain Stations
A San Francisco
B 22nd Street
C Bayshore

FIG. 3.3. San Francisco and the Mission District.

airport, in the other direction, in less than half an hour. Back then, well before the in-migration of young professionals began, the idea of making a neighborhood too convenient for its own good must have sounded bizarre. And yet, a few Mission activists had a sense of what was in store for them. "Where will we go when we are forced to leave our houses because of high rents and redevelopment?" an underground Mission newspaper, *Basta Ya*, asked in 1970. (The newspaper's name can be translated as "Enough Already.") "It is not too late for the people to wake up and oppose our enemy." Some 150 people turned out for a demonstration at the future location of the 24th Street station, chanting "BART must go" and "This is where the people's tax dollars are."[19]

The degree to which the protesters understood what might happen to the Mission is uncanny, but little action was taken. A few years earlier, before the BART tunnel was dug, a city consultant had predicted the rail system would unleash powerful economic forces and potentially displace many middle- and lower-income minorities in its path.[20] The San Francisco Redevelopment Agency proposed a plan for the Mission intended to capitalize on the potential the BART would bring while also protecting low-income immigrants. The agency, which was the San Francisco corollary of Robert Moses' Slum Clearance Committee, advocated for the rehabilitation of 70 percent of the structures within a 423-acre zone, offering loans and grants to property owners, and rental assistance for low-income tenants. At first, some Mission groups supported this plan.[21] Just 80 acres would be cleared, most of it centered around the two BART stations, where the team proposed building mid-rise apartment towers. Urban historian Ocean Howell estimates that just 4.5 percent of the neighborhood would have been razed.[22] When compared to other projects proposed by agency director Justin Herman, it was quite modest in scope.

But in the late 1960s, the San Francisco Redevelopment Agency was suffering from a lack of trust, largely because of its efforts to transform the area to the west of downtown, the Western Addition, earlier in the decade. Away went 1,280 acres of tenements, stores, churches, jazz clubs, day care centers, and other institutions in the center of the city's African American community.[23] More than 4,000 families were displaced, without much thought as to where to put them. Many of the black residents ended up in the southeastern part of the city in temporary army barracks, creating, arguably, an even worse slum. In San Francisco, the words "Western Addition" became shorthand for yet another failed urban renewal experiment.

Mission residents were far better organized than Western Addition inhabitants had been. Earlier in the century, the Mission's population was largely working class Irish and German; it was comparable to South Boston or Chicago's Bridgeport in terms of political clout. The city's longest-serving mayor, James Rolph (1912–1931), came from the Mission, and the neighborhood retained strong ties to the Catholic Church as it shifted from Irish to Latino.[24] In the late '60s, community organizer Saul Alinsky sent in one of his staff members, Mike Miller, to forge links among any and all constituencies—churches, labor unions, block associations, and nonprofit groups—and form the Mission Coalition Organization (MCO), a formidable populist force.

In its approach to business, the MCO had proudly created, in the words of a Republican official, "an atmosphere inhospitable to investment."[25] When landlords raised rents or failed to perform maintenance, tenant organizations staged rent strikes and picketed outside locations associated with the property's owner: their churches, social events, even a beauty salon one landlord owned.

The MCO was not opposed to urban renewal per se, but it would accept nothing less than veto power over any plan that the redevelopment agency came up with. Herman refused; federal legislation forbade redevelopment agencies from giving up any control to nonelected bodies. As a result, the MCO showed its muscle. The night of the vote to approve the Mission redevelopment plan, some 200 MCO members packed the legislative chamber at City Hall, and another 300 people stood outside. Under such pressure, the supervisors rejected the plan. The activists thought they had "saved" the Mission from the wrecking ball. But their short-term gain may have caused long-term pain, as the redevelopment plan would have built afford-able housing and provided rehabilitation assistance before BART's in-cursion made such remedies much more expensive.

TO BUILD OR NOT TO BUILD

With the redevelopment agency unable to help, the Mission Housing Development Corporation, a spin-off of the MCO, tried to undertake affordable housing in the 1970s on its own. (The MCO itself eventually dissolved, a result of infighting among its leaders.[26]) In its early years, the housing group had modest success constructing public housing and distributing rental assistance.[27] But then the US Department of Housing and Urban Development, under President Richard Nixon, rejected a number of the organization's applications for additional projects.[28] In one letter, HUD said the Mission already had enough low-income housing and needed more *moderate-income* housing.[29] Shortly afterwards, at the beginning of his second term, Nixon elim-inated Model Cities funding—of which the Mission was a prime beneficiary—and imposed a moratorium on housing subsidies. That effectively meant that no one, anywhere in the country, could build much housing for low-income families.[30]

The budget-cutting move came right as gentrification was begin-ning to take root across the country. Increasingly, the private sec-tor, rather than government-run urban renewal policies, was being blamed for displacing poor people. Some cities set up hotlines for people displaced by Title I projects, but they got besieged instead with calls from people displaced by private actions. In one year, the St. Louis relocation agency received 3,744 requests for housing assis-tance unrelated to public projects—a number representing almost 2 percent of the number of the city's households. Parallel agencies in New Orleans and Cincinnati also saw significant numbers.[31]

The locus of gentrification pressure in San Francisco was in Mint

Hill (now called Duboce Triangle) and Alamo Square, both close to downtown. Yet, by the end of the 1970s, the back-to-the-city spirit had spread to the Mission, where 19 percent of families lived below the poverty line and 60 percent made less than $10,000 a year. According to a report at the time, "The new owners who have sufficient capital to rehabilitate the area's Victorian three-flat structures rent their apartments at a rate prohibitively high for the Hispanic families who once lived there."[32] Even before the newcomers arrived, the Mission Housing Development Corporation described a rental squeeze that was hitting its constituents particularly hard: the typical low-income household was "rent-burdened," spending at least 25 percent of its gross income on rent.[33] Some 13 percent of units were overcrowded, and only about 15 percent of the neighborhood's residents owned their own homes. Even then, housing advocates had little faith in the market being able to deliver affordability: an overwhelming majority of new construction, the report noted, had been "more expensive and of smaller unit size," while 175 1-to-4-unit buildings had been destroyed in the previous twelve years.[34] Yet instead of trying to bring prices down by increasing supply, Mission Housing recommended the opposite: keeping the current height limits, and generally prohibiting large apartment buildings with small units. Developers would have less incentive to knock down existing buildings to build bigger ones, thereby displacing existing tenants.[35] Mission Housing said it would create 800 new units of subsidized housing in the future—yet either that number was too ambitious or the organization was too ineffective, for the development corporation did not manage to accomplish that goal until 2006.[36]

Allan Jacobs, San Francisco's planning director in the early 1970s, tried to focus City Hall's energies on increasing affordable housing. "We had almost no luck in persuading city officials to use surplus properties for subsidized housing," he wrote later. "To the contrary, the mayor on one occasion asked why we shouldn't sell a particular housing project for non-subsidized uses."[37] Both Jacobs and Mayor Joseph Alioto were constrained by the city's 300-page charter, which outlined in exquisite detail the limits and powers of different city agencies. The many checks and balances (forged at a time when local government was outlandishly corrupt) led Jacobs to joke that San Francisco had neither a strong mayor system nor a strong city council structure, but instead a "No power to anyone form of government."[38] One of the few exceptions, in fact, was Justin Herman's San Francisco Redevelopment Agency, which enjoyed a direct line of communication with the federal government. Over the next several decades, neither San Francisco mayors nor their opponents were able to do much to increase the affordability of their city, and, while working at cross-purposes with one another, they often made the problem worse.

THE BIRTH AND LIFE OF THE DAY OF THE DEAD

After La Galería de la Raza was forced out of its space on 14th Street, it was René Yañez who found it a new home. It was a storefront on 24th Street, a commercial strip right in the heart of the Latino Mission, next door to a butcher shop.[39] As a measure of gratitude, the gallery's members elected Yañez as artistic director, while his friend Ralph Maradiaga became the gallery's administrative director. As Yañez had done with street murals, he wanted to use La Galería to create a sense of community for the emerging Latino majority in the Mission. He was always looking for what *resonated* with the audience: not only did he keep tabs on how many people attended shows, but he watched them walk through exhibits, observed how they reacted, and listened, as he went about his social rounds, to what his friends, and friends of friends, said about what they saw. One day, he and Maradiaga began batting about ideas for something that could combine ceremony, ritual, and art. Yañez's father had once taken him to Oaxaca to see *El Día de los Muertos*: a macabre interpretation of All Souls Day on November 2. At the Galería, Yañez tried his own version. Along one side of the room, he set up a table with a picture, a candle and some flowers. "People went crazy," Yañez said later. "It was a very simple concept, but teachers started bringing in students and saying,

FIG. 3.4. The annual Day of the Dead exhibits at La Galería de la Raza drew visitors from around the region to the Mission District and have grown into a large procession and outdoor festival. (Photo courtesy of Shades of San Francisco, San Francisco Public Library.)

'Look at this.' So I said, 'Hey, there's something here. I should do it again next year.'" They did, this time adding a table cloth and a few more candles.

Little did he know that these efforts at community-making would, like the murals, years later serve as enticements for Anglos to visit the Mission—and eventually live there.[40] Over the years, the Galería's Day of the Dead exhibit became more and more elaborate and more and more popular, attracting viewers from all over the region. Lines would snake out the door. Schoolteachers would bring their classes and use the event to inspire students to come up with their own altarpieces. Yañez was invigorated by the attention, and by the ecumenical spirit he was able to foster. "It was spiritual. It was nondenominational. You could be Jewish. You could be Catholic. You could be black," Yañez explained. "Kids would bring pictures of their puppies or goldfish." Soon, Yañez began inviting artists from around the Bay

Area to submit works for a section of the installation called *El Museo*. It became a coveted commission. Contributors would begin meeting in June or July to figure out what they would do four months later.[41] Later, the Day of the Dead exhibit would spill into a park and evolve into a costume parade.

Yañez gave up his job as city cultural liaison for the neighborhood to focus on La Galería. Grants poured in from the National Endowment for the Arts and the California Council on the Arts. Gallerists from around the state and country came to seek advice on creating their own ethnocentric spaces. He staged one of the country's first Frida Kahlo shows in 1978, long before she was widely known, and the artist became one of the patron saints of the Mission, her image painted on far more of the neighborhood's murals than her more celebrated husband, Diego Rivera.

Shortly after that exhibit, Yañez became aware of "lowriders": souped-up cars that hung low to the ground, sometimes with hydraulic shocks that could raise and lower the chassis, to make it look like the cars were dancing. It wasn't just the cars that fascinated him; it was the entire culture surrounding them. The young men who tinkered on these cars, known as *cholos*, looked like a strange hybrid of greasers and dandies: high-waisted zoot suit pants worn with T-shirts or flannels. At La Galería, Yañez began to stock a new magazine, *Lowrider*, which featured tattoo art, risqué pictures of women, car ads, and pages of song dedications from cholos to their girlfriends. Yañez saw the stylized, showy lifestyle as proof Latinos had finally made a home in their new country, and was captivated by its energy. He wanted to put on an exhibit about it, and asked a photographer, Lou Dematteis, to help. For about fifteen months in 1979 and 1980, Dematteis spent his Friday and Saturday nights documenting the rituals of Latino youths. The cholos drove up and down Mission Street Saturday night, very, very slowly, to show off their rides to the chicas lining the sidewalks.[42] After cruising around a bit, the cholos would gather in a vacant lot at the south end of the neighborhood, smoke reefer, drink, and listen to oldies.

Dematteis, himself a second-generation Italian American, saw the lowriders as a creative way for Latinos to subvert their low status in the United States. Low-riding cars had once been the norm among poor Chicanos in the 1930s and '40s who could not afford to replace worn-out suspensions.[43] Decades later, the cholos appropriated the low-slung look of the cars, but worked on them continuously, rebuilding transmissions, replacing tires, and shining the chrome. Many of his photos could have been stills from the television show "Happy Days," except the faces are Latino: two teenage boys in a car, one wearing an undershirt, the other gesturing "Right on!"; three young women, heavily made-up and dressed to the nines, in their oversized 1950s-style coupe; a couple caught in an embrace in the back seat looking through the rear window at the camera, the man startled and angry. But the weekly parades of lowriders slowed down traffic, leading bus drivers and some store owners to complain. In the middle of Dematteis' project, the city began a forceful crackdown, handing out tickets to drivers who "jumped" their cars, and stopping and frisking the drivers. Dematteis documented that, too.

Some Latinos considered the crackdown to be racist, a desperate plot by a frightened establishment to quell an ascendant force. When Dematteis' exhibit opened at La Galería, Yañez invited the mayor, Dianne Feinstein. To her credit, she attended the show, pulled him aside, and told him that she didn't like the lowriders. She thought they were promoting delinquency, and that Latinos should assimilate. "Why set yourself apart?" he remembers her asking.

Eventually, under constant pressure from the police, the cruising stopped. For Yañez, looking back, that was the moment Latinos first learned they could not live however they wanted in the Mission District, and that the rest of the city was closing in.

FOUR

THE GOLD COAST AND THE SLUM, REVISITED: CHICAGO, 1966–1991

Old Town, on Chicago's Near North Side, gentrified in much the same way Brooklyn Heights did. It had splendid architecture, was close to the central business district, and had a tradition of bohemianism—a richer one even. That tradition went back to the city's radical days (think: Haymarket Riot), which were highly influenced by Central and Eastern European immigrants (some of whom were actually from Bohemia). Around the time of World War I, Jack Jones, an organizer of the International Workers of the World, established a bookstore in a former German gymnastics hall on North Clark Street. Called the Radical Bookstore, it quickly became a focal point of socialist and anarchist politics. In the front were the books; in the back, a stage where unpaid actors would put on a new play every week by a different playwright: Ibsen, Strindberg, Hauptmann, Schnitzler. Out in front, the bookstore put on street dances. In 1916, the bookstore spun these activities off into a new organization, the Dill Pickle Club, which set up shop nearby on North State Street. It became an avant-garde Atheneum, and hosted talks by *Poetry* magazine founder Harriet Monroe, architect Frank Lloyd Wright, and modern dance pioneers Ruth St. Denis and Ted Shawn.[1]

The Dill Pickle Club closed during the Great Depression, but it helped to turn the neighborhood, which at the time was considered part of "North Town," into Chicago's Greenwich Village. During World War II, a triangular section north of North Avenue and just west of Lincoln Park was designated a neighborhood defense unit, which enhanced the community's cohesiveness. As the war came to a close, residents of this triangle established a recreation center for children, offering boxing, ping pong, woodworking, singing, and football, for a membership fee of 50 cents a year. It was called the Menomenee Club for Boys and Girls. Three years later, the neighbors associated with that effort founded the Old Town Triangle Association to foster more youth activities and to prevent the neighborhood from becoming a slum. As Old Town had already become a sort of artist colony, it was natural that the association would put on an annual art fair, which also raised money for the club.[2]

Over the next two decades, Old Town continued to attract artists and free-thinkers, as well as young professionals attracted by its location and "middle cityscape" ambience. A *Chicago Tribune* writer noted in 1954: "Residents are frankly proud. First, that they have a pleasant section of the city in which to live, with some elements of suburban life, but without its time and transportation problems."[3] In the late 1950s, the neighborhood became the center of Chicago's folk and comedy scenes. Old Town became overwhelmed with tourists, and then with hippies, and then with tourists who came to look at the hippies. Wells Street became populated by head shops and pornography stores, and longtime residents thought it was all downhill from there.

Like the Brooklyn Heights Association, the Old Town Triangle Association came to an uneasy truce with urban renewal. In 1954, the group joined with other nearby community organizations to form the Lincoln Park Conservation Association, which encouraged renovators and attempted to stem the area's decline. "It became a thorn in the side of zoning boards, venal and uncaring landlords, streets and sanitation people, and anyone else who threatened to increase the blight or failed to correct it fast enough," a *Tribune* writer later remarked.[4] Starting in 1960, the city cleared six blocks of low-income housing to the south. Despite objections from the Catholic Archdiocese, the city sold the land to a team of developers that built a combination of 28-story high-rises and town homes, which collectively became known as Sandburg Village.[5] At about the same time, the city began planning for the area where Old Town Triangle, and the surrounding Lincoln Park neighborhood, was situated. The umbrella group of community organizations joined in the planning. and sought to attack blight, but also maintain diversity. (Lincoln Park was one of the largest Puerto Rican neighborhoods in the city at the time.)

The plan the city devised called for clearing 59 acres in the greater Lincoln Park neighborhood, including parts of Old Town Triangle. Some 617 structures would be demolished, a stretch of Ogden Avenue would be closed, and more than 1,400 homes and apartment buildings would be rehabilitated—rehabilitation being a more common urban renewal strategy in Chicago than in New York City. Though they vociferously opposed the high-rises, the community organizations endorsed the overall plan, and later were able to add more moderate-income housing to the mix.[6] Nonetheless, by 1969, some 2,000 households and businesses had been displaced, only 400 of which were relocated in the neighborhood. A number of groups held protests and disrupted meetings—including the Young Lords, former Latino street gang members—but it didn't do much good.[7] Due to urban renewal and private-market gentrification, the demographics of Lincoln Park changed radically. Between 1960 and 1990, the foreign-born population fell from 17.3 percent to 7.6 percent; even more surprising, the total population itself shrank more than a quarter, from 88,836 to 64,320—an indication of the disappearance of rooming houses and the emergence of smaller, wealthier families.[8]

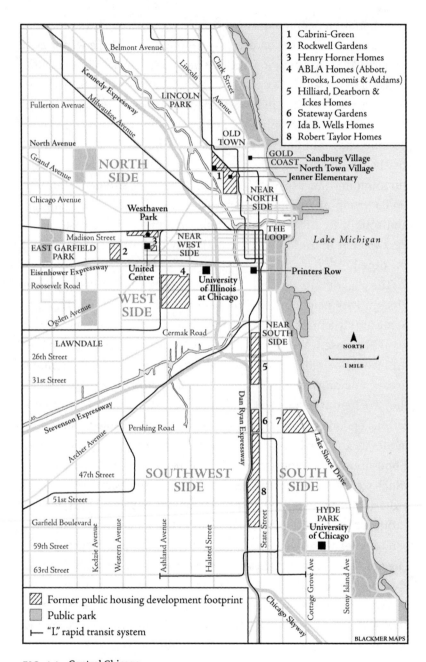

1 Cabrini-Green
2 Rockwell Gardens
3 Henry Horner Homes
4 ABLA Homes (Abbott,
  Brooks, Loomis & Addams)
5 Hilliard, Dearborn &
  Ickes Homes
6 Stateway Gardens
7 Ida B. Wells Homes
8 Robert Taylor Homes

Belmont Avenue

Lincoln

Clark Street

Kennedy Expressway

LINCOLN
PARK

Milwaukee Avenue

Fullerton Avenue

Avenue

OLD
TOWN

North Avenue

GOLD
COAST — Sandburg Village
            North Town Village
— Jenner Elementary

Grand Avenue

NORTH
SIDE

NEAR
NORTH
SIDE

Chicago Avenue

Westhaven
Park

Lake Michigan

Madison Street

NEAR
WEST
SIDE

THE
LOOP

EAST GARFIELD
PARK

2

3

Eisenhower Expressway

United
Center

4

— Printers Row

Roosevelt Road

University
of Illinois
at Chicago

WEST
SIDE

Ogden Avenue

NEAR
SOUTH
SIDE

NORTH

LAWNDALE

1 MILE

26th Street

31st Street

5

Stevenson Expressway

Dan Ryan Expressway

Archer Avenue

Pershing Road

6 7

47th Street

SOUTHWEST
SIDE

SOUTH
SIDE

Lake Shore Drive

51st Street

8

Garfield Boulevard

HYDE
PARK
University
of Chicago

59th Street

Kedzie Avenue

Western Avenue

Ashland Avenue

Halsted Street

State Street

63rd Street

Cottage Grove Ave

Stony Island Ave

Chicago Skyway

▨ Former public housing development footprint

▨ Public park

├— "L" rapid transit system

BLACKMER MAPS

FIG. 4.1. Central Chicago.

THE GOLD COAST AND THE SLUM

Chicago's Near North Side has fascinated urban sociologists since the birth of urban sociology. In *The Gold Coast and the Slum* (1929), one of the first ethnographies of the urban scene, Harvey Warren Zorbaugh wrote that Chicago's "Gold Coast"—the area between downtown and Old Town—contained one-third of the members of the city's social register. They lived, he wrote, in "imposing stone mansions, with their green lawns and wrought-iron-grilled doorways." Yet just a mile to the west lay what was then known as "Little Hell," where Italians, along with some African Americans, lived in squalor and poverty. One intersection, "Death Corner," was purported to have the highest number of murders per square foot anywhere in the world.[9] Zorbaugh recounted: "Frequently babies are found in alleyways. A nurse at Passavant Hospital on North La Salle tells of a dirty little gamin, brought in from Wells Street, whose toe had been bitten off by a rat while he slept."[10] The juxtaposition of the rich and the poor, and their simultaneous isolation from one another, he concluded, "constitute the social problem of the inner city."[11] Later in the century, as Old Town became wealthier, it would form a bridge between demographic extremes and make the gentrification of the slum next door almost inevitable.

But first, that slum would have to be destroyed—twice. In the 1940s, the Chicago Housing Authority (CHA) cleared much of Little Hell and built nearly 600 two-story row houses, christened Frances Cabrini Homes, in one of its first efforts at public housing. By stipulation, three-quarters of its original residents were white, one-quarter black. Despite the racial controls (and racial tensions), Cabrini Homes was in certain ways an ideal place to live: its low-rise character was humane and safe; its residents were heavily screened; and it was a far cry better than privately owned low-income housing of the period. But during the 1950s, money-saving requirements from the federal government led Chicago (and almost all other cities) to put their public housing residents in high-rises.[12]

By mandating such strict economy, federal and local officials were essentially preordaining the failure of public housing. Tall buildings posed three quandaries. Because playgrounds were so far away from the highest floors, architects placed long wide fenced-in balconies on each floor where children could play instead. Architect Julian Whittlesey extolled this inventive solution, calling them "sidewalks in the air," though they ended up causing as many problems as they solved.[13] Another quandary was that elevators—the circulation system of high-rises—were expensive and broke down frequently. Finally, unlike Cabrini's two-story row houses, high-rises hid vandalism and crime in vertical tubes that were opaque to anyone who wasn't already in them.

In the late 1950s and early '60s, the CHA added two sets of high-rises adjacent to the Cabrini row houses: one was called Cabrini Extension; the other, the William Green Homes. Around that time, the African American population in Chicago nearly doubled, to more than half a million, while working-class whites were moving to the city's far corners or into the suburbs. That same demographic shift occurred in public housing, though to a greater extreme. It didn't take long before Cabrini-Green became overwhelmingly black.[14]

While Cabrini-Green may have been an island amid wealth, public housing developments in other parts of the city created whole continents of black poverty. Chicago's white aldermen generally refused to allow new public housing into their districts, while black aldermen welcomed them (more votes).[15] So the CHA sited its high-rises in the Black Belt on the South Side. In 1962, it opened a two-mile-long stretch of high-rise towers along South State Street, the Robert Taylor Homes. The Chicago Urban League appealed to federal housing officials to step in; when rebuffed, it began to plot litigation. The Urban League's research director, Harold Baron, though white, felt passionately about the subject. "The Chicago Housing Authority," he noted, "has concentrated together the most vulnerable targets to be at the receiving end of American racism."[16] Baron would later liken the Taylor Homes to the all-black reservations created under South

African apartheid.[17] Because the city had not built enough public schools nearby, the Board of Education converted apartments in the complex into classrooms, with the result, he noted, "that children had to wait until third grade to get outside the reservation."[18]

WHITE KNIGHTS

Baron turned to a young lawyer, Alexander Polikoff, for help in filing a class-action lawsuit. Polikoff was an unlikely ally; he was in his thirteenth year at a prestigious downtown law firm, and while he did a fair amount of pro bono work, it had all concerned civil liberties rather than civil rights. He had very little familiarity with race issues. He had grown up on the far North Side of Chicago, where the only African Americans he knew were bus boys. "Like the furniture in the room," he later reflected, "the segregation of blacks was an accepted part of the environment to myself and many Americans."[19] Yet Polikoff had also promised himself that by the time he turned 40, he would be pursuing a more fulfilling career than commercial litigation.[20] The day he met Baron over a deep-dish pizza in Hyde Park was his thirty-ninth birthday: January 21, 1966. Polikoff was, in his own words, "a relatively young, whippersnapper of a lawyer," hungry for a challenge and a way to prove his legal intellect. And so he said yes.[21]

After their meeting, Baron began rounding up residents willing to serve as named plaintiffs in the case. One of them stuck out: Dorothy Gautreaux. A tenant leader and mother of four, she had been involved with the Urban League for a number of years and was well spoken. Not only that, but Polikoff and the four other lawyers who were working on the case liked her name, with its striking orthography and sophisticated pronunciation (gah-TROW). It was the type of name, they figured, that would get the case the attention it deserved. Dorothy Gautreaux became the lead plaintiff.[22]

Polikoff and his four co-counsels never discussed the case with any of the plaintiffs. Nor did the lawyers ask the thousands of black public housing residents for whom they were fighting just what they should be fighting for. "As the thing went forward," one of those co-counsels, Milton Shadur, remembered, "the issue arose again and again. It was always in the background." What made this situation more uncomfortable was the fact that all five lawyers were white, male, and Jewish. How could they fairly represent the interests of black public housing residents? They were not quite sure whether they could. "If there were a plebiscite, you might assume that most people in that group might opt for housing even though the aldermen in that city had placed all that housing in the ghetto of the most segregated city in the country," Shadur said later. "We resolved it, with some misgivings, by saying, 'Look, the Constitution controls. We think we are upholding the Constitution.'"[23] One member of Polikoff's team, Merrill Freed, was not convinced, and quietly dropped out of the case.

Though he did not consult with members of the class he represented, Polikoff was strongly influenced by two African American writers: W. E. B. Du Bois and sociologist Kenneth B. Clark, both of whom identified the concentration of poor members of an oppressed race as a primary evil. Du Bois likened residents of black ghettos to "entombed souls [who] are hindered in their natural movement, expression, and development." The phrase alluded to Plato's parable of a cave where men chained inside are forced to make sense of reality by watching shadows cast on the wall by things outside the cave. To Plato, the cave was a metaphor for men bereft of an education in philosophy, unable to see things for what they truly are; for Du Bois, the cave was a metaphor for ghetto life. It kept African Americans from experiencing what white people had; it kept them from even *wanting* what white people had.[24] The environment of the ghetto, he believed, affected African Americans' very psyche, keeping them subjugated, submissive, overcome with doubts of self-worth, and inclining toward anger. The cave dwellers, Du Bois continued, try to capture the attention of the world outside, but fail. They "become hysterical, screaming and hurling themselves against the glass, hardly realizing in their bewilderment that they are unheard, and that their 'antics' may seem funny to those outside."[25]

Clark's *Dark Ghetto* was a treatise that blended statistics with the author's observations from forty years living in Harlem. Clark was one of the first writers to posit that the geography of poverty inhibited African Americans' ability to climb the economic ladder. "In every one of these cities," Clark wrote, "Negroes are compelled to live in concentrated ghettoes where there must be a continuous struggle to prevent decadence from winning over the remaining islands of middle-class society."[26] Of all the cities in the country, according to Clark, Chicago was the most segregated: 65.6 percent of blacks there lived in census tracts that were 90 percent black or more. Even Washington, DC, where blacks made up a larger fraction of the city's population, was less segregated.[27]

This pattern of white people making decisions about black communities—with and without good intentions—can be found throughout urban history. It became critical when, in 1969, Polikoff won his case, but the CHA still failed to add much public housing in nonblack neighborhoods. The judge, Richard B. Austin, declared that the CHA could go ahead with building some 1,458 units that were already in the planning stages, all of which were destined for African American neighborhoods; but from then on, Austin ordered, three-quarters of future apartments the CHA built would have to go in white neighborhoods.[28] The city of Chicago, oddly enough, did not appeal the ruling; but neither did it execute the order with all deliberate speed. Through a series of legal and political maneuvers, Mayor Richard J. Daley's machine pretended to honor the order, while doing everything possible to avoid following it. Twenty-seven years later, in 1986, Polikoff told supporters, "The scattered-site part of the *Gautreaux* remedy would have to be judged as falling somewhere below zero."[29]

Polikoff was wracked with doubts about strategic decisions he made, which he recounts in his memoir, *Waiting for Gautreaux*: Should he have been less patient with the CHA's excuses, and more aggressive in pursuing remedies? Should he have negotiated rather than litigated? But in the end, he was satisfied. He had filed two lawsuits, one against the CHA, and the other against HUD. It was the second lawsuit that yielded more success, though in a roundabout way. In it, he was seeking a metropolitan-wide solution, one in which low-income blacks did not just move to other parts of the city but could relocate to the suburbs—where they would find superior schools, newer infrastructure, and an increasing number of jobs. Polikoff brought that case all the way to the US Supreme Court, where he essentially lost it. Then, oddly enough, the federal government agreed to implement his plan voluntarily. HUD and the Illinois housing finance agency agreed to give Section 8 vouchers to black families willing to move to lily-white suburbs.[30] (Under the voucher program, families pay 30 percent of their income for rent, and then the government pays the difference between that amount and the rent the landlord is asking for—within limits.) Thousands of African Americans would apply every year to make that move (partial proof that the *Gautreaux* lawyers, despite not having consulted them, *did* know what their clients wanted). Some 7,100 public housing families eventually moved out of the ghetto with these vouchers. Equally significant, these placements gave rise to some of the earliest research on the benefits of integration, and inspired HUD to enact a national *Gautreaux*-style program as well. But most important of all was how Polikoff's worldview, in subtle but important ways, set the stage for the next chapter of Chicago's public housing.

LIFE IN "THE PROJECTS"

While Polikoff fought to integrate Chicago's public housing into the rest of the city, that housing was deteriorating. The reasons were legion: vandalism, theft, poor management, lack of money. Even as early as 1958, the authority was replacing 18,000 broken light bulbs a month. In one building, thieves stole brass fire-fighting equipment, then turned on the water and flooded the nine floors beneath them. At another complex, the washing machines in the laundry room were so damaged that tenants began washing clothing in their sinks.[31] Urban historian D. Bradford Hunt ascribes the disorder to the unusually high ratio of youths to adults in CHA projects due to large families and single-parent households. Robert Taylor had 2.86 children for every grown-up, a ratio more than five times the citywide average.[32] That meant there were far too few adults to exert the subtle form of wait-until-I-tell-your-mother control that was present in more balanced communities.[33]

Then, in 1969, Congress passed a bill that capped rents in public housing at 25 percent of a renter's income. This measure was intended to help poor tenants, but it ended up isolating them. Working-class households, who were already moving out to the suburbs, had even less reason to remain in CHA buildings, for their rent increased with every salary hike.[34] As a result, only the very poor tended to remain in public housing—and since their rent was based on their income, the CHA became poor also.

By the mid-1970s, the CHA could hardly afford to fix its buildings, and even if it could, it did not have the political support to expand under the dictates of the *Gautreaux* ruling. As a result, its habitable inventory shrunk, and it did a poor job serving the city's very-low-income population. Oscar Newman, a prominent housing consultant known for his "defensible space" theory, audited the authority in 1982 and laid bare its dysfunction.[35] He blamed rampant indifference and incompetence among the authority's staff members. "In every area we examined, from finance to maintenance, from administration to outside contracting, from staffing to project management, from purchasing to accounting, the CHA was found to be operating in a state of profound confusion and disarray," Newman wrote. "No one seems to be minding the store. What's more, no one seems to genuinely care."[36]

Newman's report led to the resignation of Charles Swibel, the CHA's longtime chairman, but did little to improve the conditions under which residents lived. By this point, Mayor Richard J. Daley had died, replaced first by Michael Bilandic and then by Jane Byrne, who, midway through her term, moved into a fourth-floor apartment

FIG. 4.2. Cabrini-Green in 1998. It was probably the best-known of Chicago's public housing developments because of its proximity to the affluent Old Town and the Gold Coast neighborhoods. (Photo by D. Bradford Hunt)

at Cabrini-Green to draw attention to the complex's high crime rate. Though her relocation was widely derided as a media stunt, she explained later that she believed it was the only way to make the city bureaucracy (*her* city bureaucracy, it should be noted) care about public housing projects—a sorry statement on the indifference with which government treats its poor.[37]

Byrne's "stunt" had some beneficial effects, though her record on public housing was overall mediocre. Her successor, Harold Washington, Chicago's first African American mayor, hardly fared better. It was around this time that academics and reformers began to discuss the idea of tearing down the projects. Edward Marciniak, a former Daley aide, is often credited with being the first. In his 1986 book, *Reclaiming the Inner City,* Marciniak declared that Chicago's public housing experiment had failed; millions of dollars had been poured into education and anti-crime initiatives without making the projects any more tolerable.[38] Meanwhile, the surrounding neighborhood was rapidly gentrifying: The median income for the Near North Side grew from just above the city's median to twice that level.[39] "Inevitably," Marciniak concluded, "Cabrini-Green's high rises will be recycled or torn down, their residents relocated."[40] With uncanny astuteness, Marciniak predicted: "Sometime between now and the end of the century, City Hall will be compelled to devise a plan for the disposition of the Cabrini-Green high rises. . . . The urban revitalization slowly encircling Cabrini-Green . . . is forcing a choice."[41]

Two years later, in 1988, an advisory council set up by Mayor Washington thought the idea should be considered at the city's other public housing complexes also. "Given a long-term perspective," the council wrote, "a building-by-building assessment is required periodically to determine when CHA family high-rise developments should be phased out."[42] The advisory council suggested the city sell the land where towers are demolished and use the proceeds to build an equal amount of replacement housing elsewhere. Echoing the *Gautreaux* decision, the council said the CHA "must consider the goals of reducing social isolation and achieving an economically, racially, or ethnically integrated neighborhood."[43]

Around the same time, the Chicago Urban League had a very different perspective on the prospect of creating those mixed-income neighborhoods of which the advisory task force spoke so fondly. The League had been the group that launched the *Gautreaux* case to desegregate Chicago's public housing; now, more than twenty years later, given the mixed results of that effort, it had nearly come to accept segregation as the best the city could achieve. Yet, when Robert A. Slayton, the League's housing expert at the time, looked around, he got the sense that poor African Americans were being shut out of even those substandard housing opportunities. Slayton charged that public housing officials were warehousing units in projects that were located adjacent to gentrifying areas: not just Cabrini on the Near North Side, but also Henry Horner on the Near West Side, and Abbott Homes, near the University of Illinois campus on the Near South Side. Vacancy rates in those complexes had risen by 9 percentage points or more in a single year. Slayton wrote: "This pattern suggests that the Chicago Housing Authority may be consciously clearing out buildings in areas where land prices are rapidly rising or other pressures exist."[44]

His suggestion that the CHA was preparing for a sell-off has not been substantiated, but the high number of vacancies would make it easier when that time came. It would mean that the authority would have fewer tenants to re-house. As a result, while Slayton endorsed demolishing the high-rises, he urged the city to replace *every* unit it tore down—not just those with people in them—and to build those new units before dismantling any buildings. "Chicago has too long a history of failed promises regarding replacement housing to ignore this kind of provision," he remarked.[45]

Mayor Washington died by the time the reports by the advisory task force and the Urban League came out, advocating demolition and replacement; the mayoralty of his successor, Eugene Sawyer, was short-lived. The *next* mayor, Richard M. Daley, was Richard J.'s son. In his first two terms, Daley-fils largely ignored public housing. The head of the CHA at the time, Vincent Lane, made his name with giant, expensive police sweeps to rid the projects of gangs and crimes. At first, it seemed that the impetus to make radical changes to the city's public housing system had come and gone, and the CHA would enter another long period of dysfunction. Lane resisted the idea of tearing down high-rises, saying he would rather spend the money building new units instead.[46] It would take the death of a seven-year-old boy to change his mind.

PART TWO

RECKONING, 1972–2000

FIVE

CASSANDRAS:
1972–1981

Urban renewal in the 1950s and '60s was centralized; it was authorized by a federal law, run by a central administrative agency, and implemented by a network of city redevelopment agencies. When grassroots activists and local politicians had problems with it, they went to Congress.[1] In biological terms, urban renewal was a high-level animal, with a brain, central nervous system, and muscles and limbs. By contrast, gentrification worked like a fungus that scatters its spores, each producing more and more fungi over a widespread area. The rise of the professional class and the willingness of its members to rub shoulders with the proletariat gave birth to gentrified neighborhoods in areas as distant as San Francisco's Mint Hill and Boston's South End. This fungi-like structure presented a challenge for anyone who sought to block or reform gentrification. That person would have to fight many individual battles all over the country—or convince the federal government that it was somehow responsible.

By the 1970s, a number of activists and officials *did* warn the public of the damage gentrification would cause and tried to convince Washington, DC, to take action. But like the Greek prophetess Cassandra, they were not taken seriously. The central figure of this campaign was a young Temple University professor named Conrad Weiler, who had moved to Queen Village, a neighborhood in central Philadelphia, at the beginning of the decade. While not as fancy as Society Hill to the north, Queen Village had many of the same attributes: narrow streets, eighteenth-century brick row houses, and small windows with white trim. Many of these homes had courtyards behind them, at the rear of which was a "trinity": a three-story house with one room per floor. Queen Village was populated by Eastern European immigrants, Italian Americans, and African Americans, an estimated 70 percent of whom had been born in the area.[2] The biggest employer was the city's seaport along the Delaware River just to the east. The longshoremen had a decent quality of life: even if they did not make good wages, they could always smuggle away some of the goods that they were transferring from ship to shore—spices, coffee beans, textiles— which they would then distribute to their friends and relatives. "You would order a thousand bicycles, and by the time you got done, 750 were deliverable," explained one of Weiler's friends, David L. Auspitz, a small businessman. "The rest of them were gone somewhere, but everyone was riding around on a new bike in the neighborhood."[3] This sharing of the wealth meant the port had a greater impact on the neighborhood than just paying wages to a few hundred longshoremen. A rising tide indeed *does* lift all boats.

Though born in Philadelphia, Weiler grew up in suburban Delaware County. Still, he maintained a proclivity for city life. He had received a PhD in urban geography at Syracuse University and had spent seven months in Cologne, Germany, researching his dissertation. Cologne was a fully functioning urban center that was at once able to hold onto the urban middle class *and* preserve a twelfth-century cathedral. Weiler had read Jane Jacobs while in graduate school, and he vividly recalled how she held up Rittenhouse Square, a once-elegant section of Philadelphia's Center City, as a notable example of the "diversity of uses" (commercial and residential—what we'd call *mixeduse* today) that enlivened street life. Weiler saw neighborhoods as an important but unsung actor in civic life: they were small enough that individuals could have influence, yet large enough that the influence could matter. So Weiler joined the local neighborhood organization.[4]

Actually, he joined *both* neighborhood organizations: the Queen Village *Neighbors* Association, made up of the old-line white ethnic and black residents, and the Queen Village *Civic* Association, made up of young, newly arrived professionals (a.k.a. gentrifiers). At first, Weiler didn't realize there even were two groups and assumed, because their names were so similar, that there was just one; but then he began to notice how the Civic Association newcomers condescended to the concerns of the Neighbors Association old-timers. Though a product of the suburbs and a young professional himself, Weiler felt more at home with the old-timers. While growing up, his parents would bring him from the 'burbs back to the old neighborhood where they lived when he was born—Kensington, an Irish-German enclave in North Philly—for holidays and other celebrations. Because he had an academic's mind and a grasp of urban planning, Weiler quickly became the chairman of the Neighbors Association's zoning committee.

One of the duties of the zoning committee was to consider applications for new liquor licenses, which gave him a front-row seat for the rise of the city's young upwardly mobile professional class—and made him wary of it. Queen Village was close to downtown and therefore appealed to after-work pub crawlers. Bars meant people coming in from other neighborhoods; people from other neighborhoods meant cars; and cars meant a shortage of parking. Queen Village had narrow streets, short blocks, and relatively high population density—elements that made the neighborhood idyllic according to Jane Jacobs' theories, but a pain in the ass for the people who lived there. Parking was hard there even before the singles scene discovered it. City surveyors once found that Queen Village streets were at 137 percent parking capacity on Thursday through Sunday evenings—meaning that not only were all legal spots taken, but most illegal ones were as well.[5] Old-timers felt their neighborhood was being exploited, and at times their fears were proven right: one developer tore down two historic brick buildings and replaced them with a concrete and stucco nightclub, only to have it go bust a couple of years later. The owner let the ugly building sit fallow for years. "While from the viewpoint of economics this is just an example of a bad investment," Weiler explained, "from the neighborhood viewpoint it is a continual bad dream."[6]

Soon enough, Weiler was fielding complaints about more than just noise and parking; he began hearing about unmanageable property tax assessments. Philly's assessors, desperate to collect revenue as the city's fortunes slid, had begun aggressively reassessing neighborhoods that were getting more popular. Sometimes, homeowners were handed tax bills with a 50 percent or even 100 percent increase over the previous year.[7] For professionals climbing the career ladder and looking forward to an ever-expanding income, property taxes were an afterthought. But for elderly people who had purchased their homes decades earlier for a few thousand dollars, the taxes consumed a hefty percentage of their Social Security checks. Weiler believed the property tax increases punished those who chose not to flee to the suburbs. "Eventually," he wrote to the *Philadelphia Inquirer* in 1976, "the older lower income homeowner or the young person who grew up in the neighborhood bitterly realizes that his efforts to stay on and improve his own neighborhood have actually hurt him and helped probably only a real estate speculator."[8]

The head of the Queen Village Neighbors Association, Virginia Kelly, had become Conrad's mentor. Weiler grew close to the Kelly family, and eventually married into it (to Virginia's daughter, also named Virginia), becoming a de facto member of the urban working-class that had remained in the city, rather than one of the yuppies who had "rediscovered" it. One day, an elderly woman came running to him in tears after having received her property tax bill in the mail. Someone had moved into the row house next door and renovated it, increasing the value of all the houses around it. For a while, the woman thought that she might have to sell her house—until Weiler helped litigate a lower assessment. The fear of being priced out resonated deeply among the Kellys: the father had grown up at Third and Spruce streets in the Fifth Ward in the 1950s. When the city began to transform that district into a historic one, rechristening it "Society Hill," it bought every house within a renewal area, and sold it back only to the occupants who could prove they had the wherewithal to restore it themselves.[9] The other residents, including Virginia's husband's family, were forced to move out. The Kellys were white, but many of the displaced households from Society Hill were African American. Between 1960 and 1970, the black population in Society Hill declined by 64.2 percent, while the white population rose by 32.7 percent. (The total population of the neighborhood meanwhile shrank.)[10] Edmund Bacon, Philadelphia's director of city planning, admitted later the scheme was "cruel," but he saw no other way to revive the inner city. "It was more important to restore this area than to maintain the low-income residents," he reasoned.[11] In Weiler's view, Bacon and other Philadelphia officials made the classic mistake of so many planners of that era: they were "more interested in the look than the people," he said. "If you made something look better, you 'solved' the problem."[12]

Weiler had tenure at Temple, a flexible schedule, no children, and few other demands on his time. He got drawn deeper and deeper into the neighborhood association, eventually becoming its president. He faithfully attended the weekly meetings of the city Zoning Board of Appeals; half in jest, the board would always reserve a seat for him up front near the dais. Weiler believed that his group had to consider, and comment on, *every* application that came up in the neighborhood, including those that they favored. "We would go up to City Hall, and if we said we were for something, we were for something, and then it gave us credibility when we said we were against something," Weiler explained. "People would say, 'Oh, they are very reasonable.' That was the key."[13] The strategy required having to evaluate seventy to eighty zoning applications a year, in addition to as many as twenty or twenty-five liquor license requests. The neighborhood association never had any luck opposing the liquor licenses—those came before a state board that was impervious to community input—but Weiler attempted to use the zoning code to decelerate the pace of gentrification. To accomplish that aim, he insisted that no more than one apartment be allowed per floor in new or rehabbed buildings, thereby reducing the supply of studios and one-bedrooms.[14] (Today's pro-growth advocates, of course, might argue that by reducing the supply he was only aggravating real estate inflation.) Once, his committee successfully advocated that a former metal stamping plant be turned into a chandlery instead of into apartments. "In return," he explained a few years later, "the residents have retained a local business employing some local people, kept population and car traffic down in the area, probably kept tax assessments down as well, and helped home safety by keeping eyes on the street during the day."[15] Jane Jacobs would have been proud.

THE NATIONAL STAGE

One of the books Conrad read as a burgeoning activist was *Neighborhood Government*, a 1968 treatise that received positive attention from such notable intellectuals as Hannah Arendt and Karl Hess. The book articulated and amplified many of Weiler's own views, portraying neighborhood organizations as a crucial challenge to the centralized powers of City Hall and the White House. Its author was Milton Kotler, a Young Turk at the left-wing Institute for Policy Studies in Washington, DC.[16] Kotler had much in common with Saul Alinsky—both University of Chicago grads; both keen on church-civic collaboration; both devoted to community self-determination—but Kotler found much wrong with Alinsky's organizing approach and wanted to develop a new movement.[17] Weiler wrote a fan letter to Kotler, who invited the Temple professor to join a national organization he was creating, the Alliance for Neighborhood Government. At the inaugural meeting in 1975, representatives from forty organizations showed up, mainly from northeastern cities; a year later, 130 groups from twenty-seven cities sent delegates to Philadelphia to endorse the "Neighborhood Bill of Responsibilities and Rights."[18] Asserting a neighborhood's right to determine its own future in the mid-1970s was tricky business. At South Boston High School, dozens of white teenagers and grown-ups had pelted black students as they arrived on the first day of court-ordered desegregation in 1974. Philadelphia Mayor Frank Rizzo was channeling a similarly bigoted ideology under the guise of "local control." Weiler was well aware of the difficulty of espousing the sanctity of a community's self-determination, when that self-determination so often ended up justifying racism.

In 1976, Kotler formed another entity, the National Association of Neighborhoods, to focus on education and outreach. He took charge of that group, while putting Weiler in charge of the Alliance for Neighborhood Government, which would be responsible for lobbying Congress.[19] Mitigating gentrification became Weiler's top issue, though he preferred the term "reinvestment displacement," since he thought "gentrification" made a harsh, conflict-ridden process sound like a tweedy afternoon in the country. "Displacement," by contrast, connoted forced ouster. Well ahead of his peers, Weiler believed displacement could lead to giant migrations of whole ethnic and racial groups within a metropolitan region. After all, it was clear shortly after he had moved to Queen Village that inner cities held numerous attractions for upper middle-income whites. In 1973, the Arab oil embargo nearly quadrupled gas prices, making suburban commutes unexpectedly expensive, especially for cars getting just 15 miles to the gallon. Interest rates on mortgage loans were climbing into the double-digits, prompting buyers to look for bargains. Housing starts faltered: While in 1970, three "used" homes were sold for every new home constructed, by 1976, the ratio was six to one.[20] Two longer-term trends also came into play: the growth of the professional class—the type of person who would most likely reject suburban conformity—and the entrance of women into the workforce. (It's one thing for one parent to spend two hours commuting each day; it's much harder if both have to.) Even Carla Hills, President Gerald Ford's housing secretary, recognized the phenomenon. "Already some children of the generation that fled to the suburbs are returning to the cities," she told a gathering of mayors in 1975. "Areas that were once heading for abandonment are now being restored by families no longer willing to bear the costs and inconveniences of suburban life."[21] An Urban Land Institute survey that year found that "revitalization" efforts were underway in three-quarters of the nation's largest cities. Four years later, the organization repeated the study: "renovation" had spread to 86 percent of cities with populations of 150,000 or more.[22] Gentrification was hitting not just the coastal cities fashionable today but also places that have since been passed by, such as Hartford, Detroit, and Cleveland.[23]

The times were a-changin'. In 1963, Everett Ortner had to apply to thirteen banks before finding one to loan him money for his Park Slope brownstone. By the mid-70s, financial institutions were deeply invested in gentrification, while government officials were still largely oblivious to the trend. In Adams-Morgan, in the Northwest section of Washington, DC, developers evicted sixty-two families from three blocks of row houses in order to renovate them and re-sell at a profit. Another ninety-seven households were turned out of two large apartment buildings near Rock Creek Park.[24] Meanwhile, one African American resident, Jean Smith, applied to Perpetual Bank, the largest savings and loan in the area, for a mortgage; she was told the bank didn't lend in the District of Columbia and "hasn't done so for ten years."[25] Another black resident, Horace T. Harris, who already owned a home, applied to Perpetual for help financing a renovation. "We don't make those kinds of loans," a bank officer told him.[26] But then the Adams-Morgan Organization, a community group headed by Jean's husband, Frank, discovered that Perpetual had already awarded eighteen other mortgages in the neighborhood. Frank Smith was suspicious the bank was loaning money only to new-comers, and petitioned bank regulators to disclose the addresses of its borrowers. Although that petition failed, Frank Smith put the bank on notice that it was encouraging gentrification by white in-movers at the expense of the neighborhood's longtime black residents. Perpetual agreed to other concessions, such as writing mortgages with just 10 percent down to allow households with little savings to purchase homes in the neighborhood.[27]

Across town, the residential area around Capitol Hill was also changing rapidly. A study by a small neighborhood organization tracked twenty-nine low-income families that were forced to move from their homes in the 1970s. Only fourteen of them had been able to remain in the neighborhood; most of the others, the group reported, moved to Anacostia, a poor isolated African American neighborhood on the other side of the Potomac, which the Metro system then did not even reach.[28] The district's city council responded vigorously to complaints about displacement, proposing an anti-speculation tax and an ordinance giving tenants the right of first refusal if their building should be converted into condominiums. The council's finance committee recommended that banks foster home purchases by low- and moderate-income residents. "Lending policies that undermine the ability of the great majority of the community's residents to continue living in their community do not serve community convenience and needs," a coalition of neighborhood groups asserted.[29]

In these areas, the old vestiges of redlining were overlapping with the new realities of reinvestment. Federal policy makers were much keener to counter redlining—the practice of literally drawing lines on a map around minority neighborhoods and refusing to make loans in them. The campaign against redlining had been building for years; it encompassed both consumer advocates like Ralph Nader and community activists like Gale Cincotta, an organizer in Chicago. One of the leaders in the fight, Monsignor Geno Baroni, was even appointed an assistant secretary at HUD after President Jimmy Carter came into office. The anti-redlining forces had already scored one victory—the Home Mortgage Disclosure Act in 1975—which required banks to provide information on where they were giving out mortgages. The data showed that banks were dramatically underfunding Northeastern cities in favor of Sunbelt states. Dime and Williamsburgh, for instance—two prominent New York City savings banks—received more than 70 percent of their deposits from the five boroughs, yet awarded fewer than 20 percent of their mortgages there.[30] Those disclosures laid the groundwork for the second campaign by redlining opponents: The Community Reinvestment Act, introduced by Senator William Proxmire in early 1977. The CRA, as it came to be known, would require banks to be good citizens, and pump back money into the same communities where it took deposits.

TWO HEARINGS

Weiler was invited to testify on the CRA in March 1977. Speaking on behalf of the Alliance for Neighborhood Government, he praised Proxmire's efforts, but told the senator, "Our overall concern is not reinvestment so much as reinvestment for whom?" The bill did not require that banks give loans to longtime homeowners in poor neighborhoods, merely that banks make loans in those neighborhoods. Hence, financial institutions could fulfill the requirements by feeding gentrifiers capital while denying existing residents the chance for a renovation loan. "It has been such an exhausting and overwhelming struggle to reverse the trend of urban decline that we never dreamed that our success might generate even worse problems," Weiler noted.[31] Though he did not say it at the time, Weiler believed the bill committed the same mistake Philadelphia planners had made with Society Hill: the CRA might save the physical neighborhood but not the "community" writ large. Weiler suggested the bill be amended to require that government agencies take action if lending caused displacement, and also to make sure, through the reporting guidelines, that the federal government would be able to measure whether the act itself caused displacement. A few other speakers voiced similar concerns. "We're all for constructive change," said M. Carl Holman, the African American president of the National Urban Coalition, a now defunct civil rights organization. "But we also believe that it should be possible to stabilize, conserve, and revitalize urban neighborhoods without dispossessing or dispersing all of the residents already in place."[32]

Following the hearing, Weiler got a private meeting with Senator Proxmire and the key committee staff member on the bill, Robert Kuttner. Proxmire, though sympathetic to the threat of displacement, wasn't sure he could get the bill to the Senate floor if it was amended.[33] But Weiler persisted. After he returned to Philadelphia, he sent a thank-you note. "Though I agree that possibly the Community Reinvestment Act is not the best place to solve the problem of economic dislocation in redeveloping neighborhoods, it certainly is an opportunity to get at the problem," he wrote.[34] Weiler also lobbied Pennsylvania Senator John Heinz as well as two congressmen from Philadelphia. But it was no use. The final bill, which passed later that year, did not include any of Weiler's suggested amendments, which is one reason why it has been hard to measure the impact of the Community Reinvestment Act on gentrification.[35]

Still, Proxmire was sufficiently moved by Weiler's arguments to hold a hearing on "neighborhood diversity" in July. An iconoclast who swore off campaign contributions, Proxmire loved taking on issues that required both courage and intelligence.[36] He ran against Lyndon B. Johnson for Senate majority leader (and lost), opposed the Vietnam War early on (to no avail), and regularly chastised the Defense Department and other federal agencies for profligate spending by giving out periodic "Golden Fleece Awards." In his opening statement at the neighborhood diversity hearing, Proxmire said: "With affluent families finding cities attractive once again, our urban communities could become thriving, diverse, healthy places to live. Or they [could] turn into resegregated enclaves for the wealthy, as the poor are compressed even more tightly into ghettos."[37] The hearing lasted two days. Weiler and Holman testified once again, as did Robert Schur, the former New York City housing official who had founded "sweat equity" co-ops earlier in the decade. (See chapter 2.) After being forced out of city government, Schur had founded the Association of Neighborhood Housing Developers, an umbrella organization for twenty-eight not-for-profit housing development corporations in New York. Those development corporations were first-hand witnesses to the widespread displacement that was already occurring, especially in Brooklyn. In his written testimony, Schur stated:

> From Brooklyn Heights, the middle-class rejuvenation has spread and is still spreading in ever widening circles. It has largely engulfed the neighborhoods known as Boerum Hill and Cobble Hill to the south and Park Slope to the southeast, and is evidently encroaching into Fort Greene and Clinton Hill on the east, as well as into the next ring of communities— Prospect Heights, Crown Heights, Carroll Gardens, and Windsor Terrace.

Schur predicted that "the movement will continue its spread south and east to parts of Bushwick and ultimately into Bedford-Stuyvesant, as well as further into South Brooklyn"—which is exactly what has happened in the past forty years. He assumed that there was a direct correlation between this "middle-class rejuvenation" and displacement: "Short-term leaseholds are not renewed, statutory tenancies are terminated, and the poor, the minorities and the elderly are forced to move." Schur even asserted that private reinvestment was wreaking as much havoc on African American communities as urban renewal had two decades earlier.[38]

Officials from the Department of Housing and Urban Development also testified at the hearing. Robert Embry, the former housing commissioner for Baltimore, had become the assistant secretary for community development at HUD. At times, he seemed sympathetic to concerns about displacement. One of HUD's goals, he stated, should be to "strive to achieve economic and racial diversity in . . . central city neighborhoods by maximizing the opportunities available to those residents in danger." But he cast doubt that displacement was a widespread problem, pointing out that more middle-class people were moving from cities to suburbs than the other way around, and that little information was available about the negative effects of gentrification. Ultimately, Embry said, HUD's main priority would be to "encourage private reinvestment by upper- and middle-income home buyers in central city neighborhoods where that will benefit the city as well as that neighborhood and its residents"—but he gave no indication how HUD would make those judgments, or how it would balance a city's need for property tax revenues against the desires of residents to stay put.[39]

Privately, Embry was much more consumed by his responsibility to develop President Carter's urban policy, and specifically creating what would become the Urban Development Action Grant, an early public-private partnership program to entice commercial development in inner cities. He was also convinced, as was civil rights attorney Alex Polikoff in Chicago, that the greatest evil lay in keeping minority children in areas of concentrated poverty—and that any movement to break up that poverty by an in-flow of gentry could not be that bad.[40] (Polikoff, discussed at length in chapter 4, would end up consulting with Embry in 1991 when the Chicagoan drafted federal legislation to move public housing families to white neighborhoods.[41])

Yet, in the weeks following the hearing, Embry *did* try to get more information about displacement—namely by calling up Conrad Weiler and commissioning a report from him. Over the next five months, Weiler alternately worked from HUD's offices and from his home in Philadelphia. In December, he produced the first-ever full-length report on "reinvestment displacement" in the US, arguing that alleviating displacement was a federal responsibility. Reinvestment was not, he wrote, an entirely private process. In certain cases, urban renewal funds set the stage for modern displacement: for the Society Hill redevelopment, the feds had bought out homeowners and spent $100 million to sink Interstate 95 to preserve the view of the Delaware River.[42] "The heavy public involvement in the reinvestment process creates an additional public responsibility to see that reinvestment does not serve the interests of only one social group to the detriment of another," Weiler wrote.[43] In addition, the Federal National Mortgage Association had launched a public relations campaign—including a film titled *The Time Has Come*—to urge the middle class to move back to the city, a clear example of Washington stoking gentrification.[44] Far from seeing private sector reinvestment as a countermovement to Robert Moses–style redevelopment—the way the young marrieds had in Brooklyn Heights—Weiler believed one resulted from the other (as arguably occurred also in Chicago's Lincoln Park).

Weiler believed that local officials could hardly be trusted to rectify the situation because they were hungry for the tax dollars that gentrifiers would bring. Nor were existing federal housing programs sufficient. Section 8 vouchers were oversubscribed. Section 312 rehabilitation loans were a good idea, he wrote, but presupposed that those being pushed out were not tenants but homeowners.

To encounter Weiler's report today is like reading the work of H. G. Wells in the late twentieth century, though instead of describing the inventions of the future, Weiler foresaw the dramatic impact that the return of the middle class would have on the urban fabric. He predicted that newcomers would call for better public schools, better public libraries, free trees, cobblestone streets, and the removal of public housing from areas they had resettled. Weiler also predicted that the task of moderating gentrification would only get harder as business interests learned how to profit from the repurposing of the inner city. "The time to act is now," he wrote—in 1978.[45]

Some of the possible remedies Weiler prescribed, such as community land trusts, still appear on "solutions to displacement" lists being published forty years later as if they are new ideas.[46] Other policies he supported back then, such as rent control, have receded, a result of successful lobbying by landlord groups. Above all, Weiler wanted the federal government to begin keeping track of, anticipating, and addressing displacement before it got too late. "The more successful cities are in attracting middle-income residents, the more displacement will become the dominant issue of housing policy," he wrote. "As time goes by, corrections and reforms will become more difficult, not easier, to make."[47]

After Weiler submitted the report, he did not get a response from Embry. Weiler became curious, then nervous, about the silence and the lack of interest in publishing his work. The following spring, he asked the HUD assistant secretary whether the National Association of Neighborhoods might release the report itself. Embry said yes, "as long as you claim full responsibility for its contents."[48] At that point, Weiler and his allies launched an all-out effort to draw the public's attention to displacement. In April, the National Association of Neighborhoods distributed Weiler's report at its conference in Philadelphia. Titled "Displacement in Urban Neighborhoods: Saving the City for Whom?", the event attracted 200 housing activists from around the country. In one session, Brendan Walsh, the director of St. Ambrose Housing Center in Baltimore, compared historic preservation to a neutron bomb. "It preserves property values but doesn't do a damn thing for people."[49] Jim Wilcox, the head of a community development corporation in the Germantown section of Philadelphia, counseled, "The key to displacement is getting in before it happens." His colleague, Milton Street, described how he was able to move displaced families into abandoned buildings in North Philadelphia, renovate the properties, and in many cases get the title turned over to the new occupants. "We have reversed the legal process," Street told a workshop. "We put people in the houses and let the speculators take us to court."[50] (Street, once a hot dog vendor, later became a state assemblyman and state senator before becoming embroiled in a corruption case involving his brother, Philadelphia Mayor John Street.)

DISPLACEMENT UNDER STUDY

With some exceptions, the leaders of the anti-displacement movement (like the lawyers for the *Gautreaux* plaintiffs) were incongruously white men. That made the National Urban Coalition, the civil rights group headed by the African American Carl Holman, a key ally. On July 31, Holman's group released the results of the first national survey on displacement, based on responses from leaders in sixty-five neighborhoods across the country. The survey found that "rehabilitation" significantly reduced the number of blue-collar workers, minorities, and elderly residents in a community.[51] "People who are dislocated from improving neighborhoods do not vanish into thin air," the group stated. "Those who are poor take their poverty with them when they move. An improving neighborhood in one part of a metropolitan area will probably mean declining neighborhoods elsewhere."[52]

The survey had obvious defects, principally that it was based on the impressions of city officials and community leaders rather than hard data. But it made the point that displacement, just like gentrification, was not restricted to a few northeastern cities, and that government, in Holman's words, had failed to heed "the needs, the frustration, and anger" of the displaced.[53] Some of that frustration and anger was already surfacing in the African American media. Baltimore's black paper, *Afro American*, called gentrification "The Re-invasion." An editorial declared, "White families . . . know this city is a good place to live and know the name of the game is to move us out and themselves back in."[54] In September 1978, *Ebony* magazine quoted the head of a Philadelphia affordable housing organization who called gentrification "a conspiracy" to reverse the city's growth from white to black. "This is the story of our life since slavery," the director, Shirley Dennis, said.[55] Titled "How Whites Are Taking Back Black Neighborhoods," the article highlighted the huge demographic shift that occurred when Washington, DC's Georgetown became restored: In 1940, it was 90 percent black; by 1978, it was less than 5 percent.[56] "The descendants of former slaves and slave masters are exchanging residences in downtown Savannah," the author wrote—even though Savannah is often considered the paragon of equitable historic preservation.[57]

Yet mainstream civil rights organizations, with a largely middle-class membership, kept their distance from the displacement debate. They had made integrating the suburbs their number one priority and were therefore trying—as Alex Polikoff was doing in the Chicago suburbs with *Gautreaux* Section 8 vouchers—to move minorities to the suburbs, not keep them in the city. Weiler offered different counsel: blacks should buy property in their neighborhoods and hold onto it. Once whites moved *back* into those inner-city neighborhoods, he argued, those African American homeowners would see their wealth rise substantially. "Sometimes the suburbs just become a false symbol that all problems have been solved," he once said. "As energy becomes more expensive, it might be more wise to hold onto energy-efficient inner-city housing."[58] But Weiler also recognized how untrustworthy he must have seemed in the eyes of his intended audience. He was, after all, a white man telling blacks to stay in ghettoes.

Nonetheless, Weiler continued to raise red flags about reinvestment in any forum that would have him: at the National Urban League conference in Chicago, numerous church meetings, even one of the Back to the City Conferences that Everett Ortner had organized to *encourage* gentrification. The agitation by Weiler, Holman, and others culminated in a small provision in the 1978 Housing and Community Development Act that required HUD to study displacement and come up with some solutions for it.[59] Over the following three years, at least five federally funded studies of gentrification were produced. In one of them, statisticians from the University of Michigan concluded that about 1 percent of the nation's urban population was forced to move every year.[60] It was an incredibly rough figure, and there were multiple weaknesses in the methodology.[61] But if the estimate was anywhere near correct, and if the pace of displacement has neither increased nor decreased, then somewhere on the order of 80 million people have been forced to move in the forty years since that study was published—a number that would leave no doubt as to the toll gentrification has taken. In addition, while HUD argued that crime and blight displaced far more people than did gentrification, another analysis of American Housing Survey data found the opposite: only one-quarter of forced moves were due to disinvestment; the rest were due to reinvestment and other cost pressures.[62]

The other HUD studies included a national survey that contrasted gentrifying and non-gentrifying areas of six cities; and a full-length

examination of displacement in just one San Francisco neighborhood: Hayes Valley, near Haight-Ashbury. The Hayes Valley report
provided a rare statistical picture of urban change up close, since the
researchers were able to track down and interview forty-seven former
residents who had scattered throughout the city and its environs. The
authors estimated that 10 percent of the neighborhood's inhabitants
had been dislocated over the previous three years because of private
reinvestment—that is, their rent was raised prohibitively high or
their landlord wanted to convert their apartments to condominiums.
All of those who got displaced were renters. More than half of them
were low-income blacks and lacked any higher education. One-half
of the displaced ended up outside of Hayes Valley and its adjacent
neighborhoods. By contrast, in-movers tended not to have high incomes—a result, perhaps, of their youth and choice of professions—
but they were far more educated than those who moved out. All of
this, by the way, was going on at a time when Hayes Valley was still
overwhelmingly black and low-income, suggesting that gentrification begins before it is even visible. (Now, it is a very fashionable part
of the city.) If just over 3 percent of residents had to move each year,
almost the entire population of a neighborhood would have been
forced out and replaced by newcomers within 30 years. Other studies
around that time, undertaken by city governments, confirmed such
conclusions: in Seattle, as many as 7 percent of households were displaced in 1978 (not even counting those that moved outside the city);
in the Quaker Hill section of Wilmington, Delaware, three-fifths of
displacees were black or Hispanic.[63]

A FEDERAL ROLE

Within HUD, deep disagreement between two competing camps—
those opposed to redlining and segregation, and those opposed to
displacement—hindered the federal response to gentrification. Karen
Kollias, a policy specialist, organized a day-long intradepartmental

workshop featuring some of the top researchers on gentrification at the time.[64] HUD began work on an "early warning system" that would detect which neighborhood would gentrify next.[65] (Early warning systems are still seen as innovative approaches to displacement today.[66]) Kollias, who was previously a community organizer in Northwest Washington, recognized that local officials would not adequately address displacement on their own. "Local officials in larger cities are in great need of the tax revenues which private development and reinvestment promise," she wrote.[67] Yet HUD's policy division was not interested in adding new requirements for grant recipients—by, for example, forcing cities to use a certain percentage of their federal funds to counter displacement. Feather O'Connor Houstoun, then-head of policy development in HUD's Office of Policy Development and Research, feared that imposing anti-displacement requirements would "constipate" economic development.[68] In November 1979—nearly three years after Weiler first broached displacement during the Community Reinvestment Act hearings—HUD released its much-anticipated recommendations on the matter. The department assigned the federal government two major roles: (1) provide research and technical assistance to localities, and (2) undertake efforts to minimize displacement that is caused not just directly, but also *indirectly*, by federal spending. As part of that approach, the department funded twelve pilot programs around the country to help low- and moderate-income residents remain in gentrifying neighborhoods.

Implementing even this limited role proved challenging. That same month, Iranian students stormed the US Embassy in Tehran and took fifty-two Americans hostage. As the Iranian crisis dragged on, Carter's reelection prospects dimmed. That, in turn, hampered the administration's clout. Members of Congress who opposed Carter's agenda knew they could defeat it simply by dragging their feet. Kollias developed a small grant program for "self-help" projects (another term for "sweat equity"), but even securing that money required go-

ing back and forth with key members of Congress to get authorization, write the regulations, and get the regulations approved. "By
the time all that happened, and we were able to commit for different
groups, it was almost at the time we were shutting down," she said.[69]

Kollias maintains that President Carter's appointees would have
deepened and furthered their efforts had they been given a second
term.[70] But in November 1980, Ronald Reagan won the presidential
election in a landslide and soon began a systematic knee-capping of
HUD, reducing its staff by half. The following October, E. S. Savas,
the new assistant secretary for policy development and research, issued another report on displacement that essentially reversed HUD's
November 1979 policy paper. Savas referenced the report from the
University of Michigan researchers—the one that concluded that
1 percent of US urban households are displaced each year. He did not
contest the findings, but downplayed them, calling 1 percent "not
large" (ignoring the fact that over forty years, such a rate of displacement would have meant that 40 percent of the urban population
would have been forced to move).[71] Savas seized upon local variations
in displacement rates as proof that no single policy could apply to
all communities. Because of this, Savas wrote, "the department believes that displacement can be dealt with most effectively at the local
level."[72] As a result, the federal government did nothing.

Weiler, meanwhile, dropped out of the picture for a number of
reasons. He was exhausted from leading a successful fight to block
highway ramps from being built through Queen Village, and turned
his energy back toward Temple's political science department, becoming chairman in 1981. At the same time, the National Association
of Neighborhoods, his main vehicle for organizing and lobbying, was
taken over by a faction that was far less interested in self-government
than in the traditional liberal agenda of redistribution of resources—
that is, grants and programs. And, most significantly, Weiler was mad
at how little traction his report to HUD had received and how the
Carter administration had seemed to lose interest in neighborhoods
and cities. In fact, Weiler was so disenchanted with the president that

he went to work for Senator Edward M. Kennedy's short-lived presidential campaign in 1980.[73] Nor did Kotler or Carl Holman from the National Urban Coalition fill the vacuum left by Weiler's retreat. Interest in the issue moved from the public sphere to academic circles, where the rhetoric about it became increasingly heated, though to limited effect.

SIX

ADAPTIVE REUSE:
NEW YORK AND CHICAGO, 1975-1997

How did certain cities dig themselves out of the bad old '70s to become the economic engines—and the crucibles of gentrification—they are today? After New York City's near-death experience in 1975, the local government cleaned up its fiscal act by laying off thousands of workers and freezing the hiring of others. Then, in a three-way agreement, municipal labor unions invested their pension funds in the city's bonds, investment banks were forbidden to cash in certain notes early, and Congress agreed to loan New York up to $2.3 billion.[1] But the problems the city faced were deeper than mere mismanagement and needed bigger solutions. New York had been, from the late nineteenth century until the 1950s, a great manufacturing city, where smoke stacks lined the East River and immigrants with very little English could still find work sewing clothing or making clocks. In 1947, it had more industrial jobs than Philadelphia, Detroit, Los Angeles, and Boston combined.[2] But by the early 1970s, New York was losing industrial jobs at the rate of eighty-three per day due to mechanization and cheaper labor (and lower taxes) elsewhere.[3] In the 1960s, it began losing its white-collar employment as well. Between 1965 and 1975, one-third of the Fortune 500 companies that had their headquarters in New York moved out, merged, or otherwise disappeared.[4] At the same time that incomes and property values fell, city spending grew, leading Mayors John Lindsay and Abe Beame to borrow just to cover daily operating expenses—a cardinal accounting sin that caused investors to lose confidence in the city's credit.[5] At bottom, New York had a jobs problem, and nothing in the mid-1970s suggested the economy would recover.

Then, an amazing thing happened. The Fortune 500 companies that moved out of the city continued to employ the same accountants, lawyers, bankers, and advertising firms that they had used when they had worked near one another, just a short walk or cab ride apart.[6] The same advances in technology and transportation that sent corporate headquarters to the hinterlands—the telephone and jet airplane—made it easier for far-flung chief executives to communicate with these corporate service firms in Manhattan. The service firms, by contrast, found great advantage in being close to one another and stayed put. Economist Matthew P. Drennan noted, "Mergers and acquisitions require teams of highly specialized lawyers, investment bankers, and consultants. Media campaigns require teams of advertising executives, artists, and media specialists."[7] Multinational corporations like PepsiCo and GE were large enough to pull off moves from midtown Manhattan to Westchester County or Greenwich, Connecticut. But the firms that serviced them were smaller; if they wanted to expand, they were better off staying in Manhattan, where they would be close to a pool of talent. The same attribute that made New York City such an attractive place to locate a manufacturing business in the late nineteenth and early twentieth century—its dense concentration of population and businesses—helped save it in its darkest hour. After World War II, the Garment District became a famous exemplar of the benefits of co-location. A clothing maker could walk out his door and find the world's largest assortment of buttons and zippers and ribbons within a short walk. The sidewalks became trade routes, with workers pushing racks of clothes from one building to the next, to be finished, boxed, or shipped off to all corners of the globe. In the

1970s and '80s, corporate service firms experienced a similar type of synergy. Even if their employees wore suits and ties and did not mingle on the street in the same way that garment workers did, they could meet a potential client for breakfast, attend an event at a business association for lunch, and have drinks with a former colleague after work. A big city supplies endless opportunities for networking, and networking supplies endless opportunities.

New York's corporate service economy grew rapidly. In fact, the decline of blue-collar jobs that so devastated its manufacturing areas ended up benefiting its trade and commerce sectors. Thanks to globalization, companies in Hong Kong and Taiwan took manufacturing jobs away from American companies, but those companies parked their money in New York banks, or used New York bookkeepers to balance their ledgers.[8] In 1983, the largest accounting firms received almost half of their revenues from multinationals; major advertising firms made nearly a third of their money off of foreign accounts. Alongside this growth in the corporate support sector came an increase in the "cultural professions." Employment in educational services increased by 50 percent in New York City between 1977 and 1989, to nearly 100,000 jobs; the social service and nonprofit sectors grew even faster, from 111,000 to 178,000 jobs over the same period.[9]

In a variety of ways, the new corporate and cultural professional jobs set the stage for gentrification. For one, they tended to pay more than the blue-collar jobs they replaced, which brought greater prosperity to the city (if also greater income inequality). For another, there is some evidence that the worldview of *professionals* made them comfortable living in cities, just as that of *managers* in large corporations had steered *them* toward suburbs after World War II. In 1956, *Fortune* editor William H. Whyte called Park Forest, Illinois—a planned suburb established on the then-outskirts of the Chicago metropolitan area—"the dormitory of the new generation of organization men."[10] Whyte (who would go on to become editor to Jane Jacobs and share many of her urbanist views) explained that just as corporate middle-managers saw themselves as part of a giant machine at work, so too did they plug into the myriad of hobby clubs, affinity groups, and charity organizations that Park Forest–style suburbs offered their residents.[11] The creative worker, by contrast, did not want to belong—at least not to the mainstream dominant culture. Canadian geographer David Ley observed that the professional sought to distinguish him or herself from the masses by choosing a unique, distinctive, iconoclastic locale. To gentrifiers, Ley wrote, "the suburbs are too standardized, too homogenous, too bland, too conformist, too hierarchical, too conservative, too patriarchal, too straight."[12] In communities that had begun to gentrify in the 1970s, Ley found that professionals in education, the social sciences, and medicine were overrepresented by 29 to 48 percent; managers were also overrepresented, but only by 14 percent.[13]

But there was no person more important to the origins of gentrification than the artist, even if he or she also often became its victim; the artist has generally led educators, nonprofit workers, lawyers, accountants, and other professionals into neighborhoods occupied by working- or even under-class residents. And it so happened that in New York City in the 1970s, the number of writers, artists, and entertainers boomed, rising by 32 percent—faster even than the number of white collar professionals.[14] The city was an attractive place for artists. In the 1930s and '40s, Gilded Age heirs such as Solomon R. Guggenheim (the founder of the Guggenheim Museum), his niece Peggy Guggenheim (a collector and gallery owner), and Abby Aldrich Rockefeller (cofounder of the Museum of Modern Art) had laid out the welcome mat through their extensive patronage of contemporary artists. Then, during and after World War II, Manhattan wrested the title of world art capital from Paris. In 1955, there were 123 art galleries located in New York; by 1965, there were 246.[15] By 1983, the arts (including music, theater, and dance) were considered a $5.6 billion industry in the metropolitan area.[16]

David Ley's explanation of gentrification, by the way, is considered a "consumption model." It holds that the consumers of real estate—artists, nonprofit workers, and professionals—drove the demand for inner city space, while city officials and developers responded by making those areas habitable and palatable. Yet in the late 1970s and throughout the 1980s, a faction of urban theorists took a different approach, arguing that it was the city officials and developers—that is, *producers* of real estate—who were driving gentrification. They posited that "global capital" (presumably banks and investors from abroad) wanted to squeeze profit from urban areas that had been intentionally neglected for decades. In fact, the "disinvestment" that occurred in cities from the 1930s through the 1960s was the first phase of this plan, and helped drive property values in the city down to create better investment opportunities later on. The most famous of these theorists, Neil Smith, popularized the notion of a "rent gap": the difference between the value of a property as it is, versus its potential value. "Gentrification occurs," Smith wrote in 1995, "when the gap is sufficiently wide that developers can purchase structures cheaply, can pay the builder's costs and profit for rehabilitation, can pay interest on mortgage and construction loans, and can then sell the end product for a sale price that leaves a satisfactory return for his investors."[17] (Put another way, developers buy low and sell high.)

Smith was not the only academic to propose a production-side theory of gentrification, but he was probably the most vehement about it. Gentrification, he wrote, constituted "violence," a "class conquest" that real estate boosters tried to camouflage with the rhetoric of "pioneers" valiantly taming "the urban frontier."[18] He suggested—though did not explicitly state—that there was some sort of conspiracy among investors, developers, and government officials to, first, engage in the "devalorization of capital" in the mid-twentieth century, and then reinvest in inner cities four or five decades later. Smith's theory has several shortcomings. For one, there was no evidence of such collaboration. For another, he failed to distinguish between unscrupulous behavior and smart investments. At one point, Smith described how real estate sharks bought Lower East Side buildings cheaply in the 1970s, only to flip them a few years later at a profit. But does that mean the buyer was unethical, or that the landlord who sold him the property simply did not have enough confidence that New York would come back?[19]

Smith allows that gentrification proceeded "as often as not" by consumer preferences as by real estate interests—but asserts those consumers' desires were shaped by marketing.[20] In his book, *The New Urban Frontier*, he reproduced one newspaper ad for a luxury condo building in Manhattan on West 42nd Street. "The Armory Celebrates the Taming of the Wild Wild West," it reads.[21] While the ad demonstrates that the developer tried to present gentrification as a frontier-style adventure, it's not clear whether that message resonated among consumers. Perhaps, the people who moved into the building simply wanted to live close to their Midtown offices and, given the changing Zeitgeist, felt more comfortable living in the city than the Organization Man had. Certainly, newspapers enabled gentrification through their many stories about "up-and-coming" neighborhoods, but it is hard to imagine that such buzz *governed* individuals' decisions. In fact, some evidence suggests gentrifiers are more likely to move to "emerging" neighborhoods due to word of mouth rather than the mass media.[22] Nonetheless, it is fair to say that scholarship around this time reflected more cynicism toward gentrification than in the more innocent days of Everett Ortner and Martin Schneider, and it fueled awareness that the real estate industry could help shape the desire for city living, even if it could not create it.

RAGS TO RICHES

An excellent example of the interplay between the forces of consumption and production is New York's SoHo. (The name was both an acronym of *south of Houston* Street and a play on London's one-time red-light district, Soho.) A commercial slum known in the mid-twentieth century as "Hell's Hundred Acres" because of the frequent fires that broke out in its rag and bulk paper bins, the area between Canal and Houston streets became successively attractive to artists, gallerists, tourists, retailers, and, eventually, movie stars and fashion models in the decades since. The architecture consisted of three- to six-story cast-iron warehouse buildings, which were ideal for New York's industrial economy in the nineteenth century. Their flexibility was key: the high-ceilinged spaces could serve as storage areas, or as factory floors for light manufacturing operations. Heavy machinery could be moved in or out as one garment shop left and a printing firm replaced it. The lofts were also flexible enough to serve as live-in studios where artists could unfurl giant canvasses on which to practice the large-scale abstract expressionism that came into vogue in the 1960s. As this transformation occurred, the industrial economy was still viable: some 650 firms, employing 12,700 workers, made clothing and toys; recycled textiles and paper; and printed books and advertising material.[23] But some of the features that had earlier made the cast-iron buildings attractive in the past—a steam power source in the basement and an elevator to move goods from one floor to another—were obsolete. The metropolitan electric grid obviated the need for steam power and electric fork lifts made it easy to navigate large, single-story warehouses in more distant neighborhoods or suburbs. In 1962, about 15 percent of the floor space in the district was vacant—not a significant amount, but enough to lead landlords to rent to anyone, including artists.[24]

The artists both worked and lived in these lofts, pioneering a new style of residential living that would become widely imitated elsewhere in New York and, eventually, across the country: open floor plans with few distinct rooms, high ceilings, and a bare brick wall or two to remind the occupants of the building's "authentic" industrial past. With their own version of "sweat equity," these artist-pioneers cleared away trash, sanded floors, and installed sheet rock, learning the skills they needed from friends and neighbors who were there before them.[25] Their verve and craftsmanship posed a conundrum for city officials, for while the artists gave loft buildings a second life, the area had not been zoned for residential use, nor had the buildings been constructed to meet residential fire codes. Originally, zoning was intended to segregate factories, which emitted pollution and caused other nuisances, from residences; but zoning also came to protect industrial employers from being outbid by residential developers and the resultant job losses.

Eventually, the Koch administration legalized loft living in large parts of Manhattan, including SoHo—part of the mayor's canny embrace of "urban pioneers." While the intent was to give artists legal rights in their fights against landlords, it is impossible to target laws to one constituency as opposed to another, and soon, even established real estate investors like Harry Macklowe bought buildings in the area.[26] (Sandy Hornick, a longtime city planning official, speculated one reason for the appeal was that converting a loft building into apartments cost less than building from scratch.[27]) Lofts became luxury items, in part because of the way upper-middle-income professionals idealized the counter culture. (More on this in chapter 10.)

One of the investors who saw opportunity in industrial warehouses was David C. Walentas, a developer who grew up in upstate Rochester. His father was paralyzed when David was five, after which his mother sent him off to work as a farm hand for seven years. Even decades later, Walentas complained bitterly about the experience—which he said entailed "shoveling shit and milking cows, going to school, coming home, shoveling shit, and milking cows"—but he also credited it with making him determined to do better. He earned a ROTC scholarship to the University of Virginia. After a brief detour to Europe and Morocco, Walentas returned to Charlottesville, earned an MBA, and then landed a job at the consulting firm Peat Marwick in New York.[28]

Walentas was attracted to the urban landscape at a young age, and once even considered a career in architecture.[29] As a single man in New York, he spent his evenings wandering around the city's rougher edges, looking for a good investment. He didn't have any cash, however, so it wasn't until he befriended Jeff Byers—the grandson of William R. Grace, a wealthy businessman and one-time mayor—that he was able to buy property.[30] Together with the friend who introduced them, Walentas and Byers invested in a rent-controlled building in

Manhattan Valley, a then-marginal neighborhood south of Columbia University and north of the Upper West Side.[31] They named their
company Two Trees after Byers' grandmother's estate in South Carolina. Byers lined up the capital, while Walentas managed the buildings. In 1971, the company bought a building in the heart of SoHo,
at Broome and Wooster streets.[32] Byers himself was an art collector,
a trustee of the Museum of Modern Art, and the cofounder of the
Bykert Gallery. (Artist Chuck Close once said Bykert was known for
showing "the purist pure, nonobjective kinds of work."[33]) Later, Byers
would come to Walentas begging for money, but Walentas thought his
partner was profligate and refused to give him any. On December 31,
1977, Byers fell to his death from his fourteenth floor apartment on
the Upper East Side, leaving behind a note complaining about business problems. Afterwards, Walentas bought out his late partner's
stake in Two Trees for $1.8 million.[34]

As a young landlord, Walentas told his brokers to make all female
applicants come by his Park Avenue apartment for a personal interview. One of them, Jane Zimmerman, became his wife. She was the art
director at the Estée Lauder company Clinique.[35] It was through her
that he met Ronald and Leonard Lauder; the two brothers invested in
his purchase of a twelve-story loft building in NoHo, a small warehouse district north of Houston Street that was absorbing some of the
spillover demand from SoHo.[36] Walentas asked some young artist-
types hanging around that building where the next SoHo would be.
One replied, "Dumbo"—an acronym for "Down Under the Manhattan Bridge Overpass."[37] Dumbo was across the East River in Brooklyn, on a flood plain to the north of Brooklyn Heights. It was the first
time Walentas had heard of the neighborhood. Shortly afterwards,
Walentas drove his red Mercedes-Benz convertible over to have lunch
at the River Café, an isolated high-brow outpost on the far side of the
Brooklyn Bridge, not far from Brooklyn Heights. Afterwards, he ram-
bled along Dumbo's cobblestone streets.[38] The views were far better
than any in a Manhattan loft, in part because they were *of* Manhattan, in part because both the Manhattan and Brooklyn bridges ran

high above the neighborhood, opening up in a way that seemed to reveal the whole world. The buildings were also much larger than in SoHo—as many as sixteen stories high, and a full block wide—and much cheaper. The 43-year-old Walentas decided this was going to be his big bet. In 1981, Two Trees, with help from the Lauders, bought eleven buildings for $12 million.[39]

Until the nineteenth century, most of Dumbo had been under water; Front Street had marked the landward side of the neighborhood, and Water Street, New Dock Street, Main Street, and Plymouth Street were just marsh.[40] Then, Robert Fulton chose it as the place to dock the ferries that he shuttled to and from Manhattan—as many as 1,200 vessels made the crossing each day—inspiring the need for buildings in which merchants could store wares. Hence, the area got the name "Fulton Ferry."[41] Decades later, box manufacturer Robert Gair erected some of the earliest reinforced concrete structures a little to the north; he christened his collection of edifices "Gairville." Though the box company dissolved, manufacturing remained a stronghold in the neighborhood, in part because it offered easy truck access to Manhattan and the Brooklyn-Queens Expressway, which could bring goods out to Long Island, or up through Queens and the Bronx to the rest of the continent. But as the buildings became tenanted by multiple manufacturers instead of just one owner-occupant, fights would break out over who got to use the elevator and when, making the upper floors much less desirable for industrial use.[42]

It was on the high floors of Dumbo's lofts where artists and other like-minded adventurers began to roost, a similar pattern to what happened in SoHo.[43] One of them, Crane Davis, had looked for an apartment in Fulton Ferry when he decided to leave his job as a public television producer and go freelance. He lived on the Upper West Side and knew he'd need a cheaper place; he saw an ad in the *Village Voice* for a 2,000-square-foot loft space next to the Manhattan Bridge for $500 a month. When Crane showed up, the landlord, who owned a burlap bag factory that occupied four floors in the same warehouse, put Keith Jarrett's *The Köln Concert* on the phonograph, lit up a joint, and passed it to Davis. The place, the young television producer decided, was perfect.[44]

In 1976 when Crane moved in, between 150 and 200 people lived between the Brooklyn Bridge and the decommissioned Navy Yard, which formed the northern boundary of what was then called Fulton Ferry. They were artists, writers, hangers-on, and even a renegade banker. It was a tight group; even though it was an active and bustling manufacturing area during the week, there weren't many living souls to be found between 5 p.m. Friday and 9 a.m. Monday. On weekend evenings, the residents would convene for giant loft parties and make all the noise they wanted.

Even before Walentas arrived, Crane got the sense that real estate developers were hoping to make Fulton Ferry the next SoHo. He asked his brother Monte, who also lived there, what they should do. Monte responded, "You stand in the bushes and make noises like the crowd."[45] To that end, the small group of committed loft dwellers began to organize in any way they could, creating new organizations, each with its own stationery, to make it seem like there were far more people resisting development than there really were. Monte formed Brooklyn Loft Tenants to make sure Manhattan's loft law would extend across the East River. Another friend organized the manufacturers.

When a couple of lawyers tried to create a local development corporation to "improve" the neighborhood, Crane and his friends planned a counter-offensive. They secretly went door-to-door, up and down the staircases in all the warehouses in the area and asked each tenant or business owner to sign proxy forms handing over their right to cast votes for the corporation's board of directors. The night before the deadline for the corporation election, Crane and his friends showed up at the home of one of the lawyers. They endured a long lecture about voter participation drives that the lawyer had led in the South during the civil rights movement. Then, the lawyer proudly produced forty proxy forms to show how much work he had done; he smugly declared he would be representing the area. Crane and his friends then pulled out their *two hundred* proxies and declared that *they* would in fact be representing the area. These artist-pranksters had hijacked the development corporation from the very men who had tried to found it! That's how Crane Davis, freelance journalist, became president of the "Fulton Ferry Local Development Corporation."[46]

Crane and his friends had little interest in attracting investment to the area the way most local development corporations did; in fact, they tried to do the opposite, because they wanted to keep their digs cheap and available. A little while later, they decided to come up with a new name for the neighborhood. Davis later wrote:

> After much sitting around and drinking beer, to a point where none of us could remember who had suggested what, we came up with two alternatives:
>
> DUMBO: Down Under the Manhattan Bridge Overpass
>
> DANYA: District Around the Navy Yard Annex
>
> The choice was presented to the community at a huge loft party and the results weren't even close. It was DUMBO by a landslide. Everyone agreed that it had just the right kind of Dadaist anti-marketing positioning to protect our turf from developers: who, after all, would spend a million dollars for a loft in a place called DUMBO?[47]

They were wrong, of course. The zany name would just add to the area's appeal. But Davis et al. did buy themselves some time. Walentas at first did not take to the name "Dumbo." Instead he used the name "Fulton Landing" to refer to a massive development proposal that would convert some of his buildings to residential, and some publicly owned property into restaurants, a farmer's market, entertainment complex, hotel, and marina.[48] Davis did everything he could to derail the project. A Vietnam veteran, he was suspicious of the narratives that can build up around momentous events. The idea that manufacturing was "dead" in Dumbo—which developers insisted was true— did not sit right with what he saw every weekday morning, as hundreds of blue-collar workers, most of them minorities, got off the subway and arrived at their jobs.

Davis convinced the City Planning Commission to undertake a survey of industrial businesses in Dumbo and volunteered to do the research. His team found that more than 5,000 workers were employed in the neighborhood at 150 firms, and that absent the space that Walentas was holding off the market, the vacancy rate was 1.74 percent.[49] Davis and his friends collaborated with the garment unions who represented many of the workers and organized a "Save the Jobs" rally in October 1982, right outside the main Gairville building, a sixteen-story monolith with a giant four-faced clock on top. Some 2,000 workers attended, as did gubernatorial candidate Mario Cuomo, who had staked his campaign on preserving manufacturing jobs. In turn, they got state assembly members, city Comptroller Harrison J. Goldin, and then finally Mayor Ed Koch on their side. Walentas would later contend that Koch's deputy mayor, Kenneth Lipper, opposed the Fulton Landing proposal out of spite because he had been close to Fred Byer and blamed Walentas for his friend's suicide.[50] Even the nation's biggest city is a small town sometimes.

Because of resistance to his proposal, Walentas lost the designation as the developer of the publicly owned property along the water in February 1984. He called it the beginning of his "Stalingrad period," during which he had to subsist on industrial-level rents, which were far lower than what he would have gotten from office or residential. In reality, though, the $2 a square foot he received from manufacturers each year should have provided a sufficient return on his investment, which had been $6 a square foot. But he had no interest in renting to manufacturing tenants. The local development corporation found that in the prior three years, twelve firms with 293 employees reported either being forced to leave or not being offered renewals.[51] Davis and his team kept close track of tenancies and determined Walentas shifted around the manufacturing companies so that none of them occupied spaces with views of the East River. Crane presented these findings to the local community board and pretended to be puzzled as to why industrial companies would be intentionally avoiding the river views. "We have to understand why manufacturers hate the river so much," he exclaimed in mock seriousness.[52] In reality, Crane suspected that Walentas was intentionally keeping units with good views vacant so as to make it easier, if a rezoning succeeded, to convert them into apartments. On the other hand, there was no law against keeping space vacant; in real-estate parlance, that practice is known as "warehousing." Walentas was warehousing warehouses.[53]

In reality, Walentas' "Stalingrad period" lasted less than a year. In December 1984, Mario Cuomo, after winning the gubernatorial election, agreed to move more than 1,000 state employees from the World Trade Center to the clocktower building and pay $10 million a year in rent; in return, Walentas would consolidate his remaining manufacturing tenants in his other buildings and keep them on for up to ten years.[54] In 1997, after the state's ten-year-lease expired, Mayor Rudolph Giuliani and the city council rezoned Dumbo from primarily industrial to primarily residential and commercial. Within a year, Two Trees had converted the clocktower building at 1 Main Street into condominiums. On the ground, Walentas and his son Jed, who had joined the company after an internship with developer Donald Trump, worked feverishly to make the notoriously quiet area lively. They owned such a large portion of Dumbo—approximately 40 percent of the five million square feet of built space—that they would be able to define the character of the entire neighborhood.[55] Unlike the Vegas-style extravaganza the elder Walentas had planned for the area in the early 1980s, this time they followed Jane Jacobs' principles.

According to those principles, articulated in *The Death and Life of Great American Cities*, what makes a neighborhood pleasant and safe is street life; a city creates street life by mixing uses. In three of the most celebrated pages of urbanist literature, Jacobs described the scene outside her home in the West Village as an intricate sidewalk ballet that played out from early morning until late at night. Teenagers dropped candy wrappers on their way to school; shopkeepers opened up their businesses; well-dressed men and women walked to work; longshoremen gathered at the White Horse Tavern; and mothers pushed their baby carriages.[56] One reason it worked was that the diversity of uses made sure that there were "eyes on the street" at almost any hour of the day to discourage people from acting out of line. Jacobs believed that porous busy villages, rather than the fortresses of urban renewal, suited modern civilization best.

David Walentas meticulously planned his neighborhood so as to replicate the conditions that appeared to arise organically in Jane Jacobs' West Village. Because Dumbo was so desolate on weekends, Walentas sought ways to bring more of the city in. Walentas gave away ground floor retail space for free or little rent to grocery stores, restaurants, a hardware store, and art galleries, in order to make Dumbo an attractive place for residents as well as a destination for visitors.[57] Before he could legally convert those warehouses to residences, he carved them into artist studios and rented them out, conscious, having been a landlord in NoHo, that artists confer cachet upon a neighborhood. Along the same lines, much later, Walentas' wife Jane bought and restored a wooden carousel, sanding the paint off the horses herself, then placed it in a giant acrylic box designed by Jean Nouvel. The carousel acted as a magnet to draw in more visitors and broke up the monotony of green. (Like Jane Jacobs, David Walentas was wary of large parks; among other reasons, they become empty wastelands in winter.)[58]

As the neighborhood's streets grew livelier, Walentas' buildings gained value. He picked through his holdings and strategically decided which building to convert when, biding his time, making sure he had financing lined up and that demand was sufficient. In order to convert the buildings, however, he had to kick the artists out. Like the manufacturing companies before them, they were renters, and did not have any legal right to expect that their leases would be renewed. Nonetheless, some artists felt used, as if they were being cast aside after having lent the neighborhood their cachet. (Unlike in Soho, very few artists had arrived in Dumbo pre-1981, the year when the Loft Law

FIG. 6.1. Washington Street in Dumbo in 2018. The Manhattan Bridge is in the background. Once the home of a cardboard box factory, Dumbo is now one of the most expensive neighborhoods in New York City. (Photo by Matthew L. Schuerman)

went into effect; only those buildings with three or more units occupied by artists in that year were protected. When necessary, Walentas fought them in court or bought them out.)[59] The sculptor Tom Otterness, known for his miniature bronze cartoon sculptures, saw rent on his studio triple in 2002, and left for Gowanus, another industrial part of Brooklyn. "I wanted to be treated better after fifteen years there," he told the *New York Times*.[60] Walentas was, however, not a sentimental person; he once yelled profanity during a public meeting at a woman who opposed one of his plans and he proudly considered himself a misanthrope. "People get displaced," he explained once. "We displaced a lot of Indians when we changed Manhattan island and it evolved to what it is today. There's a public good that evolves out of short-term disruption."[61]

The 1997 rezoning, and Walentas' careful curation of the neighborhood he dominated, made him a rich man. The industrial properties he had bought for $6 a square foot in 1981 became worth 100 times that amount as luxury residences. The J-51 tax incentive, revived in 1975 during a desperate attempt to goose the housing market, helped, too; Walentas vigorously employed it while converting his warehouses to residential lofts. Over the past twenty years, his residential properties have received at least $14,488,072 in tax abatements and exemptions.[62] In 2014, Walentas made it onto *Forbes'* list of the 400 wealthiest Americans; his net worth is now estimated to be in excess of $2 billion.

MANY SOHO'S

Dumbo was just one of numerous SoHo spinoffs around the country. In the late 1970s—even before Walentas crossed the East River in his red convertible—the award-winning architect Harry Weese began to renovate printing buildings just south of Chicago's Loop to create what he called "SoHo West." He said once: "I'd like to change the rules of lofts making it a constitutional guarantee a person can live and work where he wants."[63] He essentially did, convincing the city to relax zoning codes to allow people to sleep as high as 120 feet off the ground in loft buildings. (That was as high as a fire truck ladder could reach.)[64]

A once vibrant center of Chicago's printing trade, the area emptied out as businesses migrated to the suburbs and the train passengers who once came into neighboring Dearborn Station took to airplanes or were diverted to other stations after it closed. The Pacific Garden Mission and nearby transient hotels along South State Street attracted down-on-their-luck single men, hobos, alcoholics, and the mentally ill, some of whom ended up squatting in the printing houses after the presses were cleared out. (A few of their bodies were found during renovations.) Weese and his fellow developers christened the area "Printers Row," in the fast-emerging tradition of naming redeveloped neighborhoods after their past use. Unlike Dumbo, there is little indication that any artists had been working and/or living in the South Loop until the elegant tall-ceilinged buildings had been properly converted. In general, though, Weese and his peers redeveloped the area with more serendipity than Walentas did Dumbo. For instance, one of Printers Row's inaugural events was an exhibition in a loft of Judy Chicago's installation "The Dinner Party" in 1981. This work was one of the iconic feminist art pieces of that era—a triangular dining table with thirty-nine place settings for historically famous women. But while Walentas might have gone out of his way to cultivate Ms. Chicago's friendship and give her free space to exhibit the work in one of his buildings (with the expectation the investment would pay off in free publicity), the work ended up in Printers Row more or less by chance—because the artist's backers couldn't find anywhere else to host it.[65]

Weese, a respected architect whose more dubious accomplishments included the "play corridors" in CHA housing, also converted buildings in another of Chicago's warehouse districts (rechristened River North), once taking on a former cold storage building that had miles of steel refrigerant pipes and insulation made of horsehair, cork, and Styrofoam, over a foot thick.[66] Developers in Atlanta,

St. Louis, Pittsburgh, Omaha, San Francisco, etc., followed suit with similar projects—aided by the historic preservation tax credits awarded to conversions. (A prominent booster of Printers Row, Cerf Hill, went so far as to say that the Tax Reform Act had made that neighborhood's redevelopment "viable.")[67] Whereas brownstoning appealed to newcomers with charm and history, loft living evoked glamour and the sense of reinvention. "Lofts are romantic places," writer Felicia Eisenberg Molnar observed in 1999. "Banks of windows and towering ceilings speak of unusual heights, intense luminosity, open spaces, and personal freedom in cramped city environments. A loft offers a tabula rasa where an urban dweller can cast a wide net in seemingly endless space."[68] Which is probably how Crane Davis felt when his landlord put on Keith Jarrett and passed him a joint.

OLD VS. NEW URBANISM

These redeveloped industrial areas, even when undertaken by someone with the meticulous (and manipulative) intentionality of David Walentas, strike a dramatic contrast to the way suburbs had been laid out following World War II. In preplanned settlements such as Park Forest, Illinois, one part of a town was residential, another part commercial, and other areas were devoted to schools, a public library, or an office park. In the suburbs, residents couldn't walk from one place to another; there were no delis on street corners; the baker's family didn't live above the bakery. In fact, there were no homes above stores, only HVAC equipment.

Dumbo and its ilk differed as well from the products of New Urbanism, a school of planning that caught on in the 1980s and 1990s, and which ostensibly rejected suburbia by promoting street grids, front porches, sidewalks, Main Streets, and other features intended to increase the community's walkability and neighborly feel. But in reality, it didn't: most New Urbanist communities were subdivisions, built on farm land on the outskirts of metropolitan regions. "An avalanche of magazine and newspaper articles, books, and tele-

vision shows preach that New Urbanism will save us from our suburban sins," writer Alex Marshall noted. "But these new subdivisions
cannot cure the ills of sprawl. They are sprawl." Marshall observed
that even the retail areas were not doing well, for though they were
close enough for residents to reach on foot, people simply preferred
to drive to a mall or big box store.[69]

While redeveloped industrial areas were sometimes derided as
"Disneylands," one New Urbanist community—Celebration, Florida—
actually was *created* by Disney Corp. Celebration, like New Urbanism
generally, took as its model not the big city, but the small town. In
contrast, Dumbo, Printers Row, and similar areas had an urban heritage; they were examples of adaptive reuse. That meant that residents
could tap into the existing subway and bus network rather than drive
to work. In addition, Walentas and Weese made some smart choices:
they converted some of their properties into office space as well as
residential. The offices fed retailers customers throughout the work-
day, and kept the areas from becoming bedroom communities. But
perhaps their biggest advantage over New Urbanist developments
was density: The 8- and 10- and 12-story warehouses housed far more
people and businesses than could the 2- to 3-story zoning of the suburbs. Dumbo residents did not even need to walk to the center of town
to pick up a newspaper; they could often just go downstairs.

SPOILS OF VICTORY

One would think that all of this gentrification would be good for the
tax base by increasing the values of properties.[70] But during this era,
two other developments limited such benefits in San Francisco and
New York City. In 1978, California voters approved Proposition 13,
by a 2-to-1 margin, in part because inflation was increasing the value
of homes, and elderly Californians in particular were having a hard
time paying the rising property tax bills that resulted. This measure
prohibited localities from increasing the taxable assessment of a given
property by more than 2 percent a year. Yet capping assessments not

only choked off revenue needed for public schools and other services, it also limited the ability of municipalities to redistribute wealth. If a neighborhood rose in value, the public would benefit from that appreciation only if a property changed hands, at which point its assessment would be adjusted to market value, leading to commensurately higher tax revenue. Commercial properties were able to avoid even that adjustment if the new owner took an ownership stake of less than 49 percent. (In the 1980s, San Francisco imposed an "impact fee" on new buildings in part to compensate for the loss of revenue from Proposition 13, but at times, the city failed to collect it.)[71]

In 1981, the New York state legislature imposed its own, lesser known, tax increase cap of 6 percent a year on one-, two-, and three-family homes in the five boroughs. In 2006, the city's nonpartisan Independent Budget Office determined that over the preceding twenty-four years, the market value of New York City's real estate had grown by 559.7 percent. Yet the "net levy"—the amount the city collected from property taxes—rose only 239.7 percent, or less than half of what it could have been without tax caps, breaks, abatements, and exemptions.[72] In Park Slope and Carroll Gardens, Brooklyn, the tax bills on 98 percent of the one-, two-, and three-family properties were "capped"—meaning their owners did not have to pay the full levy—because their market values had risen faster than 6 percent annually.[73] In other words, if you live in a gentrifying neighborhood, there's a good chance you pay a lower effective property tax rate than you would if you owned a similar house in a non-gentrifying neighborhood. During the 2017 municipal election campaign, Republican mayoral candidate Nicole Malliotakis pointed out that she paid more in property taxes for her Staten Island home, valued at $549,000, than did Mayor Bill de Blasio for his Park Slope row house, valued at $2 million—all because of protections for owners of rapidly appreciating properties put into place decades earlier.[74]

Given this inane system, it is a wonder that New York City's treasury has done as well as it has since the fiscal crisis of the 1970s. The reason once again proves that gentrification is more a symptom than a cause. New York City, like just a handful of other localities in the country, taxes personal income; between 1980 and 2015, revenues from that tax rose nearly twelve-fold, while revenues from property taxes rose just six-fold. As a result, the city's income tax has been paying for a larger and larger share of the city's expenses.[75] It's the revitalized economy—as expressed in the growth in the number of jobs and the incomes those jobs are paying—that has been propelling the city's fiscal health, rather than the appreciation of real estate values.

It is even possible to argue that New York City's property tax cap encourages gentrification. Residential property tax rates in the city are far lower than in the suburbs, giving people capable of owning property yet another reason to buy in the five boroughs rather than outside of them.[76] But regardless of that argument, the 6 percent cap shortchanges the city from collecting all the revenue it should be entitled to receive—revenue that could go toward building affordable housing that would mitigate the displacement that gentrification causes. Instead, in places where property tax limits exist, private homeowners benefit the most from the appreciation in home prices: they can sell their property at a substantial profit and share very little of that, if any, with the government.[77]

SEVEN

SUPPLY AND DEMAND: SAN FRANCISCO, 1981–2000

Toward the end of the twentieth century, activists in San Francisco generally considered the city's main housing problem not that it had too little supply, but rather that it had too much demand. The origins of that belief date back to 1975, when a number of community groups—not just housing organizations—held a "People's Congress."[1] The People's Congress platform demanded that the city's housing policy should be to "preserve and expand housing opportunities for people who presently live in the city."[2] That goal—to protect those who currently live in the city—has driven San Francisco's left-wing politics ever since.

In New York and Chicago, an anti-growth *neighborhood preservation movement*, consisting of neighborhood associations and historic preservationists, evolved separately from an *affordable housing movement*, consisting of nonprofit community development corporations. At times, these two groups fight: one way to create affordable housing, after all, is to go tall and wide. Yet in San Francisco, the two movements have been unusually closely aligned in large part due to the leadership of Calvin Welch, a pony-tailed hippie who founded the Coalition of Community Housing Organizations out of his Haight-

Ashbury row house. Welch's group represented nonprofit housing development corporations, including the Mission Housing Development Corporation. But the coalition took a strict no-displacement approach, rarely endorsing any zoning proposal that would permit taller or bigger buildings, even if it would encourage the construction of affordable housing. To do so, according to Welch, would entice developers to tear down existing buildings to make money off of bigger ones. That would be, he thought, urban renewal all over again. The bulldozing of the Western Addition had left a deep scar on the city's psyche.[3]

Welch was instrumental in prompting the city to downzone Haight-Ashbury in the early 1970s—that is, limit the heights and bulks of new buildings to something lower and smaller than previously allowed. Other neighborhoods began to call for their own downzonings, and some got them. The planning commission, seeking to avoid having a patchwork of zoning plans, developed its own citywide proposal that would largely limit the height and bulk of residential neighborhoods at their then-present positions, freezing San Francisco's growth potential.

The planning commission held numerous special meetings around the city in early 1978 on the proposal. Most neighborhood organizations spoke out in favor: the Inner Sunset Action Committee, the Pacific Heights Association, the Glen Park Association, the Potrero Hill League of Active Neighbors. A citywide anti-development group, San Francisco Tomorrow (which had fought against the Transamerica and US Steel skyscrapers downtown), even asserted the city's plan did not go far enough, because it adopted as the maximum density "the highest prevailing density" within a neighborhood instead of the lowest. "We believe in the need for additional housing units in San Francisco," the group said. "We do not believe they should be created at the expense of the existing houses and San Francisco's neighborhood ambience."[4] The League of Women Voters of San Francisco said the downzoning "will maintain and improve the quality of life."[5] Even SPUR, the former urban renewal advocacy group that is a prominent pro-development voice today, spoke in favor of the height limits, arguing it would stop the flight of middle-class white families from the city.[6]

Opposition to the plans came from a curious corner: the Asian American community, which at the time was seeing a large influx from Hong Kong, Vietnam, and Laos. Some speakers expressed concern about low-income housing, others owned property they wanted to develop. Jenny Lew of the Chinatown Coalition for Better Housing objected to the "special review criteria" to which proposals for new housing could be subjected, such as whether the building would block views or alter the existing character of a neighborhood, because they would add delays. "These delays only succeed in encumbering massive cost increases often threatening, if not destroying, the entire economic feasibility of a project even before it gets through the review process."[7] Another speaker, Mel Ling Ho, put it more plainly: downzoning would increase housing costs, which would force people out of the city, and lengthen their commutes. Pius Lee, the head of the Richmond Hill Republican Club and a landlord, interpreted the proposal in class terms: "We want the residents in $300,000 homes to understand we support their decision to down zonings [sic] in their own neighborhoods, but we also want them to spend some time studying our special problems in Chinatown North Beach."[8]

Nonetheless, the plan passed the Board of Supervisors overwhelmingly. Future mayor and US senator Dianne Feinstein, then a supervisor, called it "the single most important neighborhood issue of the 1970s."[9] Advocates of community preservation cheered: they thought the vote would preserve their way of life into the indefinite future. Consultants working for the city, however, estimated that the downzoning reduced San Francisco's capacity for growth by 180,000 new units.[10]

COMMERCIAL ENCROACHMENT

Welch's coalition, and the 1978 downzoning, have been blamed for blocking housing construction and driving up housing costs, but that argument tells only half the story. True, housing construction between 1967 and 2006 was anemic: just 60,000 new units, or an annual increase of just about 0.5 percent of the existing stock. However, the rate of production was not significantly less anemic after the 1978 downzoning than it was before. And at the same time that the city's builders weren't building much, the city's leaders were tearing down what little residential stock San Francisco had—to make way for a convention center and the expansion of hospitals and universities. Hence, the *net* gain was even lower: only 46,000 units over those four decades.[11] Meanwhile, households were getting smaller due to the increasing frequency of divorce and parents' decisions to have fewer children; the city needed more homes to house the same number of people. Between 1970 and 2010, the number of households in the city grew 36 percent faster than the population. (New York saw an even more dramatic change: the number of households grew three times as fast as the population in that period. In Chicago, population fell during that period by nearly 25 percent, while the number of households dropped only 9 percent.)[12]

Welch has maintained that his coalition was in fact *pro*-housing, but that City Hall wasn't. "San Francisco in the mid-70s through mid-80s counted on suburban counties to house its workforce," he said recently. "We were pleading with the city to do residential development and limit commercial development."[13] Even as late at 1992, when the city began to redevelop former railroad yards known as Mission Bay, planning officials advocated building a massive office complex in their place; it was only after coaxing by housing groups that they added 6,000 apartments to the plan.

Unable—or unwilling—to do much to increase the supply of housing, Welch tried to reduce demand. In 1985, Mayor Dianne Feinstein's administration issued the "Plan for Downtown." It was intended to respond to a backlash against the downtown building boom by limiting the size of new structures in the Financial District. But it would also allow commercial development to expand deeper into the South of Market area, which consisted of a mix of residential and industrial uses at the time. Welch became convinced that the plan would end up reducing the city's housing stock by prompting landlords to replace apartments with office buildings. (It would also, however, add new housing units, albeit pricey ones, in and around the Financial District.) He was able to rally enough supporters to get a ballot question—Proposition M—passed in 1986, limiting the amount of new office space that could be built each year to 475,000 square feet (later changed to 950,000 by a subsequent ballot measure).[14]

At this point, it wasn't just hippie hangers-on who opposed growth. According to political scientist Richard de Leon, many of the professionals who had come to call San Francisco home in the 1970s and '80s supported Proposition M as well. "These new San Franciscans," he wrote, "were affronted by the overbuilt and congested environment in which they worked and lived."[15] In other words, some of the same individuals lured to San Francisco by the growth of its commercial sector became anti-development after they arrived. Like the 1978 downzoning, Proposition M was a way to bottle and preserve San Francisco the way it was. Unfortunately, it left a few loopholes that were just big enough for the type of economy that was emerging to slip through.

DOT-COMMERS

This new type of economy started in 1995, with the advent of Netscape. Though it may seem like just another Internet browser today, Netscape was different. First, it made it possible for users to shop on the Internet securely through a new protocol (SSL). The ability to exchange money over the Web in turn launched a giant industry of easy-to-build, easy-to-operate dot-com companies like E-Trade, Excite, Ask Jeeves, and Commerce One. They required little capital compared to manufacturing—a few computers and a server cost a lot less than the machinery needed to assemble automobiles—and were attractive to investors. For the most part, these start-ups clustered in San Francisco, particularly in the two-square-mile area south of the city's financial district, encompassing South of Market (rebranded

SoMa), Potrero Hill, and the northern end of the Mission. There, they would be close to venture capital firms in the financial district, and also draw from the thousands of college-educated workers who had been drawn by the San Francisco lifestyle to create their websites and write their copy. Second, Netscape's initial public offering was the first big IPO of the era, yielding twice as much revenue as expected and spurring venture capital firms to invest even more in dot-coms.[16]

Employment in the information-related industries, including web media companies, grew 25 percent between 1994 and 1998. By 2000, it had nearly doubled, with a net gain of 18,000 employees. Other sectors—such as professional services, tourism, food service, and retail—also grew substantially.[17] All of these companies needed places to operate, and with ballot propositions limiting the amount of new office space to come onto the market to less than a million square feet a year—only enough to house about 4,000 office workers—they had to be creative.

That's where one of the loopholes came into play. When city officials implemented Proposition M, they did not count the conversion of industrial buildings to office buildings as part of the city's 950,000-square-foot annual quota. Housing advocates protested the exception, but city officials maintained that those warehouses had already existed and that changing their use would not damage the skyline. Yet, changing the function of those warehouses from manufacturing to office use *would* burden the transit system, housing stock, and public schools—for the simple reason that office-based companies could employ three to four times as many people in the same space. (The rule of thumb is that a company needs 250 square feet for each of its office workers, compared to 700 to 1,000 square feet per industrial employee.)[18]

In other words, if the intention of Proposition M was to relieve pressure on San Francisco's housing stock, the way it was implemented failed to do so. In fact, the city's decision increased pressure on another aspect of "old San Francisco": the industrial district south of downtown. Just as in Brooklyn's Dumbo, these warehouses were not necessarily bereft of industrial tenants, but when dot-coms offered to pay several times what a factory or processing plant could afford, they became that way. (Over five years, the per-square-foot rent for these industrial properties doubled.) Besides, there was an aesthetic attribute that made warehouses more attractive to dot-coms than downtown office towers ever would have been. "Multimedia companies loved these buildings because they're decidedly non-corporate," said Shannon Tobin, the president of a firm that rented space in South of Market. "They're low-rise yet have great views of the city. They have high ceilings, wood floors, and open loft-style floor plans."[19]

The prosperity that the dot-com boom (and other developments in the entertainment and hospitality industries) brought to the city was significant. In 1994, San Francisco's unemployment rate was 6 percent; by 2000, it had dropped to 3.4 percent. Yet it was also true that at least some of those jobs created during the dot-com boom weren't for longtime San Franciscan residents, and that therefore, this prosperity wasn't equally shared. By 2001, more than one-fifth of all San Franciscans had moved into their present apartment from outside of the Bay Area, sparking innumerable conflicts between newcomers and old-timers fighting over scarce housing resources.[20]

THE GOLDEN ERA

In the Mission District, the 1980s were glorious days. At the start of the decade, the neighborhood was 50 percent Latino and growing ever more so. It was a melting pot not just for Mexicans—who had been the primary Latino group there before—but for Central and South Americans fleeing civil unrest, reinforcing the notion of la raza nueva, in which the particularities of political borders melted into one common mestizo heritage. Patricia Rodriguez, a prominent muralista, invited any number of refugee artists to crash on the floor of her rented bungalow. People of all nationalities would congregate at a Nicaraguan bar on Mission Street, El Tico Nica, where they would drink rum and trade stories about their old lives. "And like any *pueblito*, everyone knew everyone, and you'd bump into friends at receptions, parties, street fairs, or just shopping for pan dulce," the poet Alejandro Murguía remembered. "Or I'd walk down Twenty-Fourth Street and hear the Spanish inflections of the entire continent—Nicoya slang, Chicano *caló*, rapid-fire *cubanismos*, the elegant phrasings of Chileans."[21] (The Chileans—refugees of the brutal Pinochet regime—were known as the intellectuals of the bunch.)

The strenuous politics back home in Latin American seeped into the murals of this period. In 1984, muralist Ray Patlan organized a group of painters to turn their brushes on Balmy Alley, one of several alleyways that cut the Mission's large blocks in two. The idea of tackling such a large amount of space was a departure from earlier murals, which had been mainly confined to the exterior walls of "friendly" spaces such as schools or community centers. This time, they had to convince dozens of disparate property owners to give them permission to paint on their garage doors or back fences. It was no mean feat given that the designs the artists proposed for Balmy were harshly critical of US foreign policy. In his contribution, Patlan offered a bird's-eye view of two women passing each other on their way to and from the market, automatic rifles hidden beneath their shawls. Soon, muralists decorated other alleyways in the neighborhood; walking down them was like traversing a funhouse hallway, with people alternately yelling, crying, screaming, and singing on either side.

Murals had, by that point, taken on a cultural life of their own. René Yañez was no longer needed to cultivate the art, and he spent less and less time with muralists and more and more time on La Galería, putting up shows that blended art, pop culture, and social justice themes. (One exhibit presented *pañuelos*, handkerchiefs drawn on in exquisite detail by prisoners for their girlfriends.) Yañez settled down with painter Yolanda Lopez, and they moved into a small one-bedroom on the top floor of a Victorian row house in the Mission. In 1980, they had a boy, named Rio. Shortly afterwards, Yañez met the marketing

FIG. 7.1. Balmy Alley, 2016. The first of a series of alleyways that Mission District artists began painting in the 1980s. (Photo by Matthew L. Schuerman)

director at the Asian-American Theater, Cynthia Wallis, and fell in love with her. He and Yolanda decided, however, that they wanted to remain close. She moved into the apartment next door with Rio, while Cynthia moved in with Yañez.

Yañez's relationship with La Galería went through a similarly tepid divorce, especially after his longtime business partner, Ralph Maradiaga, died of a heart attack at age 54. Yañez jumped around from job to job. He curated a show at the San Francisco Art Commission. Then he joined an ill-fated experiment in multiculturalism: Festival 2000, which was to be a celebration of a new generation of artists of color in October 1990. Instead, it turned into a giant three-week-long extravaganza with thousands of acts and a sound and light show—or it would have if it hadn't run into money problems first.[22] Yañez was laid off with the rest of the staff before it ever started.[23]

By the late 1980s, the *San Francisco Chronicle* noticed a shift in the

Mission District. It started at the northern end, furthest away from
the heavily Latino 24th Street corridor where La Galería was located
and where Yañez lived. On the one hand, the *Chronicle* called the
plaza above the 16th Street BART station "the heroin-selling capital
of the Bay Area," adding: "It is also *the* spot to buy stolen Muni bus
transfers." At the same time, the newspaper noted the rise of cafés
and used bookstores, along with an underground night club or two,
and asked whether gentrification could be far behind. Twelve years
later the rival newspaper, the *Examiner*, answered in the affirmative,
describing a territory where the working-class past had been supplanted by the dot-com present. A tavern known for fist fights became the retro Beauty Bar, with old-fashioned hair dryers along one
wall; an Italian restaurant turned into a jazz club with a 500-gallon
fish tank; a French bistro that showed foreign films in its courtyard
supplanted a taqueria and a thrift store. The neighborhood's Latino
flavor lent credibility to the idea that the Mission was the real thing:
in 1994, a pair of locals bought an old school bus, outfitted it with
Christmas lights, and took outsiders on hop-on, hop-off nightlife
tours of the *barrio*. A 45-year-old homemaker from Marin County
explained that fancy restaurants further north on the peninsula
lacked "the sex appeal and the sizzle" to be found in the Mission.[24]

The most overt conflicts during this time were not between Latinos and white newcomers, but between the (largely white) proto-
gentrifiers who had arrived in the late 1980s and the (largely white)
gentrifiers who arrived shortly afterwards. Take the Yuppie Eradication Project: In 1998, a man in his 30s, Keith Keating, was sitting
at a café when he heard a man sitting next him, as he later recalled,
"talking very animatedly with this kind of bovine hubris on his cell
phone to some guy he keeps referring to as 'Jeffster, dude.'" Keating,
who was working as a mail clerk at an office while writing a novel on
the side, decided to do something. He put up a series of posters on
lampposts around the neighborhood announcing the Mission Yuppie Eradication Project. "Yuppie scumbags have crawled out of their
haunts on Union Street and the suburbs to take our neighborhood

FIG. 7.2. René Yañez (behind mask) and his performance troupe, Culture Crash, one of a series of artistic endeavors, in 1985. (Photo by Lou Dematteis)

away from us," one of them read. (Union Street is a thoroughfare in the upscale Russian Hill neighborhood.) "This yuppie takeover can be stopped and turned back." The signs chastised outsiders who drove into the neighborhood after dark to patronize fashionable bars and restaurants, and urged neighbors to vandalize Porsches, SUVs, and Jaguars parked along their streets. The posters ended up attracting a fair amount of media attention—they were an expression of the hostility that first-comers often feel toward those who arrive later—but failed to ignite the type of revolution that Keating had envisioned. He did, however, end up getting arrested and having property confiscated.[25]

Another Mission writer, Laurel Rosen, took the Yuppie Eradication Project to task in an op-ed published around the same time, and exposed the subjective nature of most, if not all, anti-gentrification movements. "'Yuppie' no longer means BMW, dinner at Stars and overpriced Chardonnay. Nowadays it simply means 'them,'" she noted in the *Chronicle*. "If you work in the service industry, it's those computer people who are the yuppies. If you're part of the digerati, the investment bankers are your yuppies. If you're a banker, your organic-food-eating, pot-smoking parents are the real yuppies."[26]

No social type was more associated with the urban "renaissance" than the yuppie. The first time the term appeared in print was in 1980, when *Chicago* magazine writer Dan Rottenberg used the term to describe the "chic upper-middle-class families" who were moving from the suburbs back to the city's lakefront neighborhoods.[27] (The name stood for "young upwardly mobile professionals.") In some ways, yuppies were the descendants of the "young marrieds" of the 1950s, and part of a long lineage of social types that mirrored the transformation of the nation's economy from manufacturing to corporate to information-based. These social types were not counter-cultural, but neither were they mainstream; at times, they took aspects of the counterculture and, because of their power and influence, *made* them mainstream.

Yuppies quickly became hated: status-conscious, rich, and overly conspicuous. Even by the time the Yuppie Eradication Movement had launched, the term was outdated. In its place, came "hipsters," a revival of the term coined in the late 1940s to describe the bohemians of New York's Greenwich Village. The original hipsters smoked marijuana, listened to bebop, and adopted African American slang. They were connoisseurs of popular culture, but also aloof from it, as if they were too cool to enjoy it, or enjoy anything.[28] The hipsters of the early 1990s wore trucker hats and drank Pabst Blue Ribbon, forging an ironic allegiance to blue collar culture over the ostentation of Yuppie consumerism. (Gen Xers, slackers, and grunge were intermediary stages.) The goatee came back into vogue, and ambition was frowned upon (as in the movies *Slacker* and *Reality Bites*). Some hipsters were conscious of their heritage. In 1995, a reporter writing about the Mission noted young men walking around wearing black berets, smoking Camel nonfiltereds, and using words like "cool cats" and "dig."[29]

At first, hipsters had little purchasing power, but as they entered their 30s and then 40s and climbed the career ladder, the Yuppie aesthetic was replaced with a studied authenticity: Out went balsamic vinegar and sun-dried tomatoes, flown from halfway around the world; in came locally grown organic produce. David Brooks would call this species the "bobo," for someone who combined the material success of the bourgeoisie with the anti-establishment values of bohemians.[30] Bobos were anti-status, but in a status conscious way: "Everything about you must be slightly more casual than your neighbor," a practice Brooks refers to as "one downsmanship."[31] While Brooks never connected bobos to gentrification—the locus of his sociological observations was suburban Wayne, Pennsylvania—he did call Jane Jacobs a patron saint of bobo-ism because of her ability to marry the bourgeois obsession with order and the bohemian infatuation with freedom. Brooks noted: "A city street, she argues, looks chaotic but is really quite orderly."[32] Hipsters liked the Mission because they felt free there. There was something appealing about forgetting one's class origins. One 29-year-old told the *Chronicle* in 2000 that in the Mission, "You don't have to fit [into] a certain socioeconomic class."[33] At first, the newcomers, the intermediaries, and the indigenous in neighborhoods like the Mission all shared similar politics and worldviews. They favored a pro-urban agenda; liberal immigration policies; and higher spending on education, mass transit, and social services. They liked locally owned stores, street life, and whatever gave a community its unique feel. Sometimes it was difficult to tell one group apart from another; at other times, each group was blind to its own hypocrisy. It came back to the observation made by Roger Starr in 1970s New York about urban professionals: because of their education and confidence in their ability to make ends meet, hipsters had "eminent social distance" from the poor, and no fear of living close to them. The hipsters in the Mission did not necessarily share the wealth or jobs that New York's pioneer class did, but they were part of a series of transitions—from Latino to white, from working class to upper-middle-income—that were so subtle that it is hard, looking back, to see when one phase ended and the next began.

Eventually, once too many people became "hipsters," it turned into a pejorative and protean term, just as "yuppie" had. And as too many hipsters moved to the Mission—and they grew older, and wealthier, they "ruined" the neighborhood—even in their own eyes. "There are too many people who look like us," an Internet business developer, Mark Sole, admitted. "Despite the fact we're a part of it, we lament the city losing its grit."[34]

THE RENT CONTROL DILEMMA

The impact of the dot-com boom on housing values was enormous. The median monthly rent for a 2-bedroom in San Francisco in 1995 was $1,100; by 1999, it had more than doubled, to $2,500. By 2000, the US Department of Housing and Urban Development concluded that a minimum wage worker would have to work 24 hours a day, 7 days a week, 52 weeks a year, and still not be able to afford the median rent.[35]

How did the city ever manage to function with such high rents? The short answer is that it didn't; about half of all renters were paying below-market rates. They were protected by the city's rent control ordinance or other regulations, and saw their rents rise by a cost of living adjustment each year.[36] San Francisco's rent control ordinance had been passed amid a statewide rental shortage in 1979, spurred by high interest rates that had stifled new home construction. Yet it had many loopholes, and the higher market rents went, the more tempting it was for landlords to take advantage of them. For example, a building owner could evict a tenant if he wanted to use the apartment for himself or a family member. San Francisco had a hard time policing this exception. In the mid-90s, two reporters from the *San Francisco Bay Guardian* knocked on the doors of apartments that, according to building records, had recently been renovated because of an owner move-in. In 18 percent of the cases where reporters could establish the unit's history, they found that the apartment had been re-rented to someone unrelated to the owner, for significantly higher rent.[37] (An anonymous city official told the newspaper that he actually suspected as many as 60 percent of owner move-in claims were fraudulent.) The Bay Guardian also tracked down the evictees, and determined they were paying on average 71 percent more to rent places that were typically smaller and in less desirable neighborhoods.[38]

Between 1996 and 1998, as the city's economy boomed, the number of owner move-in evictions nearly tripled, from 433 to 1,253 a year.[39] The Bay Guardian's report, as well as some well-publicized cases, led voters to pass a referendum that protected many disabled and elderly tenants from owner move-ins. Landlords then began taking advantage of another loophole, known as "the Ellis Act." In 1985, California state senator Jim Ellis introduced a bill to benefit a 23-year-old Santa Monica man, James Nash. Nash had received a building as a gift from his mother, but he quickly became disenchanted with the rental business. In court, he said he wanted to evict "the group of ingrates inhabiting my units, tear down the building, and hold onto the land" until he could sell it.[40] The state Supreme Court blocked Nash from demolishing the building because of a Santa Monica law that regulated the removal of rental properties from the city's housing stock. The following year, the state legislature passed Ellis' bill, which permitted evictions if the landlord wanted to "go out of business."

"Going out of business" was not well defined in the law. In many cases, instead of throwing up their hands and getting into some career other than real estate, as James Nash did, landlords invoked the Ellis Act, evicted tenants, and then converted the building to condominiums or tenancy-in-common, a California version of a cooperative building. But tenant activists found several cases where a landlord supposedly "went out of business" by converting a building to a co-op, and then went on to buy another property and repeat the whole process. One such research effort, undertaken in 2014, found that 78 percent of Ellis Act evictions take place within five years of a landlord buying a property, and that a good number of landlords continue owning other properties even after they sell off one of their buildings as a cooperative.[41] These landlords could hardly be considered to have "gone out of" the real estate business.

Between 1995 and 1999, the number of Ellis Act evictions rose from 14 to 664 a year.[42] The actual number of displaced tenants was likely several times that, since each case involved an entire building. That's what makes an Ellis Act eviction worse than an owner move-in: it empties out the whole building, not just one apartment. In other words, those well-meaning voters who tightened one loophole pushed landlords toward another, more detrimental one.

The real estate industry defended the use of the Ellis Act as a rational response to overly restrictive regulations. "Often the longtime owners of properties are not prepared to evict tenants whom they have come to know over the years," Andrew Zacks, a real estate attorney who popularized Ellis evictions in the late 1990s, said recently.[43] "So that presents an opportunity for the purchaser to clear out the longtime tenants who have been paying drastically discounted rents and bring the rents up to market rates." Another landlord attorney, Daniel Bornstein, said the Ellis Act "is usually invoked where you have . . . a statistical differential between what rent is being paid for your rent-controlled property, and a neighbor's house. Someone may be paying $4,000 a month and in this other house, a person is paying only $600 for the same space and amenities. What you have is a situation that a third-party objective observer may say, 'Hey, that's patently unfair.'"[44] Tenant leaders have countered that San Francisco landlords knew it was a heavily regulated industry before they got into it.

RENÉ'S GENTRIFICATION

René Yañez had been following the gentrification of the Mission all along, as an observer and then as a victim. As early as 1989, he collaborated with the cofounder of Artist Television Access, Marshall Weber, as well as the community newspaper, *North Mission News*,

FIG. 7.3. Cartoon in the community newsweekly *North Mission News*, in April 1990, accompanying an article about the "Project Mission: Who's the Landlord" multimedia collaboration that Yañez produced with Marshall Weber to bring attention to gentrification.

for a multimedia project called "Who's the Landlord." Then, in 2000, the elderly Irish man who owned Yañez's apartment building, Michael Dolan, died. Dolan had lived in the Castro and was always kind toward Yañez. He liked what Yañez did with the small garden plot out front and admired him for his involvement at the Galería. Yañez figured that whoever bought the place wouldn't be as sentimental and would try to get him out one way or other. Waiting was painful: each time a prospective buyer came through, Yañez gauged his chances for staying. After it was sold, the new property manager told him that the buyer was planning on evicting all the tenants. Yañez could not imagine leaving the neighborhood and decided to use his connections. He went back to the *North Mission News* and told his story to the iconoclastic editor, Victor Miller, because he wasn't afraid to pick fights with developers and landlords. The coverage produced enough negative attention that the landlord backed off, selling the property within months to Sergio Iantorno, an Italian immigrant who had invested shrewdly in real estate.

As summer moved into fall and fall into winter, everything changed. As quickly as the early Internet economy, with all its excitement and hyperbole, had boomed, it faded. The NASDAQ dropped by more than 50 percent over 10 months. The IPO market was beached. Dot-coms closed by the hundred. Thousands of college-educated white folks living in San Francisco lost their jobs and went on unemployment.

No one seemed to worry about gentrification any more. It would be several years before Yañez heard anything more about the Ellis Act.

EIGHT

THE RISE AND FALL OF RENT CONTROL

There is apparently nothing economists hate more than rent control. In 1990, a team of researchers surveyed members of the American Economic Association and asked whether they agreed with a set of forty statements. No question gained more support than the proposition, "A ceiling on rents reduces the quantity and quality of housing available."[1] In one of the earliest essays on the subject, the future Nobel Laureate Friedrich August von Hayek wrote, "We pay too little attention to the phenomenal rise in demand for homes which must occur every time rents fall below the level at which they would settle in an unfettered market."[2] He was writing in 1929, about Vienna, which had been suffering from a housing shortage since well before World War I and the imposition of rent control in 1922, largely because construction costs outweighed the ability of the proletariat to pay for suitable shelter.[3] Nevertheless, it was clear that rent controls at the time further stifled housing production, which then had to be taken over by the state. Hayek, a self-described "Old Whig" who has been embraced by the political right over the years, argued that government would be able to afford to build only modest homes for the poor, which would then boost rents on the private market.[4] "A large number of people will therefore inevitably settle for a home of poorer quality than they would have occupied if rents had shown a smooth progression instead of such a disproportionate variation."[5] Curiously, Hayek supposed that once the government stepped in, it would be able to meet demand for housing; his main complaint was that well-off renters would settle for lower quality housing than they were willing to pay for. (Today, Vienna's system of social housing has become a model for other cities.[6])

The ongoing dislike of rent controls among economists has sometimes muddied the debate around gentrification. Shortly after World War II, Milton Friedman and George J. Stigler assessed rent controls, which had been imposed on New York City, San Francisco, and other "defense rental areas" by the Office of Price Administration. They argued that an unfettered market could produce enough supply to meet demand and used as an example the case of San Francisco after the 1906 earthquake and fire, a devastating event that destroyed half of the city's housing stock. For evidence of the free market's resilience, Friedman and Stigler looked at the classifieds in the May 24, 1906, issue of the *San Francisco Chronicle*—about five weeks after the catastrophe—and counted eighty-three offers of apartments and houses, versus five ads requesting shelter. It is odd that two eminent University of Chicago professors would use such a self-selective, incomplete sample as a basis for a "scientific" conclusion. Yet they did, asserting "new construction proceeded rapidly" to meet demand after the fire, when there was plenty of evidence to the contrary.[7]

The news pages of the *Chronicle* that spring and summer described how 100,000 people had moved across the bay to take refuge in Oakland.[8] Thousands of others were camped out in Golden Gate Park, the Presidio, North Beach, Jefferson Square, and Ingleside. Dozens of displaced persons ended up in a cemetery in the Mission District, "where manure and garbage have been deposited to add to the possibility of disease-breeding conditions," until city officials moved them to a high school. Glen Park, a largely undevelopable canyon in the middle of the city, was turned into a refugee camp.[9] The city's Housing Committee was empowered to "take possession of any vacant houses and flats, and to permit their occupancy by refugees."[10] In an editorial, the *Chronicle* asked "our Eastern and European sympathizers" to loan the city's banks $50 million for recovery efforts.

The laws of supply and demand, far from kicking into gear, seemed to have gone into a state of shock. "No hard and fast rule is to be laid down on the real estate situation," the *Chronicle* noted in August.[11] While it would *seem* like there would be high demand for housing, it was unclear whether anybody could pay for it, no matter the price. People were not only without homes, many of them were without jobs as well. One of the "apartment wanted" ads Friedman and Stigler must have seen offered caretaking services in lieu of rent.[12] "Realty men," as landlords were called at the time, feared prices would actually *decline* despite the housing shortage. In June, Mayor Eugene Schmitz proposed buying up cleared property in the destruction zone and building 20,000 homes for sale, yet by August, as leaders worried about getting thousands of families permanent shelter in time for the autumn rains, that plan was foundering. Instead, relief funds were put to work to erect one-tenth as many temporary cottages on publicly owned land. What private development there was took place on previously undeveloped dunes in the western districts (which are, it goes without saying, no longer available for development to address the housing shortage in the early twenty-first century). San Francisco's elite fretted that if the city failed to create enough housing, refugees would continue to flee, shrinking the workforce needed to rebuild the city.[13] Far from demonstrating the robustness of the free market, the earthquake and fire proved the importance of government intervention in times of crises. Friedman and Stigler make passing reference to the chaos that followed the fire, yet state, "*At all times during the acute housing shortage in 1906 inexpensive flats and houses were available*" (emphasis theirs).[14]

The historical accuracy of Friedman and Stigler's statements is important insofar as they saw an unregulated market as working even in the most extreme housing shortages. At the time they wrote, Friedman and Stigler wanted to persuade the Truman administration to loosen war-time price controls on rents. Their reasoning was nuanced. It had less to do with the severe housing shortage generally — which they argued was caused by rising incomes that prompted Americans to leave multigenerational households in favor of nuclear ones. Rather, because price controls did not apply to for-sale houses, Friedman and Stigler noted that homeownership units were plentiful but expensive, while rental units were scarce but cheap. Consequently, they complained that rental housing was being rationed by "chance and favoritism" — for example, it went to families who had been living in their apartments since before the war, or to those willing to devote excessive time to apartment-hunting — rather than to the highest bidder. Once price controls were lifted, they predicted, rents would go up about 30 percent within the first year; some poorer families would have to double-up until supply increased and prices dropped again. But Friedman and Stigler were not concerned with those consequences; they counseled that society should address income disparities by addressing inequality directly, rather than through price rationing.[15]

In 1947, Friedman and Stigler got their wish; the federal government removed price controls on housing. In New York, however, state legislators quickly jumped in with an amended version of rent control that would apply to New York City. This version took a page from free-market theory and imposed price ceilings only on existing buildings; therefore, developers would have enough incentive to construct new buildings and increase supply — an important concession. This is what's known as partial control — a regulated market next to an unregulated market, and it introduced the additional question of whether controlling the rents of some apartments caused rents on others to rise — a question that has not been thoroughly answered.

Under this hybrid regime, New York City enjoyed its largest years of housing production since the 1920s. In 1960, 35,348 units were created; in 1963—right before a new zoning code imposed growth controls—the number exceeded 60,000.[16] Yet even that pace of building failed to meet the need for safe and sanitary housing. At the end of the 1960s, the *New York Times* noted that "the city's poor remain housed in 800,000 substandard units."[17] Beginning around that time and into the early 1970s, New York City's rent laws underwent more revisions and took their modern shape. Apartment buildings constructed between 1947 and 1974—which had been unregulated until then—were put under a system called "rent stabilization." Stabilization allowed landlords to increase rents according to a rate decided by a city board (roughly the rate of inflation); owners could also charge additional amounts to cover improvements. This move infuriated landlords who owned such buildings, since it basically capped their profits. Several of them filed suit, unsuccessfully.

In and around the 1970s, numerous other cities and states passed some version of rent controls: Boston, Cambridge, and other Massachusetts cities; Washington, DC; Connecticut; New Jersey; and numerous municipalities in California including Los Angeles, Santa Monica, and San Francisco. Canadian provinces also adopted rent controls as part of the country's wage and price control program.[18] In many ways it was an odd time to impose price controls on a commodity—inner city housing—that seemed to be less and less desired as middle-income families moved to the suburbs. But property companies, for a variety of reasons (inflation among them), were hiking rents by as much as 30 or 40 percent in a single year, and an antiestablishment tenor remained in the air from the 1960s.[19] In eastern cities, the residents left behind were often poor minorities, less able to bear higher rents and yet more compelled to pay them. In California, tenants' anger was particularly acute, since voters had passed Proposition 13—a 2.5 percent cap on property tax increases—in the belief landlords would pass along some of that savings to them; but that didn't happen. In all, an estimated 10 to 15 percent of rental units across the country were covered by some form of rent supervision.

RENT REGULATION AND GENTRIFICATION

In 1988, the eminent economist Arthur Downs concluded that "temperate" rent laws did not inhibit the construction of housing, because they applied only to older buildings and/or gave developers the chance for some profit.[20] That was the case in New York City as its economy strengthened after the fiscal crisis. In the 1970s, fewer than 10,000 units a year were being put on the market; in 1985, the number exceeded 20,000. Yet, even though most of this new supply was unregulated, a substantial portion of the city's housing stock consisted of stabilized or controlled rentals. As a result, the city had two housing markets: a New Yorker who had lived in a rent-regulated apartment for a while enjoyed relatively modest housing costs, while new entrants had to compete for a relatively small pool of market-rate apartments.

Or at least, such a bifurcated housing market existed in prime sections of Manhattan. In large parts of the city, rent regulation was unnecessary: landlords were not able to get even the legal maximum rent because the market rate was lower. One study from the 1990s predicted that rent-stabilized tenants in south-central Brooklyn (Prospect Heights, East Flatbush, and Crown Heights) would not see much of a change at all if they had to pay the market rate. But in more attractive areas of the city (the Upper West Side, Greenwich Village, Park Slope) eliminating rent regulations would increase rents on stabilized units by as much as 50 percent.[21] What would happen in those choice locations? Presumably deregulation would force tenants there to move to the next proximate affordable neighborhood—Yorkville, Chelsea, Crown Heights—causing rents to increase in *those* neighborhoods, and so on, like dominoes falling. But if the long-term residents of those neighborhoods had rent protections, they could sit pretty. In other words, rent regulations not only protect tenants in expensive neighborhoods, but they also protect tenants of nearby neighborhoods from encroaching gentrification. In fact, in a full-page ad in the *New York Times* in 1985, the Real Estate Board of

New York, the umbrella group for the city's largest developers, cited rent regulations as the reason why the public did not need to fear that gentrification would cause displacement of low-income households.[22]

Nonetheless, the Citizens Budget Commission (CBC), an organization founded in the Great Depression by leading businessmen, lawyers, consultants, and real estate developers, became concerned about the two-tiered market. Its board members were in charge of multinational companies that recruited employees from across the country, if not the world, and had a keen interest in making sure New York's housing costs were reasonable; otherwise, these companies would have to pay new hires more. In 1991, the commission argued the time was ripe to relax rent regulations. The stock market crashes of 1987 and 1989 had hit New York's housing prices hard; for the first time, the vacancy rate among rental apartments had reached 4.2 percent, an extraordinarily high number for New York.[23] The CBC recognized that deregulation would cause sudden shocks, but that acting during a lull in the market would ease the transition to a more "rational" free market.

The CBC acknowledged that New York's rent laws at the time had no perceivable impact on supply. "Economists generally agree that rent regulations have adverse effects on new construction, but the consensus is based more on theory than empirical investigation," the writers concluded.[24] Still, the CBC levied two criticisms of rent laws that rang true. One was that they effectively required landlords, rather than government, to subsidize low-income individuals.[25] What's more, in the 1970s and 1980s, there were no income limits on who could take advantage of rent stabilization. Since middle- and upper-middle-income households tended to inhabit higher-value apartments in attractive neighborhoods—even rent-regulated apartments—landlords paradoxically ended up giving larger subsidies to them. Poorer renters, who made up the bulk of rent-regulated tenants, received smaller subsidies because they tended to live in poorer neighborhoods, where market rents were lower.[26] This observation, the CBC concluded, suggested the need to cap the income levels of households that qualified for rent protection.

There was one other, less prominent, but arguably more important reason to act in the 1990s: many owners of rent-stabilized buildings were opting to convert their properties to cooperative buildings, in part because they thought rent regulation was a dead end.[27] In a co-op conversion, landlords could sell their property to its tenants. Between 1981 and 1986, landlords filed plans to convert 205,000 units, and the CBC expected the number to rise to 300,000 by 1991.[28] In that way, the city was on track to lose about 25 percent of its rent-regulated stock. It looked like the city was going to lose affordable apartments either through co-op conversions or through relaxed rent regulations. The only question was which route was the best one to take.

The CBC wasn't the only outfit lobbying for rent reform at the time; the real estate industry had been hard at it for a while. Their main vehicle was Joseph L. Bruno, a state senator from upstate Rensselaer County who was the head of the Legislative Commission on Public-Private Cooperation. In 1993, Bruno proposed "luxury decontrol"—ending rent regulation on vacant apartments renting for $2,000 or more a month and for tenants with incomes of more than $100,000 a year.[29] Since rent regulation existed only at the mercy of a state law that authorized it for a few years at a time, Bruno threatened to block renewal of *any* sort of rent regulation in order to get his way.[30] By the early 1990s, the tenant movement had begun to lose its political clout—its numbers depleted by co-op conversions, among other factors—right as the real estate lobby was gaining power. (The Senate Republican Campaign Committee received $222,500 from landlords' political action committees in 1993.[31]) Opponents warned that "luxury decontrol" would lead landlords to harass tenants, knowing that once a unit was vacant, renovations could eventually elevate the rent above the $2,000-a-month threshold. Bruno's legislation passed, largely unchanged, and without any provisions to protect tenants; the one concession to tenants was that rent regulations were extended for four years, instead of just two.[32]

Four years later, Bruno was back. Crime had fallen, the economy had rebounded, and the soft market under which the CBC had called for a humane and gradual dismantling of rent regulations had vanished. Yet somehow the will to undo rent restrictions was even stronger. "I am here to tell you that on June 16, 1997, rent laws will cease to exist," Bruno promised a crowd of landlords before the legislative session began.[33] He said the law of supply and demand would keep building owners from gouging tenants, and speculated that deregulation would spur enough construction to end the housing shortage.[34] Bruno proposed phasing-out rent regulation over two years, and again threatened to block any contrary legislation from getting to the floor. "I don't need any votes!" he told reporters proudly.[35] All he had to do was sit there, let the law expire, and win. Or so he thought.

Even supposedly impartial actors—newspaper editorial boards—soured on the idea of price controls in a way they never had before. "Rent regulation has not served New York City well," the *New York Times* concluded. "It has discouraged investment in the upkeep of old properties and the construction of new ones."[36] Neither of these claims holds up under scrutiny as serious problems.[37] Yet *Newsday* went further, tying rent regulations to the widespread abandonment of the 1970s and "the loss of hundreds of millions in tax dollars annually"—a gross simplication of history, as shown in chapter 2.[38]

One reason for the shift in attitudes since 1993 was that, as prosperity returned, the rental market had rebounded, widening the gap between regulated and market-rate rents. That development made stories about dirt-cheap rents in prime locations all the more scandalous, and also made the prospect of deregulation all the more attractive to landlords.[39] In 1997, real estate groups gave $700,000 to state Republicans—more than twice what they had four years earlier.

This time, however, Bruno had overplayed his hand. Rent regulations were part of New York City's value system and fared well in polls, even among homeowners. Tenant advocates warned that ending rent control would end "any kind of economic integration."[40] Even pro-market economist Susan Wachter cautioned, "Low-wage workers

FIG. 8.1. Then: A street fair in Park Slope in the 1970s. (Photo by Anders Goldfarb; courtesy of Brooklyn Public Library)

could be priced out. This could have consequences for the availability of blue-collar and service workers for the general economy."[41]

Democrats refused to pass the state budget until the rent laws were renewed, a ploy Bruno apparently had not considered. At one point, Bruno reported receiving a series of threatening phone calls, and fires broke out in two trash closets at the upstate building where Bruno had his district office.[42] He blamed tenants groups, but they denied any wrongdoing. Governor George Pataki, a free-market Republican but a fairly pragmatic one, ended up persuading Bruno to accept a far more modest set of reforms. According to the new rules, "luxury decontrol" would kick in when a household earned $175,000, down from $250,000. The amount landlords could hike the rent between regulated tenants, meanwhile, was raised from 16 percent to 20 percent.[43]

The Times called it "a molehill of rent reform," but the 1997

FIG. 8.2. Now: The same intersection, at Seventh Avenue and 2nd Street, in 2018. (Photo by Matthew L. Schuerman)

changes had far-reaching consequences.[44] About 12 percent of all rent-regulated units became vacant every year, the price for which landlords could now boost by 20 percent. Plus, after each tenant left, the landlord could make cosmetic renovations, the cost of which they could then pass along to their tenants. In New York, it is easy to spend $10,000 renovating a bathroom, and $25,000 on a kitchen; at a ratio of $1-a-month extra rent for every $40 spent, the landlord could tack on $875 a month after remodeling. Altogether, the landlord could bring a $1,000/month two-bedroom up to $2,075, which would then qualify the apartment for deregulation, after which the landlord could raise the rent as high as the market could bear.

Between 1994, after the first set of reforms took effect, and 2017, some 155,664 units exited regulation by exceeding the rent threshold. Another 6,346 units were lost because their inhabitants earned too much. Some 49,640 homes were converted to co-ops or condos. Another 41,341 were deregulated when their J-51 or 421-a tax breaks expired. All in all, the city lost 290,958 rent-regulated units in that period, or approximately 25 percent of the rent-regulated stock, each one representing what had been, at one time, a fairly affordable place to live.[45] The city tried to make up for that loss by giving incentives to private developers to build new affordable housing, or by making deals with landlords who voluntarily kept their units regulated. But Mayors Michael Bloomberg and Bill de Blasio had to fight two trends: laws that made it easier to escape the rent-regulation system, and economic forces that were making the city more desirable. Every time New York lost a rent-regulated apartment, it was increasingly expensive to build a new one.

THE BOSTON MODEL

Even though so-called temperate rent laws did not seem to impede housing construction, many economists suspected that they nonetheless inflated the prices of the unregulated apartments. When rent laws applied only to older housing, they reasoned, the supply on the free market was constrained. In addition, occupants of rent-regulated apartments tended to stay longer in their units, reducing turnover, and re-creating the conditions observed by Friedman and Stigler during and after World War II, under which tenants landed good deals through "chance and favoritism."[46]

The degree to which market-rate rents would fall if an entire metropolitan area were deregulated was hard to predict and depended on a variety of factors. For instance, an area where most rents are regulated might logically see its market rents decline considerably, while deregulating a small number of units would seem to have a negligible effect. The neighborhood itself also matters greatly.[47] Oddly enough, a study commissioned by the Rent Stabilization Association, which represented landlords, discounted the idea that rent regulations inflated market-rate rents. Consultant Charles W. de Seve wrote that, except in prime areas, regulated rents were "already near their free-market level, given the condition of regulated apartments." The main consequence of rent regulations, de Seve concluded, was that it led to less investment; he predicted that 70 percent of the rent increases that might follow deregulation would be spent on improvements.[48] But did that mean that regulated units were substandard, or did they simply not have finishes as nice as luxury buildings did? The city's 2017 Housing and Vacancy Survey found that only 0.2 percent of rental buildings in the city (regulated and non-) were dilapidated and that more than half reported having no maintenance deficiencies.[49] Those numbers suggest that, while landlords may be withholding investments in rent-regulated properties, they are not as a rule letting them crumble. So, if renters are willing to accept an apartment with outdated décor that, say, looks out onto a ventilation shaft, so long as it's inexpensive, is that a problem?

The best real-life experiment showing the impact of partial rent control took place in Massachusetts. In 1994, voters repealed rent laws in Brookline, Boston, and Cambridge, the last three municipalities in the state that had them. Cambridge, the home of Harvard University and the Massachusetts Institute of Technology, had had a strict form of rent control on units built before 1969. Throughout the 1970s and '80s, property owners there had tried lawsuits and political pressure to relax the laws, but the city council refused. Finally, in 1994, the Small Property Owners Association of Cambridge got the question on the state ballot. (The local rent laws were predicated on a state law allowing a "local option.")

The arguments against rent control were based more on notions of justice and fairness—that is, against "chance and favoritism"—than on economics. A survey of Cambridge noted that 30 percent of beneficiaries were poor, while others were students—only temporarily poor—or even well off. Even the city's mayor and a Supreme Judicial Court Justice enjoyed rent protections.[50] "All of my tenants are affluent, every one of them," one landlord told a newspaper reporter.[51] Malcom Peabody, another landlord who asserted he was renting to professionals and college graduates, said, "It's kind of silly that I should be subsidizing these people who make perfectly good incomes. . . . It's just bad public policy." Talk show host Glenn Koocher predicted the measure would get sizable support because of voters' distaste for liberal elitism. "Some people may vote against rent control just to screw Cambridge," he quipped.[52]

Voters statewide opted to abolish rent control by 51 to 49 percent. Next came a frenzied few months in which elected officials in the affected cities scrambled to find ways to extend rent laws and then, when they failed, to wind them down gradually. Within two years, rent control on privately owned apartments had vanished from the commonwealth. In Boston, 5,000 of the approximately 60,000 regulated households were evicted. Suffolk County Housing Court was seeing 400 cases a day, an increase of 29 percent over three years earlier and an all-time record. The managing director of the Rental Housing Association told the Boston *Herald*, "Maybe we're talking about the lawyer living in the rent-controlled unit whose rent increased to the point where he was evicted. Some might have sympathy for that and others might not."[53] Except that the well-off individual who was abusing rent control would be best situated to hold on and weather increases; it was the poor who would most likely be displaced.

A survey of Cambridge in 1998 found that median rents in formerly controlled units had risen by 40 percent. That was not surprising. Yet the same study found that rents for formerly *un*-controlled units had risen also—by 13 percent. The findings refuted the commonly held belief that abolishing rent control would bring housing costs under control. Of course, it is hard to determine whether deregulation alone caused market rates to increase, given the bullish economy at the time. But another team of researchers concluded that the repeal of price ceilings had led landlords of all stripes to renovate their stock, and therefore raise their rents accordingly (as consultant Charles de Seve had predicted in his study for the Rent Stabilization Association in New York). The authors saw this price appreciation in a positive light, for it increased Cambridge's tax base by about $2 billion. They even noted that as owners improved their rental buildings, housing values throughout their neighborhoods increased.[54]

All of this makes perfect sense, even if it is counterintuitive. Even some free market economists admit that the typical supply and demand curve breaks down when it comes to luxury goods—a Mercedes-Benz derives its high price not from its scarcity but from its high status. While one might assume that adding 16,000 apartments to Cambridge's housing supply should lower rents, that's treating housing like a commodity—like corn or oil or sugar, where one bushel or gallon is identical to another. But housing isn't exactly a commodity: its desirability is based on location, amenities, and other characteristics. During the 1980s, Cambridge housing in particular had become something of a luxury good; it was close to two top tier universities and a promising biotech hub at Kendall Square. Just as producing a few thousand more Mercedes won't substantially lower its price, deregulating a few thousand more housing units in Cambridge won't bring rents down. Landlords will be inclined to spiff up their buildings so that they appeal to this new demographic looking for luxury goods and can command the highest price possible. The abolition of rent control in Massachusetts suggests that, at least in a rising economy, the quality of housing will change to meet a market price, rather than having the market price fall to meet the quality of housing.

In recent years, there has been a revival of interest in rent control. In 2016, the town of Mountain View, California, where Google's headquarters is located, as well as Richmond, an East Bay community that has seen an influx of gentrification refugees from San Francisco and Oakland, adopted rent-control ordinances. In 2017, the city council in Portland, Oregon, got around the state's prohibition against rent regulations by requiring landlords to pay tenants up to $4,500 if they evict them without cause—discouraging exorbitant rental hikes that would displace residents.[55] In March 2018, 75 percent of Cook County voters approved a nonbinding referendum to eliminate Illinois' prohibition against rent control, while a victory by Democrats in the New York State Senate that November led to a successful campaign to restore the protections that tenants lost more than twenty

years earlier.[56] Yet resistance to rent control is still firm. Two years
after Mountain View passed its law, a group of landlords fought, albeit unsuccessfully, to repeal it.[57] Also in 2018, a Washington State
bill to repeal a ban on rent laws died in legislative committee, while a
California ballot initiative to allow localities to strengthen rent regulations also foundered.[58] Rent control is increasingly being seen as
a tool to reduce displacement, even though it is still far from being
widely accepted.

PART THREE

CONFLICT, 1992–2018

NINE

MIXED-INCOME MIXED BLESSINGS: CHICAGO, 1992–2014

The undoing of Chicago's public housing began on a clear autumn morning in 1992 when 33-year-old Anthony Garrett climbed into the bathroom of an empty apartment on the tenth floor of a Cabrini-Green high-rise and stuck an AR-15 semiautomatic rifle out of the window. He pointed it down toward the entranceway of the next tower over, 502 West Oak Street, and looked for rival Vice Lords to pick off. Garrett was a high-ranking member of the Cobra Stones, and the two gangs were warring for control over Cabrini. An Army veteran, he was known as "Carbine" and taught younger gang members how to scurry across the open balconies of the high-rises on their stomachs while also cradling a gun—the same balconies approvingly called "play corridors" thirty years earlier. Sometimes, Garrett would randomly shoot at 502 just to intimidate residents.[1]

The 502 building was neutral territory, but some Vice Lords lived there. That morning, Garrett had an extra reason to get one of them in his gun's sight. The night before, the Vice Lords had shot and injured two Cobras. Just before 9 a.m., Garrett steadied his arm on the window sill. Without a scope, he couldn't see very well from that far away, but when he thought he spotted a few of his rivals, he squeezed the trigger and let out at least three rounds.[2] Then he climbed out of the apartment, handed his gun to an accomplice, and ran down the stairs of the building.

A little later that morning, he entered the lobby of an adjacent building and encountered a security guard. By this time, Garrett had figured out one of his shots had hit a little boy; he threatened to kill the guard too if he tattled.[3] The boy was 7-year-old Dantrell Davis. Garrett would later say he had known the boy and had spoken with him "in a counseling role" once or twice.[4]

Dantrell had lived in the 502 building, just across the black-top from Jenner Elementary School. He had been holding onto his mother's hand on his way to class, and there was also the usual safety patrol—an assortment of volunteers from Cabrini wearing yellow jackets—ushering kids across the blacktop and into the safety of the school building. Nearby, two police officers were sitting in a patrol car. Dantrell fell to the ground, his mother crouching quickly beside him, screaming, "Please, baby, don't die." Paramedics brought him to Children's Memorial Hospital, where he was pronounced dead half an hour later.[5] Two other children died at Cabrini that year from stray gunfire, but it took Dantrell, who was the youngest, and had been holding his mother's hand and walking to school when it happened, to spur the city to take action.

The next month, the *Chicago Tribune*'s editorial board called on the city to tear down the CHA high-rises. The *Tribune* predicted the process would take a while but remarked the timing could not be better. Dantrell Davis' murder, the editorial board wrote, "still burns our civic memory"; recently signed federal legislation, HOPE VI, offered troubled public housing agencies federal funds to demolish their high-rises. "Getting private developers to chime in with market-rate units shouldn't be difficult," the *Trib* opined, "especially not at highly desirable locations like those now occupied by Cabrini-Green."[6] This was the moment many had anticipated and some had feared: the tipping point at which when one of the most notorious neighborhoods in Chicago would be gentrified.

The head of the CHA at the time, Vincent Lane, had taken office in 1988 and had received a better than average reception from the city's media and business elite. At first, he considered tearing down public housing projects a waste of money and preferred renovations and massive gang sweeps. But he couldn't seem to get rid of the gangs, and the redevelopment idea kept coming up.

Finally, after Dantrell's death, Lane applied for money from HUD's new HOPE VI grant program to demolish the middle section of Cabrini and invite private developers to build "mixed-income" communities in its place.[7] The point, Lane said, was to dilute poverty with wealth. "We can no longer isolate poor people within the boundaries of public housing," he explained.[8] In many ways he was taking the *Gautreaux* voucher program and turning it on its head: instead of moving poor blacks to the suburbs, Lane wanted to import the upper-middle class to the inner city. But because only 15 to 25 percent of the redeveloped property would be dedicated to the very poor, HUD disliked the idea. "We have legal and policy concerns about this, which perhaps can be distilled to the point that HOPE VI is about revitalizing communities, not displacing and replacing them," wrote Joseph Shuldiner, the assistant secretary for public housing.[9]

Lane was getting into ethical trouble at the time—he had allegedly given a CHA security contract to a Nation of Islam security firm in exchange for help with a struggling shopping center he had owned—and was soon forced out. The US Department of Housing and Urban Development took direct control of Chicago's housing authority, putting none other than Joseph Shuldiner in charge.[10] Shuldiner put a lot of energy into straightening out CHA's management—reducing CHA's workforce, outsourcing its voucher program, and unifying its contracting practices. He continued to work on Cabrini's redevelopment, and the scope of the plan expanded beyond what Lane had proposed. The density of the complex—long considered a source of its barbarity—would be slashed in half. Some 1,324 apartments would be torn down, replaced by only 650 units; and only half of *those* would be reserved for the type of very low-income households that were living at Cabrini. In other words, the redevelopment plan provided for only one-quarter as many apartments for CHA residents as would be torn down.[11]

This revised schema struck some CHA residents as even worse than Vince Lane's proposal, even though there would be more very low-income units, and other apartment buildings would be built in the surrounding neighborhood for other CHA residents. "It doesn't add up," the president of the local advisory council, Cora Moore, responded. "CHA plans to leave us out in the cold."[12] Others pointed out that the CHA was trying out this mixed-income experiment in the public housing complex closest to the wealthiest area of the city. "They've been trying to get this property for the longest," one resident, Leon Maddox, said of real estate developers. "That's all they've been talking about since I've been here. They've been trying to move these people out."[13] The local advisory council, a board elected by Cabrini tenants, enlisted the Legal Aid Foundation, and they sued the CHA to gain a bigger role in the process.

"THE TOUGH STUFF"

Before too long, an aide to US Housing Secretary Andrew Cuomo called Julia Stasch, the city's housing commissioner, to tell her the federal government was ready to relinquish supervision of the CHA. The aide suggested a media event in which Cuomo would come to Chicago and make some symbolic gesture—such as presenting Mayor Daley with a giant key—to signify the return to local control.[14] But the Daley administration did not see regaining its public housing as something to celebrate, but rather something to fear. Stasch conferred with the mayor; the two of them realized they would gain some leverage by refusing to take over the housing authority right away.[15] If they *had* to own the CHA, they wanted to do so on their own terms.

Richard M. Daley was a slimmer, better groomed, and more restrained version of his father, Richard J. Daley. If Daley-père acted like a union boss, his son governed like a corporate manager.[16] During his first two terms, Daley-fils put himself in charge of the city's public schools and the Chicago Park District, both notorious rabbit holes of inefficiency. In many ways, the CHA was a similar institution: a quasi-independent agency that had long operated in the shadows and thrived on patronage and mediocrity. Many of his advisers thought getting involved in public housing would cause him lots of grief and yield few, if any, rewards. But Richard M. believed that Chicago would never be considered world-class if it had such a miserable blemish on its record—a blemish that his own father had allowed to grow.[17] At one point, during deliberations over how to respond to HUD, Richard M. told Stasch: "Of course we're going to do it. Why am I mayor if I don't take on the tough stuff?"[18]

Meanwhile, Stasch took a good look at the city's public housing stock. She toured Stateway Gardens, one of the developments on the South Side, and edged up and down pitch-black staircases guided by tenants who had memorized the number of steps between landings because the lights were always out. Although many of the low- and mid-rise buildings could be rehabilitated, Stasch considered the "open gallery" style high-rises—the ones with the once vaunted "play corridors"—to be beyond salvation; their exposed pipes sometimes froze and burst during winter, covering stairs and balconies with ice. She also came to believe that the CHA bureaucracy was deeply flawed and relished the idea of outsourcing most of its functions, privatizing the management of the agency's properties, and shrinking the size of its staff.

Stasch was able to get HUD to make two major concessions before the city would agree to resume control of the CHA: regulatory relief that HUD normally reserved for only the very best housing authorities; and permission to repurpose money the federal government normally gave Chicago for capital improvements.[19] With those commitments in hand, she designed what would be called "the Plan for Transformation," the official name for tearing down CHA's high-rises and replacing them with low-rise, mixed-income buildings.

Stasch and her team made three crucial decisions. First, the whole thing would be done in ten years. Second, as had already been proposed for Cabrini, the redeveloped sites would have only half the population density of the old projects. Third, the new complexes would be mixed-income. Each decision had its own rationale, but taken together, they would require the CHA to relocate massive numbers of its residents in a short period of time, opening the process up to a number of unintended consequences.

The tight time frame was little more than a lark. After Stasch had been promoted to Daley's chief of staff, the new housing commissioner, Jack Markowski, told her that the transformation would likely take twenty to thirty years.[20] He advised Stasch not to publicize a deadline at all. Stasch thought that approach lacked credibility. "I can assure you that we're not going to say the housing commissioner told us to drop all references to time," she told him. She had her reasons for wanting to move quickly. For one, she did not want to spend money to maintain high-rises that were going to be torn down later. For another, nearly all the CHA's units had failed HUD's "viability test," which meant it would cost more to rehabilitate them to federal standards than they were pulling in on rent. But Stasch, and Mayor Daley, had proved adept at getting around other federal regulations in the past; the entire Plan, in fact, was predicated on receiving twenty-nine waivers to federal regulations—that was the regulatory relief she had sought as condition for taking the CHA back.[21] (It presumably helped that Mayor Daley's brother Bill worked in the Clinton administration.[22])

Amazingly, in the final version of the Plan, submitted in January 2000, the CHA told HUD it would complete the entire redevelopment in *five to seven years*, and simply needed ten years of federal subsidies to get the job done.[23] Such a statement took a lot of bureaucratic chutzpah: Most of Chicago's public housing had been constructed over nearly thirty years, between 1937 and 1965. Yet, now, in an age of voluminous environmental regulations, advocacy groups, and conflict-hungry media, the city's housing authority was promising to tear down, rehab, and/or rebuild that housing in one-sixth the time.

In its submission, the CHA asserted it could demolish 168 high-rises in just ten months. Then, it would remediate the contaminated sites, solicit bids from private developers, select the developer, have the developer design its buildings, and get planning approval for them—all with "extensive resident and community input"—over the following four years.[24] "Nobody thought ten years was realistic," Tim Veenstra, a mid-level CHA manager at the time, later recalled. "But nobody would believe it if you said it could be done in five years, and fifteen or twenty would seem too long."[25] Ultimately, the ten-year deadline was a strategy: Stasch later explained she wanted a timeline that was tight enough to "galvanize" all the players involved, even if they did not make their deadlines.[26]

The problem with such an overambitious schedule became apparent in the following years. The CHA tore down high-rises faster than they could replace them, leading the agency to rely on Section 8 vouchers—rechristened "housing choice vouchers"—to shelter residents in privately owned buildings in the meantime. Even at the beginning, there was skepticism that these vouchers would work. An independent study estimated that across the city, two low-income households were looking for each affordable unit that was available.[27] HUD and the city commissioned its own survey, which was, predictably, more optimistic. Yet even one of the leaders of the government study, Susan J. Popkin, was skeptical of its conclusion: "At least on paper, Chicago's neighborhoods could offer enough units to house all the residents who might choose vouchers for their replacement housing," Popkin, a senior fellow at the Urban Institute, later wrote. "But in focus groups we conducted with CHA residents, they raised real concerns about whether they would be able to find those units— and whether landlords would be willing to rent to them."[28]

TIPPING POINTS

Alexander Polikoff, the public interest lawyer who had begun battling the evils of concentrated poverty thirty years earlier, had reason to be wary of certain aspects of the Plan for Transformation. Polikoff had based his 1966 lawsuits on the same principle at work here: that housing poor people together in certain areas of the city stifles their spirits and degrades their educational and occupational opportunities. One lawsuit blocked the CHA from continuing that practice; the other lawsuit propelled HUD to use vouchers to move people out of public housing and into white suburbs. While the HUD program was successful, it had shortcomings that made Polikoff pause when, in 2000, the city decided to employ vouchers as it dismantled the highrises. First, the *Gautreaux* voucher program was small, serving just 7,100 participants, far smaller than anything the Plan for Transformation would require. Second, only the most generous landlords were willing to rent to African Americans with vouchers: only onefifth of the CHA residents who qualified for the program ended up signing leases.[29]

Even before the CHA announced the Plan for Transformation, it had begun to demolish a handful of its high-rises, giving the residents vouchers to find housing elsewhere. Polikoff sued to intervene. He argued the CHA should make sure it was not merely pushing the tenants out of the projects and into all-black neighborhoods, for doing so would violate the spirit of the 1969 court decision he had won. But the judge assigned to the case, Marvin E. Aspen, rejected the argument, stating that the vouchers, and the segregated housing patterns they were likely to reinforce, did not have anything to do with the discrimination that had formed the basis of the earlier ruling.[30]

Aspen's decision threatened to sideline Polikoff from the most meaningful chapter of Chicago's public housing since the high-rises were built. Yet, he still had some legal and moral authority left, and he aggressively used it. In late 1999, Polikoff came out largely in support of the Daley administration's efforts. "There is much to praise about the CHA plan," he wrote. "First is its commitment to economically integrated communities, to communities that include public housing but are not public housing communities."[31] As for the voucher families, he urged the city to undertake "compassionate relocation" and give tenants sufficient notice before they would have to move.

Though legally powerless to control whether vouchers pushed tenants toward high-poverty neighborhoods, Polikoff still had some authority over the redeveloped mixed-income CHA properties. On this point, he wanted to limit the number of very low-income CHA families who were allowed to move in. This may sound punitive, but he did not want the new developments to be anything like the old highrises; he also did not want the new developments to be so dominated by CHA residents that no middle-class families would want to move in. His insistence introduced a conundrum: if only a small fraction of the displaced CHA tenants were allowed to return to the mixed-income developments, where would all the rest of them go—except into neighborhoods where there already was concentrated poverty? In essence he chose to "save" the small number of families who made it into the mixed-income developments, rather than risk dooming all CHA tenants to continued segregation and negligence.

Polikoff's avatar in the execution of the Plan for Transformation was The Habitat Company, the development company appointed to act on behalf of the *Gautreaux* plaintiffs. Habitat Co. (no relation to the nonprofit Habitat for Humanity) intervened in the redevelopment of three CHA complexes, in each case seeking to lower the number of public housing residents who would move back.[32] Valerie Jarrett, Habitat Co.'s general counsel (later one of President Barack Obama's most trusted advisers), argued that very-low-income residents should make up no more than 30 percent of a mixed-income neighborhood.[33] In some instances, Polikoff's legal outfit joined the court efforts, siding with City Hall and outright battling other public interest law groups representing CHA residents.[34] In general, those groups were fighting the city to allow a higher proportion of mixed-income developments to be devoted to very-low-income, so that CHA tenants could remain in neighborhoods where they—and in some cases, their parents and grandparents—had grown up.

These legal fights were in essence debates over gentrification: how do you keep low-income residents from being pushed out so they may stay and reap the benefits of better schools and better city services that middle-class areas enjoy? "Revitalization must benefit our residents and allow us to have a meaningful voice in our future," declared Cora Moore, the president of Cabrini's Local Advisory Council.[35] The nonprofit LAF (formerly the Legal Assistance Foundation), which represented Moore and other Cabrini tenants at the time, argued that mixed-income communities should reserve 50 percent of their units for public housing residents. The CHA meanwhile thought that 30 percent should be the maximum in order to maintain "middle-class norms." Polikoff inclined toward that number also, as did the developers who were going to build those mixed-income communities; they were afraid potential buyers would perceive the new developments to be ghettoes were they more heavily poor or black.

With litigation, the tenants were able to nudge up the share for former CHA residents to 33 percent in some complexes; at one portion of the former Henry Horner Homes, it was settled at 50 percent.[36] Yet, Polikoff's influence on the Plan for Transformation continued to be felt. The city included a member from his nonprofit legal outfit, BPI, to sit on the working groups that helped formulate the redevelopment program for each housing complex. That gave him an opportunity to influence the income mix even before it became public. Later, Polikoff even sued to fight an attempt by LAF to reserve the Cabrini row houses entirely for CHA residents. LAF lawyers argued that the posh neighborhoods surrounding the low-rises would provide sufficient integration and opportunity, but Polikoff strenuously objected, claiming that 600-plus low-income families, even in the middle of the Near North Side, was still too many to be living close together. Under a settlement reached in 2014, the fate of the low-rises was left up to the private redeveloper.

SECOND THOUGHTS

The Plan for Transformation unleashed forces that were unpredictable and uncontrollable. In some cases, speculators bought up substandard apartments in Chicago's poorer neighborhoods, evicted the old residents, and fixed them up just enough to qualify to house voucher families. (Depending on the area, landlords could make more money by renting to a voucher tenant than on the free market.) Yet, the biggest problem CHA tenants encountered wasn't unscrupulous landlords, but the absence of landlords willing to rent to them in the first place. One early study found that only 38 percent of voucher households found private-market housing within twelve months.[37] The places where they did find apartments had above-average poverty levels.[38] In 2003, an outside monitor declared that the CHA was "converting its vertical ghettos into horizontal ones," and asserted the agency was purposely overstating the success of its results.[39] The next phase of the Plan—in which mixed-income developments would be constructed on the site of Cabrini and other demolished projects— was slow in coming, meaning that tenants were not able to return to their neighborhoods, and hundreds of acres of city-owned land were laying fallow. What's more, because the CHA sites were being redeveloped less densely than they had been when poor people lived there, the chances of moving back were quite slim.

Polikoff had been something of a cheerleader when the Plan for Transformation launched.[40] But as facts about the relocation process came out, he believed the experiment had gone awry. In 2003, after the Sargent Shriver Center and LAF sued the CHA over its relocation process, the city agreed to revamp its system, promising to give tenants more warning before displacing them and offering more support services. Most significantly, the CHA hired many more relocation counselors to guide residents, so that instead of having to help 300 residents, each employee had to help only 25—a manageable case load that also ended up attracting a far higher caliber of social worker to work for the authority.[41]

A hierarchy of relocation emerged: the most capable residents—the ones with jobs, and whose family members had clean criminal records and no drug habits—qualified for the few CHA slots in the new mixed-income housing; a second tier of residents who couldn't make that grade ended up in private apartments with vouchers; a third tier with little chance of renting on the free market were moved to low-rise buildings that the CHA continued to own. Only 17 percent of CHA tenants moved into mixed-income developments, about half of them took vouchers, while the remaining third ended up back in highly segregated public housing.[42] Given those results, it is hard to reconcile the Plan for Transformation with the ideals the *Gautreaux* settlement had sought. Yet by 2011, at least the most extreme abuses of CHA housing—the high-rises, with, as Polikoff put it once, "their incalculable damage to both residents and society"—had come down.[43]

TWENTY YEARS LATER

The first affordable housing developer to attempt to build one of these mixed-income developments for the CHA was Peter Holsten. In the late 1990s, he was operating a small real estate company out of an office on the Near North Side when he heard of a request for proposals for a seven-acre parcel nearby, part of the former Cabrini-Green complex. The city would pay for the environmental remediation and some infrastructure, while the developer would have to guarantee that it would offer 30 percent of the units to public housing residents, and another 20 percent at reduced rates to low- or moderate-income households. The rest could be market-rate. The bidding materials also stipulated there should be a mix of rentals and condos.

Holsten had been managing small affordable apartment buildings in Chicago's neighborhoods for more than a decade; he was familiar with the array of financing packages that could facilitate such an enterprise, but he had never done any new construction. He and his employees had sixty days to submit their proposal, but they dithered for the first thirty, torn between excitement and fear. Finally, the excitement won out, and they had to put their bid together in half the time available.[44]

First, Holsten called up Richard Baron, a partner in McCormack Baron and Associates, the developer that did the first HOPE VI mixed-income project in Atlanta. Next, Holsten read about what had been done elsewhere and visited the high-rises at Cabrini with tenant leaders. One of the things he heard was that the elevators were always breaking down, which made it hard for mothers with young children to move between their apartments and the playgrounds.

He found a partner, Kenard Corp., who would take care of the for-sale side of the development; Holsten would take care of the rentals. They put together a site plan with a mish-mosh of building types one might find in an organically grown Chicago neighborhood: a seven-story mid-rise, some townhomes with yards, a few coach houses with apartments on top. In some cases, the two developers could not agree. Holsten wanted to put in a splash pad and a couple of play lots, but Kenard thought that the sight of black kids playing in water spray would turn off middle-class home buyers. Holsten dropped the idea but was able to see through some of his other treasured planning choices. He put family-sized rentals in the walk-up buildings, so mothers didn't need to rely on elevators and could keep an eye on their kids playing below. The mid-rise was devoted to smaller units for singles and couples. Holsten also promised to bring over a regimen that he had begun in other affordable apartment buildings: drug tests for tenants every time they signed or renewed a lease. He would require the tests for both market-rate and moderate- and low-income tenants, though could not for legal reasons require the same for the condo owners.

Before Holsten submitted his bid, he asked Cabrini's local advisory council what residents needed. They had a realistic sense of what life would be like in a mixed-income complex and asked for help in getting to know their market-rate neighbors. They also wanted basic information about how to run a dishwasher, microwave, and garbage disposal—all items that would be new to them. Holsten had put $600,000 into his budget for resident services, but he couldn't find nonprofit providers who would do the job for less than $3 million. So Holsten decided to have his company do it all.

Holsten and Kenard ended up winning the bid—but that was the easy part. The tenant screening process was so intense that Holsten estimated just one out of every five applicants from the CHA pool was accepted.[45] More challenging was what happened after everyone moved in: a complex set of tensions and emotions arose when residents who had experienced the trauma and pathology of Cabrini life lived side-by-side with neighbors who came from privileged backgrounds.

Holsten had gone out of his way to design the complex, called North Town Village, so that the differences among the three types of tenants would be invisible. The units appear the same inside and out, no matter the type of occupant.[46] Each hallway, corridor, and stairwell was integrated economically, such that a CHA resident lived right next to a professional paying market rate. Yet, some rules—imposed either by the CHA or by the condominium association that later governed the complex—highlighted class differences. For example, homeowners could grill on their rooftops; CHA renters, because of liability issues, could not; they had to either use electric grills on their balconies or grill in the park with charcoal.[47] Nor were residents allowed to congregate on porches. Simply the fact that teenagers tend to be loud and mobile exacerbated tensions; they would walk home from school in large groups, spout swear words, and act tough. Neighbors would call the police, or the condo association, making the former CHA families feel bullied.

The social difficulties of mixed-income living were examined in 2011, when two researchers, Robert J. Chaskin and Mark L. Joseph, conducted a series of surveys and focus groups at three of the "transformed" developments; they found widespread disenchantment with the idea of economic integration among subsidized *and* market-rate residents. A CHA resident on one panel said she would try repeatedly to be cordial to her neighbors but received only stares in return. "The grown people look at you just like you're trash," she said.[48] Meanwhile, market-rate renters complained that the former public housing residents exhibited "ghetto" behavior, such as banging on someone's door long after it was clear that no one was home. Yet, the CHA stigma worked both ways: some homeowners believed residents on subsidies would label *themselves* as "CHA."[49] These observations reflected a tragic paradox: the Plan for Transformation was intended to disrupt the pathology of poverty by placing the very poor in a new environment, but it somehow reinforced it.[50] "They have a sense of pride about who they are," one female homeowner at a focus group noted of her CHA neighbors. "They're very territorial." A male homeowner said that during community meetings, all the CHA residents sit together.[51] The self-imposed segregation is surprising in part because public housing residents who qualified for mixed-income developments had met stringent standards of employment and behavior; they were presumably more *assimilable* than the typical CHA resident. Yet, they nonetheless clung to their past identities.

Peter Holsten was personally disturbed that his developments were more bouillabaisse than melting pot. He lay awake at night trying to figure out how to integrate the two income groups—or really, two racial groups, as he saw the greatest tensions rise between upper-middle-income whites and very-low-income blacks. One morning, his executive assistant—a former CHA tenant who had moved into North Town Village—came to work in tears. She told him she had had friends over for a birthday party for one of her children. Each time her guests arrived at the entrance to the complex, security guards would stop and question them—or, they felt, hassle and intimidate them. Holsten became furious and confronted the head of the condo association, who defended the guards. The incident, Holsten believed, reflected deep-seated prejudices about race and crime.

Holsten felt obligated to make sure everyone got along. He organized community events around the holidays and other times, so that residents of different backgrounds could get to know one another.

He engineered a way to get a CHA resident onto the condo board. In 2009, he held a community meeting where a theater troupe played the different roles of white homeowner and black renter to break the ice. The event was well-attended but appeared to change little. "I'm a little frustrated," he told a reporter later. "I don't feel the community-building thing is anywhere near where it should be."[52]

"DEMOLITION BY NEGLECT"

To some CHA residents (the term refers to former CHA tenants whose rent continued to be subsidized by the housing authority), the feeling of not belonging in the mixed-income developments defeated the whole purpose of economic integration. Latrice Hudson grew up in the Henry Horner Homes on the Near West Side in the 1970s, as the eighth of eleven kids. (Large families were common in Mississippi, which was where her mother, Lois Hudson, came from.) The apartment had only three bedrooms: one for her parents, one for the girls, the other for the boys. The kids' rooms had double bunk beds in them, and the youngest children would share the bottom bunk: six girls in one room, five boys in the other. Latrice, however, did not find the conditions crowded. "Our apartment wasn't large but I think that our mother did everything to make it feel as large," she recalled many years later. "She was a very intricate housekeeper."[53]

Her father, Elighia Harris, held a steady job at the General Electric plant nearby. He kept his presence secret from the CHA in order to hide his income and save on rent, which was calculated as a percentage of one's income. It was not an uncommon arrangement. Harris would not, for example, appear at school events with the children, or community picnics, even though he slept every night at their apartment.

In the 1970s, street gangs and crack had yet to make much of an impact on Horner, and the family felt it was a safe place. In the early 1980s, that began to change. Drug dealing became more visible and more violent. Two of Latrice's brothers were shot. In 1985, at age 14,

FIG. 9.1. The Henry Horner Homes under redevelopment in 1999: the mid-rise building in the background is a relic from an earlier era; the rowhouses in the foreground housed low- and middle-income residents, as well as some former Horner tenants. (Photo by D. Bradford Hunt)

she moved with her family to Lawndale, a West Side neighborhood where much of the 1968 rioting took place, and which was still littered with abandoned lots and charred ruins of three-flats. Finally, seven years later, they moved to the suburbs, which had been her mother's ultimate goal.

By her early 20s, Latrice Hudson had three kids of her own but was still living with her mom. She knew she needed to move out. She couldn't afford the suburbs, however, or pretty much anything else. The only place she could afford was public housing. She signed up for CHA's waiting list, and waited. It took more than five years; part of that was because she was waiting for a spot back at Henry Horner. For safety reasons, she didn't want to go anywhere else. Residents of a housing project are often viewed as extensions of the gang in control. When she was growing up in Horner, the Vice Lords were in charge, and she feared she would be targeted as an infiltrator if she had moved to a complex affiliated with the Stones or Disciples. Memories among CHA residents are long, loyalties deep.

It was 1999 when Hudson returned to Horner as an adult. She was placed in a seven-story mid-rise across the street from Chicago Stadium, the home of the Chicago Bulls and Blackhawks sports teams. There were more gangs, more drug dealing, and more violence than there had been when she was growing up. (Alex Kotlowitz's book about Horner in the late 1980s and early 1990s, *There Are No Children Here*, reflected the violence of that era.) And yet the culture of trust persisted, sometimes getting the better of people. One morning, a 12-year-old girl knocked on her aunt's door to pick up two younger cousins and walk them to school. When no one answered, the girl let herself in, and discovered her aunt, the aunt's boyfriend, a family friend, and the two cousins on the floor dead. They had been stabbed repeatedly the night before by two acquaintances whom they innocently had let in. Hudson learned later that the acquaintances were drug addicts who had heard the family had received a sizeable Social Security settlement; when they couldn't find any money, they went into the kitchen, grabbed the two largest knives they could find, and cut up the family in rage.

Hudson began seeing flyers from the housing authority announcing that they were going to tear down most of Henry Horner and replace it with a set of row houses and low-rise apartment buildings; moderate-income families would live next to CHA households. This was due to one of the lawsuits that had predated the Plan for Transformation: in 1991, the Sargent Shriver Center, a nonprofit legal outfit, had sued the CHA for failing to maintain the complex. The lawyers claimed that the failure to maintain was effectively "demolition by neglect," and that the authority had not gone through the proper procedures to get federal permission to demolish what was in essence a public asset.

This was a very different sort of lawsuit than *Gautreaux*: the Horner plaintiffs wanted CHA to fix up the housing, not build more elsewhere in wealthier or "whiter" neighborhoods. In addition, the consent decree—reached in 1995 after four years of legal wrangling—put public housing tenants in charge of the remedy. On all aspects of the redevelopment, the private company that took over management of the complex would have to reach agreement with the Horner Residents Committee, made up of seven elected representatives from the complex and counsel from the Shriver Center. The residents insisted on phasing the demolition in order to reduce the amount of displacement—tear down one building, replace it with new row homes, then move onto the next parcel. The committee also designed the screening criteria for residents who wanted to return to the new or renovated buildings. (By contrast, at other developments around the city, the CHA tended to demolish the high-rises all at once, figuring that would make the land more attractive to commercial developers.[54] The screening criteria for the mixed-income developments that replaced other CHA towers were also far stricter than the ones adopted at Horner.[55])

In many ways, the Horner settlement was a blow against gentrification. In the late 1980s, the Wirtz family, which owned Chicago Stadium, had begun thinking of building a new arena. That announcement sparked a wave of real estate speculation in the area. The first Horner settlement, by devoting half of the new units to public housing residents, was intended to ensure that the city's poor would benefit from the neighborhood's resurgence without getting pushed out.

The contrast with *Gautreaux* was deliberate; the lawyer behind the Horner settlement, William P. Wilen, was skeptical about Polikoff's legal strategy; Wilen thought BPI had essentially blocked the construction of public housing by insisting on racial integration. In the 30 years after the *Gautreaux* ruling, just 3,000 units of public housing had been built or acquired in Chicago, most of it in heavily black or Latino neighborhoods. "[J]ust as the Holy Roman Empire was reputed to be neither holy nor Roman," Wilen wrote later, "this type of fair housing is in actuality neither 'fair' nor 'housing.'"[56] The rivalry between Wilen and Polikoff became legendary in Chicago's affordable housing circles: two prominent advocates who shared similar goals but differed dramatically on strategy. Polikoff contended that both men saw mixed-income communities as the solution to concentrated poverty, it was just a question of what the right mix was. In response to Wilen's charges, Polikoff wrote: "Neither honest disagreement about such issues, nor distortions of *Gautreaux*, should divert poverty lawyers from the real culprit—a pitifully inadequate supply of well-located housing for very low-income families."[57]

Hudson heard about the redevelopment plans for Horner casually. At first, she thought they would never really happen. Then, when the demolitions began, she had mixed feelings. Even with elected representatives involved in the redevelopment, she and her neighbors were nervous about their ability to return. "We knew that you had to just really try to make no trouble," she recalled. The selection criteria, for example, would not allow any household with a member convicted of assault or criminal damage to property to return.[58] Hudson wasn't worried so much about herself, but some of her friends were nervous.

While waiting for the buildings to be demolished and the new housing to go up, Hudson moved with her family first to a small CHA building less than a mile away, in East Garfield Park, and then, after about another year, to a second apartment, also fairly close by. During this time, she repeatedly had to resubmit her application after management told her they had lost it or needed more information. But she kept at it, figuring that the red tape was a strategy to dissuade former tenants from returning to the complex. Hudson was adept at seeking out opportunities that would let her children rise above their circumstances: she had been enrolling them in an after-school tutoring program, Chicago Lights—hosted by the Fourth Presbyterian Church on the Near North Side—and got them scholarships to parochial schools. She knew the mixed-income community that was being promised would be far better than Horner had been.

After the first phase of the redevelopment, called Westhaven, was finished, Hudson moved back to the Horner footprint, this time into a brand new four-bedroom row house, with a back door that opened onto the United Center, the venue that ended up taking the Stadium's place. "It was like a blessing and a nightmare," Hudson reflected later. "It just seemed so political to live there." Traffic increased, illegal parking became more frequent, and so, she believed, did police harassment. The new arena had made the neighborhood far more desirable, but Hudson didn't see the location as anything special: "We didn't really have much of a desire really to go to the United Center."

Shortly after Hudson moved in to Westhaven, an unfortunate incident took place. She was home with her two youngest children one day and thought she heard someone running down the stairs next door; she did not think much of it. Later, the woman who lived next door—a black professional with a small family—came home and said her house had been burglarized. She asked Hudson if she had seen anything; Hudson told her what she had heard. She felt the neighbor believed Hudson had let the burglary happen, and the relationship between the two households became icy.

Meanwhile, Hudson's three male children—Stephen and Reginald Jackson, and Andrew Hudson—were being repeatedly stopped by the police—something that rarely, if ever, happened at the old Horner, before middle-income residents moved in. Most of the stops were for dubious infractions, such as sitting on the low wall outside their home or loitering on the sidewalk. Much of the time, her sons were hanging out with friends they had made at Horner before the Transformation, children who had not managed to move back into Westhaven. Each time her sons were stopped—even if they were not charged—the officers would fill out a "contact card" with the teenager's name and address on it. Hudson believed these cards were used to slowly build an eviction case against her. The experiences also made her sons hate living at the redeveloped Horner.

One day, Reginald, who was 16, was walking through the neighborhood with a female friend. Two police officers stopped them, searched them, and found a marijuana blunt—Hudson believes to this day it belonged to the girl, but police said it belonged to Reginald. The police reported the incident to the management company of the complex, which then initiated eviction proceedings against Hudson. She got a legal aid attorney but was given little hope of holding onto the apartment because of the new screening criteria. (Hudson blamed the overly strict enforcement of the rules rather than the rules themselves.) After a year's worth of court appearances, the management company made a deal: Hudson would agree to take Reginald off the lease and not permit him to visit; in return, she and the rest of her family would be permitted to stay at Westhaven.

It was a wrenching decision for Hudson, forcing her to choose between her son and her other four children who would no doubt have a better, safer environment at Westhaven than elsewhere. She chose the latter, even though she knew she would not be able to uphold her end of the bargain. How was a mother to shut out her teenage son? Where else would he go? His only other option was a cousin's home on the West Side; Reginald had begun to sleep over there more and more to avoid the police in Westhaven, but it was a higher-crime neighborhood, and Hudson stayed up late worrying about him every time he went there.

On January 12, 2010, Hudson went to housing court to agree that her son could not return, not even to visit. That evening, her son called her.

Mom, should I come home tonight? Reginald asked.

*You **better** come home tonight,* Hudson answered.

She knew that the police officers who patrolled the complex, the management agents, the grounds crew, maybe even her neighbors would be watching her house from then on, watching when her son came and left, and if he stayed overnight. But it was the only option she could live with.

That August, the management company brought Hudson back to court, alleging she had broken the deal. This time, the court gave her another chance: if her son returned within the following year, she would be evicted. About six months later, police found Reginald back on the property. According to the management company, he threw rocks at the police and then fled into his mom's home. Hudson argued with the police. Then Reginald came out and was charged with disorderly conduct and aggravated assault. About six months after that, in December 2011, the management company said, Reginald was caught again and charged with criminal trespass, at which time he was given thirty days in jail. A month later, he was seen again at Westhaven, but got away.[59]

Hudson despaired; she began to wonder if she really wanted to live in a mixed-income community after all. She fell behind on rent and was served with eviction papers in late 2013, claiming she owed more than $1,000. She gathered up the money from friends and family and brought it to court, but the management company refused to accept it. Her lawyer, Samira Nazem, from the Lawyers' Committee for Better Housing, knew the opposing counsel from earlier cases, and called him up to see if she could work out a deal, but the response was gruff and resolute. "They were very, very clear. They were not interested in working out anything," Nazem recalled. "There was a sense that this was a problem family that they wanted out."[60] Hudson assumed it was because of Reginald. At that point, she knew she would lose the case, as well as all rights to federal housing benefits for the rest of her life. She tried to keep that fact from her son. She knew he had a big enough burden to carry around.

In early October 2013, Reginald, who had been working on and off since high school, decided to pull himself out of the doldrums and get into college any way he could. That meant attending community college, working on his grade point average, and then applying to a four-year school. He felt relieved, elated by the decision to move forward with his life. There was a two-year school in the same exurb as a four-year college that his girlfriend was going to attend; he would move out there and find an apartment where he could live with his girlfriend. His mother said she would help him do that, and he was planning to visit the college a few days later.

A couple of days later, on October 9, Reginald turned 22. The following day, he was walking through an alley in West Garfield Park, near his cousin's house, when he was shot in the back.[61] He died almost immediately. Police told his mother it was a random, drive-by shooting, without any apparent motive, and they did not have any suspects. Hudson felt like her breath was knocked out of her; when she returned home from the hospital, she didn't go inside her house. Instead, she began to walk. She walked all the way east to Lake Michigan, until she got tired out. Then she turned around and went home to bed.

A few weeks later, Hudson and her lawyer went back to court and agreed to stop fighting the eviction; in return, the management company let her stay in her apartment for free until the following April, giving her time to find a new place and save up for a security deposit. Hudson found it nearly impossible to find an apartment large enough in a safe neighborhood. When, unable to move out April 1, she was finally evicted, she ended up in a three-bedroom home in a walk-up in East Garfield Park. The place was adequate, if also distinctly carved up from a larger apartment, with awkwardly shaped rooms and newly sheet-rocked walls. A vacant lot took up most of the block across the street, and sometimes gangs shot at each other there. Around the corner stood a row of storefronts, all boarded up except for a grocery that sold lottery tickets and beer. Further down toward the L stop, there was a set of highway guardrails where dozens of people hung throughout the day drinking out of 40-ounce bottles. This was the ghetto that prompted Chicago reformers to undertake public housing in the first place in the 1930s; which they naively re-created in vertical form through high-rises; and which they sought to avoid when creating mixed-income communities in the Plan for Transformation. But for people like Hudson who didn't qualify for mixed-income communities, or who qualified but were then evicted for extenuating circumstances, it was as if none of that had happened.

THE END OF TRANSFORMATION

Given the difficulties of integrating very-low and middle-income residents in the new mixed-income communities, it might be just as well

FIG. 9.2. The Cabrini-Green towers have been demolished, but redevelopment has been slow. Here, a large vacant area surrounded by replacement housing, between Clybourn Avenue and Division Street, in 2017. (Photo by Matthew L. Schuerman)

that the CHA's construction of them is far behind schedule. By the end of June 2018, only 3,091 units for CHA families had been built in mixed-income communities; the city had originally imagined building more than 10,000.[62] Inhibited by the Great Recession as well as the city's own outsized expectations, vast swaths of Cabrini-Green's former footprint—supposedly the most attractive land the CHA had to offer—still lay fallow. On Chicago's South Side, most of the State Street corridor was covered in grass or gravel; no signs of the notorious high-rises remained, but very little had taken their place. Instead of building the mixed-income complexes promised by the Plan for Transformation, the CHA had moved many of its residents off-site to privately owned buildings, subsidizing their rents with vouchers. In fact, more CHA residents were housed in these long-term voucher arrangements than in the mixed-income developments, which had been supposedly the raison d'être of the Plan for Transformation in the first place.[63]

For these "Project Section 8" buildings, the housing authority secures the apartment; the tenant then pays the authority 30 percent of her income while the housing authority, with federal assistance, pays the rest of the rent. This arrangement has its advantages: the CHA does not have to construct buildings from scratch, and it also gets to pare down its own staff of custodians, groundskeepers, and repairmen—the inefficiencies that once plagued CHA's bureaucracy. But neither do the residents get to enjoy the fruits of *Gautreaux* standards of integration, let alone the mixed-income settings that Mayor Daley and Julia Stasch had promised. In addition, CHA's arrangements with landlords are temporary, generally lasting twenty years, and, especially in gentrifying areas, might not be renewed.

Julia Stasch and other high-level officials in the Daley administration have admitted that the Plan for Transformation was imperfect, that many of the early assessments about how long it would take or how easily public housing residents would assimilate were wildly off. They also have, nudged by lawsuits and public pressure, instituted a number of reforms; in 2004 came a "relocation rights contact" guaranteeing former tenants the right to return to the public housing system. The following year, the CHA intensified its efforts to locate voucher holders in "high opportunity areas"—neighborhoods with lower-than-median levels of poverty, where the authority agreed to subsidize higher rents than they would normally allow.

In 2007, the city began offering extensive social services, such as drug addiction treatment, to former tenants, and relaxed the requirement that recipients of housing assistance work or be enrolled in school.[64] "We thought isolation was the problem, and the antidote was connection," Stasch recalled. "And what we learned over time was there's a swath of people for whom that is the right thing—a little motivation, a little support—but there were another couple of tiers of people who had been so disconnected from the workforce for so long, that connection had not been sufficient to put their lives on the right trajectory. And then there was another whole swath of people who were never going to function in a fully market dynamic—people with disabilities, families where the head of the household could never have a job."

More distressing than the shortcomings of Chicago's Plan for Transformation, however, are research findings that suggest the advantages of mixed-income living are mixed at best, and chimerical at worst. The small number of families who enrolled in the highly selective *Gautreaux* relocation program in the 1980s and '90s showed higher education attainment and employment levels, but only "tenuous" income benefits. A larger pool of low-income households integrated in the 1990s under HUD programs showed that participants had better health than their public housing counterparts, but no gains in employment or education.[65] In the Plan for Transformation, adults paradoxically fared better than children: half of adults under 62 years old were employed in 2011, compared to one-third four years earlier;[66] but youths did not gain access to better schools and delinquency levels stayed about the same.[67] Plus, the Plan was disruptive, academically and socially: a family might have to move out of a highrise in the middle of the school year, then might move again suddenly to find a safer spot.[68] Susan Popkin, the Urban Institute senior fellow who has studied Chicago public housing for nearly thirty years, concluded that young people "gained little more than a slightly better quality of life."[69]

TEN

ZERO-SUM GAME:
SAN FRANCISCO, 2001–2018

Add to the factors complicating San Francisco's gentrification—its small geographic size, its rigid zoning laws, its redevelopment schemes—another one: an uneven affordable housing record. In the Mission District, the organization in charge of developing below-market-rate housing, the Mission Housing Development Corporation, was debilitated by infighting right when it was needed most.

It began in 1999, when one of Mission Housing's senior staff members, Eric Quezada, allied with other neighborhood organizations to create the Mission Anti-Displacement Coalition.[1] The new group sought strategies to slow gentrification. They protested a proposal to turn an armory into a dot-com workplace. They organized a *caminata* through the Mission, leading hundreds of participants to one example after another of the effects of gentrification, such as a Latina-owned flower stand that well-off neighbors tried to shut down because it wasn't in a commercial zone.[2] They invited the city's planning director and two planning commissioners to a community meeting at a local public high school, where 500 people came to jeer at them.[3] Then, in September 2000, more than a dozen coalition members stormed the Bay View Federal Bank building, the only high-rise office tower on Mission Street. They came to protest the arrival of Bigstep.com, an e-commerce platform company that had taken over the space that once housed several nonprofits and small businesses. Fifteen activists were arrested. "We sent a message, not just to Bigstep, but to all dot-com companies, that you can't build and displace people irresponsibly," said one of the coalition members, Elly Kugler.[4]

The younger staff members of Mission Housing viewed themselves as the true children of '60s radicalism, trying to re-create the same "atmosphere inhospitable to investment" from the Mission Coalition days. (Mission Housing was a direct outgrowth of the Mission Coalition Organization.) They viewed the organization's board of directors as washed-up activists who had gone soft after getting jobs in the city's anti-poverty apparatus. One Mission Housing staffer, Lisa Pagan, said the older generation was "talking for the poor and promoting themselves."[5] They considered the nonprofit's president, Larry Del Carlo, to be the poster child of the fading old guard. His father had served on Mission Housing's board during the 1970s and 1980s, and his mother had been one of the first board officers of the Mission Coalition Organization. But he was now considered too "establishment," and staff members charged him with cronyism.

Del Carlo didn't have a problem with the radical leanings of his staff—at least at first. But in 2001, Del Carlo and other board members began talking more and more about the need to build housing for middle-income workers, as opposed to for exclusively low-income households. The idea started with a former school building at 1950 Mission Street, near the 16th Street BART station, which Del Carlo wanted to turn into housing for school district employees: teachers, clerical staff, and custodians. "What happened in San Francisco was that you had to be very poor to qualify for subsidized housing, or very wealthy to afford market-rate housing," Del Carlo said later. "The workforce could not live here anymore." Del Carlo, who was working for the school district at the time, had gotten buy-in from school officials, the teachers union, and Mayor Willie Brown's administration. The idea of "workforce housing" was still new in policy circles, and it was a departure for Mission Housing. Carlos Romero, the executive director, saw any attempt to divert resources from helping low-income households as a betrayal of the organization's purpose. In January 2004, when the board asked him to take on the development of 1950 Mission, Romero refused. Then, he was fired. What followed was a year-and-a-half of acrimony and public name-calling. Many staff members were asked to leave or quit on their own accord. Two city supervisors who had been elected with campaign help from Mission Housing staff members held hearings and called for an audit of the organization's finances. Meanwhile, Del Carlo, the board president, was worried that his organization's nonprofit status was in jeopardy, because HUD had received complaints that its employees were campaigning during work hours.[6]

Had it not been for this internal dissension, this era would have been an ideal time for Mission Housing to go hunting for some good real estate deals: The dot-com boom had busted. Bigstep.com had downsized. The developers had put the armory project on indefinite hold. But Mission Housing was too dysfunctional to take advantage of the real estate slump. The city audit, while failing to find evidence of cronyism, described an organization in disarray, confused whether it was to serve just low-income individuals, or middle-income people, too. Mission Housing had pulled out of two city service contracts and failed to win renewals on four others. One of the comptroller's investigators had been offered a job at the organization during a field interview.[7] The city, pressured by left-wing supervisors, terminated $360,000 in annual Community Development Block Grant funding.[8] Two foundations that had been major donors for years—Enterprise Community Partners and the San Francisco Foundation—followed suit.[9]

For nearly the next decade, Mission Housing limped along on an operating budget that was just half of what it used to be.[10] Del Carlo stepped in as executive director to oversee day-to-day operations; he found it difficult if not impossible to win contracts to develop land within San Francisco. In desperation, Mission Housing sought to build two single-family developments 200 miles away in California's Central Valley. (Housing corporations, even nonprofit ones, need the development fees that new projects bring in order to survive.) It wasn't until 2016, after yet another leadership change, that the housing corporation came back to full strength, and again took up 1950 Mission Street. The upshot was that in the midst of rapid gentrification, the organization didn't put any new affordable units into circulation in its home neighborhood.[11] The current executive director, Sam Moss, lamented, "We lost ten years."[12]

MISSION VS. THE TENDERLOIN

It's unfair to blame gentrification in San Francisco on just one organization. The social and economic forces driving upper-middle-income professionals into neighborhoods like the Mission were far too powerful for a $1 million-a-year operation to resist. Yet, that was a big part of the problem: for more than forty years, Mission Housing was just about the *only* group creating *any* affordable housing in the neighborhood. By contrast, the Tenderloin, a small slice of Skid Row just north and west of downtown, had three or four housing corporations, often outgrowths of religious organizations that had been ministering to the down-and-outs in the area's residential hotels. One, Mercy Housing, was a national outfit with 325 locations in 41 states. These nonprofits planned ahead. Like the best for-profit developers, they bought up properties cheaply during the neighborhood's fallow era in the late 1980s and 1990s, even though the need for affordable housing was much lower at the time.[13] As a result, twice as many affordable housing units were preserved or developed between 1970 and 2007 in the Tenderloin (4,429) as in the Mission (1,883), even though the Tenderloin had half as many residents.[14] By 2015, one-quarter of all units in the Tenderloin were controlled by nonprofits and subsidized by the city, which kept a lid on rents.[15]

Yet replicating the Tenderloin's stability in other neighborhoods proved extremely difficult. For one, the Tenderloin had the law on its side: in 1980, the Board of Supervisors made it illegal to convert single-room occupancy hotels—which tended to house the very poor—into tourist accommodations, warding off the biggest threat to the neighborhood. For another, Tenderloin real estate consists primarily of large buildings divided up into small units. The size of the buildings discouraged for-profit landlords from buying out rent-controlled tenants—it would be too expensive to pay off so many people—while also making it possible for nonprofits to rehab-in-place. (It's a lot easier to move residents from an un-renovated room to a renovated one in a big building than in a small one.)

The Tenderloin was the exception, however, that proved the rule that San Francisco has had an enormous amount of trouble creating affordable housing. Not that it hasn't tried. Unlike New York City, which can unilaterally issue bonds to subsidize construction, California has a referendum system that makes it easier to block growth than to accommodate it. Most referendum measures require a simple majority to pass—like Proposition M in 1986, limiting the amount of new office space each year—but any authorization to borrow money requires approval by two-thirds of the voters. Three affordable housing propositions in San Francisco—supported, incidentally, by Calvin Welch's Council for Community Housing Organizations—failed between 1996 and 2011, proof that residents of the nation's supposedly most liberal city can be quite stingy.

Unable to borrow, San Francisco attempted a new strategy: "inclusionary housing." It meant that developers of any large building had to subsidize affordable housing, either by dedicating 15 percent of a project to below-market-rate units, or by giving the city cash to build low-income apartments somewhere else. But, while proposed during the height of the dot-com boom, San Francisco's inclusionary system wasn't implemented until 2002, after the economy collapsed. Nor was it implemented very well. One city audit found that many for-profit developers waited five to sixteen months before advertising that they had subsidized units available. Some of the developers didn't even bother to check whether the tenants who applied for them were income-eligible. In one building, auditors found that seventeen affordable units had stood vacant for three years.[16] A change made in 2010 skewed the system further to developers' advantage. If they chose to pay the fee instead of including subsidized units on-site, developers could finish their market-rate apartments first, and then give the city its money. Yet it would take the city another two years on average to put that money toward affordable units. Builders took this build-now-pay-later option in overwhelming numbers, which meant that instead of inclusionary housing off-setting the displacement that a large market-rate building might cause in a neighborhood, it was a delayed counter-reaction. (By contrast, a New York City voucher system that was in place until 2007 required developers to complete their share of affordable apartments before they received a certificate of occupancy for market-rate units.)[17]

If anyone thought San Francisco's inclusionary program would mitigate escalating housing prices, they were quickly disillusioned. Between 2002 and 2011, only 133 apartments a year on average were constructed under the program, constituting less than one-tenth of all affordable housing production. Ironically, a much larger source of affordable housing funds came from the oft-reviled San Francisco Redevelopment Agency—the same one that had bulldozed the Western Addition in the 1960s. (The agency funneled property tax revenues on the land it owned back into housing production—rather than to the city's general fund.)[18] In another irony, the federal Low-Income Housing Tax Credit was responsible for creating even more affordable units. That program was signed into law by a Republican, President Ronald Reagan.[19]

GOOGLE'S VIEW

With the growth of Silicon Valley's economy in the early twenty-first century, the peculiarities of the Greater Bay Area economy became clear, while the ramifications for housing prices became painful. Jobs were distributed like a barbell, clustered in the north and south. But

housing was primarily in the north. In between lay former fruit or-
chards that had been turned into single-family homes, shopping centers, and wide boulevards.

The mismatch dates to World War II, when business at defense-
related contractors in the South Bay area grew exponentially. The
Department of Defense preferred non-urban locations for its contractors, because they would not put large numbers of civilians in
danger. Consequently, Stanford University developed about 3,000
acres of its land into a high-tech industrial park in 1952. Stanford
nicknamed its development "the city of knowledge," but it was in
many ways the antithesis of urbanity. Its planners tried to imitate the
sprawl of an English university campus, which was thought to stimu-
late creativity by removing the "knowledge worker" from the hustle
and bustle of the city.[20] The university stipulated low-rise buildings
with 90-foot buffer strips between roads and buildings.[21] There was
no requirement to build sidewalks and so none were. According to
one survey, just nine people walked to work there.[22]

The transformation that the Stanford Industrial Park introduced
would be the envy of most economic development directors around
the country: high-paying, low-polluting jobs. Thousands of them.
Employers made their workplaces comfortable and their hours flexible, and treated workers as partners in a grand endeavor to change
the world. Hewlett-Packard adopted "The HP Way," characterized by
mutual respect and numerous perks intended to make life outside and
inside the company seamless. Employees were offered on-site child
care, generous maternity (and paternity) leave, and—though it must
have sounded quaint at the time—a chance to co-own the company
through stock options.[23]

Facebook and Google made their homes in Silicon Valley largely
because that's where the venture capitalist infrastructure began during the HP years. But even if these companies had wanted to move to
a more densely populated, commuter-friendly, and hip urban environment, San Francisco's land-use controls would have made it hard
to grow. Google recently expanded to a 7 million square foot campus;

under Proposition M, the company would have needed eight years to secure that much space in downtown San Francisco, and then only if no other companies were waiting in line. So while these Web 2.0 companies expanded their workforces south of San Francisco, there were few places for them to live.

So where *were* all these people supposed to live? As the computer industry grew, tens of thousands of jobs were grafted onto suburban towns created in the 1950s and 1960s, when both economics and ideology discouraged high-density residential zoning. (Industrial parks like Stanford's bring in lots of property tax revenues, while single-family homes produce fewer children to be educated in public schools.) As a result, it was difficult if not impossible to build apartment buildings or even row houses needed to accommodate high population density. Neither had San Mateo and Santa Clara counties bought into the BART district in the 1960s or attempted any sort of mass transit system until much later, meaning that most of these workers had to rely on a car to get around. By the second internet boom, Silicon Valley offered only one housing unit for every three jobs located there, a ratio that meant that more than two-thirds of the workforce commuted from outside the immediate area.[24]

Even without a housing shortage in Silicon Valley, the tech industry's roots in the 1960s counterculture steered workers toward an urban environment. The ardently anti-establishment Whole Earth Catalog espoused "tools for human use"—including computers—that encouraged self-sufficiency. The Homebrew Computer Club that gave rise to Apple was an outgrowth of a weekly potluck dinner. Collaboration, tinkering, and creativity were all essential ingredients of Silicon Valley's entrepreneurialism. "The hierarchical systems of the East Coast, England, Germany, and Japan do not encourage this different thinking," the musician Bono, a friend of Steve Jobs, once said. "The sixties produced an anarchic mind-set that is great for imagining a world not yet in existence."[25] Even a Marxist might look upon these jobs favorably. Where was the alienation of labor when engineers and scientists were just as likely to get inspiration walking down the street as at their desks? In his manifesto, *The Rise of the Creative Class*, urban theorist Richard Florida writes of information workers: "They could never be forced to work, yet they were never truly not at work."[26] As with the creative professionals David Ley studied in Canada in the 1970s, it should be no surprise that the iconoclasm valued in Silicon Valley would propel tech workers to eventually seek out unconventional places to live—or at least places that seemed unconventional on the surface.

The choice of the prototypical Millennial tech worker was obvious: live in San Francisco.[27] With little night life and suburban-style living, the appeal of Silicon Valley to young single employees was limited. Yet the reverse commute was a miserable hour-long drive by car and virtually impossible by mass transit: Cal Train, which had few stops inside San Francisco to begin with, deposited people in a handful of stations in Santa Clara County, miles away from the dispersed tech campuses.

In 2004, a Google employee, Cari Spivak, thought she had the solution: a massive car-pool. Her superiors gave her time and resources to work on it. The first "Google Bus" was just a van. It made two stops in San Francisco, one at the Glen Park BART station, a bit south of the Mission, and the other at a park-n-ride lot at Candlestick Park, along the bay.[28] These buses didn't do much to reduce employees' commute time, since they were stuck in the same traffic the cars were. But they allowed passengers to do something else while commuting—in many cases, work on their laptops for the corporation that was paying their way. Spivak's idea caught on, and other suburban employers followed suit, including Genentech, Facebook, and Apple. In 2012, more than 130 buses carried 4,015 employees a day to and from San Francisco.[29] By late 2016, the daily ridership had grown to 9,800.[30] In 2014, Apple was spending $35 million a year on its transportation program; Google, with a much larger workforce, likely spent three or four times more.[31] The tech companies came to see transportation expenses as a necessary cost of doing business, even if they had nothing to do with their core missions. Google CFO Patrick Pichette said in 2011, "If we did not have this bus system, what we would have is gridlock every morning and every afternoon, with loss of productivity for employees."[32]

THE EVICTION

The influx of these tech workers was being felt in San Francisco. Landlords were turning to the Ellis Act more and more, claiming to be getting out of the real estate business as a way to evict lease-abiding tenants who were paying below market rate. Between 2010 and 2013, the number of households in San Francisco evicted under the law nearly tripled.[33] The Mission had become a favorite destination for Silicon Valley workers: it was edgy, and located closer to their jobs. Valencia Street, on the neighborhood's western edge, transformed first—an eyeglass store, a real estate agency, renovated apartments—because it was closer to the already gentrified Noe Valley.

René Yañez and his partner, Cynthia Wallis, lived near Valencia on a small side street, San José Avenue. A few days before Christmas 2012, their landlord, Sergio Iantorno, went by the house unannounced. Yañez was at the SOMARTS art center, where he was an exhibit curator. Wallis was home, resting from a recent chemotherapy treatment for stomach cancer. Iantorno told her he wanted them to move so he could turn a profit on the building. When Yañez found out, he was furious, especially because of how the news was delivered. "Listen," Yañez told Iantorno on the phone. "I don't want you doing that. Call in advance if you have business." Iantorno at first began to tell Yañez about his history: how he immigrated to this country with $15 in his pocket and worked his way up the ranks of the real estate industry through hard work. But hearing that only irritated Yañez more and they continued to argue. Finally, the landlord said, "I'm going to have my lawyer talk to you." And then he hung up.[34]

Iantorno had paid only $415,000 for the rent-controlled four-unit Victorian row house in 2000. While that might sound like a bargain today, he had expected rents to rise much more quickly than they had. Indeed, out of the seventy buildings he owned, it was one of the six lowest-performing assets. Yañez and Wallis paid just about $600 a month for their piece of it—perhaps a quarter of what the one-bedroom would command if renovated and put on the free market. Two other tenants there paid roughly the same. The fourth, a film-maker, had moved in nearly twenty years earlier—so even *he* wasn't paying anywhere near market rent. As housing in San Francisco be-came more expensive, none of his tenants could afford to live any-where else, meaning that turnover was nil.[35]

Given that the building was rent-controlled, Iantorno could in-crease the rent only a couple of percentage points a year—or invoke the Ellis Act and claim that he was getting out of the real estate busi-ness. He did so the following July, hiring Andrew Zacks, the lawyer who had helped popularize Ellis Act evictions in the dot-com era. "He had undervalued properties," Zacks said. "He was getting pen-nies in rent. He had liabilities. The costs to maintain the properties—insurance, what have you—were all going up."[36]

Yañez's first move was to find his own lawyer. He called the city's planning department for help, and was referred to the Tenderloin Housing Clinic, a nonprofit law practice that had been the bulldog in the fight over the SROs. The lawyer, Raquel Fox, was in charge of cases in the Mission, and had a good record. Fox eagerly took the case: the tenants were largely senior citizens who had lived there a long time, the type of case she cared about the most.

Fox visited Yañez and the other tenants the following week. Since the landlord had every right to invoke the Ellis Act, her strategy was to fight the case on procedural grounds, appealing whenever proper notice wasn't served, or if other rules weren't followed. Those delays would buy the tenants more time, enhance their negotiating posi-tion, and cost the other side as much in legal fees as possible. During the dot-com era, Fox had represented Lola McKay, an 83-year-old widow whose case became famous. She had been living in her apart-ment for forty-two years; her rent was a mere $100 a month. Back then, landlords didn't need to give any tenant any more than thirty days' notice, no matter what their age. Fox convinced a judge to give her an extra month, and then an extra year as the sole tenant in a four-unit building on Alvarado Street. McKay died before the year was up. Her case became famous, inspiring rallies and leading to a state law extending the notice period on Ellis Act evictions to 120 days, and a full year for the elderly. Because of their ages and disabilities, Yañez and Wallis benefited directly from that law, and had a full year to look for another place.

Landlords thought the legal strategies employed by tenant lawyers like Fox were unfair, especially once Mayor Ed Lee increased funding to legal clinics as part of his anti-displacement agenda. From landlords' point of view, Lee was using taxpayer money to persecute one class of people: landlords. It was all the more unseemly, many of them thought, that the public's money was being used for legal nit-picking to delay and delay, running up legal bills and denying landlords profits. "We are willing to do our part to house the elderly and the poor," Iantorno wrote to a city supervisor, "but we firmly believe the city is attempting to shift to us, and to similar property owners, the entire burden of housing poor and disabled people in San Francisco."[37]

THE ANTI-TECH MOVEMENT

The Ellis Act and the Google buses fueled a vicious anti-tech movement. The beginning is often traced to early 2013, when San Francisco writer Rebecca Solnit—twelve years after decrying the onset of the dot-com boom—attacked the Google buses that were shuttling "neatly dressed, uncool" employees of tech companies between their homes in the city and their workplaces in Silicon Valley. Solnit herself had bought an apartment in the Mission in the 1990s, then sold it in 2011 and moved into a rental. When, a couple of years later, she decided she wanted to buy again, she found she could not afford anything. "At the actual open houses, dozens of people who looked like students would show up with chequebooks and sheaves of resumes and other documents and pack the house, literally," she wrote. "[I]t was like a cross between being at a rock concert without a band and the Hotel Rwanda."[38] Though published in the elite *London Review of Books*, the essay was circulated widely. Activists had certainly noticed the buses before, but Solnit helped shape them into a *thing* unto its own, which had causes (Web 2.0) and impacts (gentrification). The buses quickly became objects of derision, protest, and analysis. In May, a bunch of activists made piñatas in the shapes of the buses— they were of the tinted-glass luxury-coach variety—and smashed them open.[39] Around the same time, Alexandra Goldman, a graduate student at the University of California, Berkeley, calculated that rents near the tech bus stops were about 20 percent higher than the surrounding areas—though she acknowledged that she could not prove that the shuttles were the cause.[40]

The following month saw Pride, the annual celebration in which the city's gay, lesbian, bisexual, transgender, and queer populations dress up in costumes, build floats, and march down Market Street from downtown to the Castro District. Once a countercultural assertion of gay rights, the event had by 2013 gone mainstream. Corporations, including many Internet companies, bought space in the line-up to signify their embrace of alternative lifestyles. Some housing activists saw this corporatization of a grassroots event as a type of gentrification itself. So they decided to put a faux "Google bus" in the parade.[41]

The activists raised $1,500 through the crowdfunding website GoFundMe, rented a coach like those used for employee shuttles, and affixed to its side a giant vinyl scroll that read "Gentrification Eviction Technologies OUT" (GET-OUT) in a font and colors resembling those on Google's home page. Volunteers cut out giant teardrop-shaped pieces of cardboard and colored them red to look like the drop pins that Google Maps uses. There was a hole near the top of each cardboard cut-out where the carrier's face could show through, and above it, the word "Eviction." (A few weeks earlier, activist Brian Whitty had made a map of all the known Ellis Act evictions from the previous fifteen years.[42]) The marchers followed behind the bus and passed out flyers calling for an eviction-free summer.

The morning of Pride, the activists ended up near Google's official entry in the march's line-up at the top of Market Street. "At first, when we were waiting before the march to begin, Google employees thought we were with them," Leslie Dreyer, one of the leaders of the group, remembered. "Then, they read the sign more closely and there was a debate over the reasons for eviction and what the tech companies had to do with it." When their bus neared the reviewing stand near Cole Street, the live television feed cut to the program's anchor so viewers at home wouldn't see the GET-OUT bus.

As the eviction figures continued to increase, the activists planned a more disruptive action. Dreyer discovered a law prohibiting unauthorized vehicles from using the city's bus stops, which carried a $271 fine per incident. Dreyer multiplied that amount by the number of stops she figured the Google shuttle had made over the previous two years and came up with a total of $1 billion in outstanding fines. The group wrote out a giant ticket for that amount, donned reflective vests, and called up the news media. "When a double-decker bus came through at 9 a.m. at Valencia and 24th Street, there were forty to fifty people lined up to take the bus," Dreyer recalled. "We stopped the bus, put up the blockade, and gave them the citation."

The press coverage was overwhelming. "Bemused Google workers spent about a half hour sitting on the bus until the protesters disbanded, many of the workers sending Tweets about the incident," went a Reuters report picked up by hundreds of publications and websites around the world.[43] Local television stations and newspapers, the *Toronto Globe and Mail*, the *New York Times*' technology blog, BBC's website, and dozens of other outlets did their own stories. Some of the stories were critical: it was simplistic to blame tech workers and their shuttle buses for high housing prices. But that interpretation was itself a simplistic view of the protest—especially for anyone who knew anything about Saul Alinsky's methods. It was a stunt that was meant to be a stunt: confrontational, visual, and even a bit funny. And it worked. Other groups followed with their own Google bus protests, in San Francisco and in Oakland, where one demonstrator climbed on top of a shuttle, vomited down its windshield, and broke the glass. The tech industry—and city government—were put on the defensive. One of Mayor Ed Lee's closest backers, venture capitalist Ron Conway, pledged to use his tech lobbying group, sf.citi, to "engage" on affordable housing and technical education.[44] A stream of computer donations and adopt-a-school events followed.

Tech companies were stunned at being targeted. "Everyone at the companies thought that these buses were a good idea," said Adrian Covert, a senior vice president at the Bay Area Council who represented Silicon Valley employers on this issue. "Why were people upset about it?"

Yet there were legitimate, concrete problems caused by the employee shuttles, beyond their theoretical impact on housing prices. When the buses loaded and unloaded passengers at public bus stops, they often forced public buses to wait. Other times, the shuttles double-parked, trapping public buses and blocking car or bike lanes. They idled too much and were awfully big, at 45 feet long and 18 feet high, to go hurtling through the narrow hilly streets in the northern reaches of the city. There was also a push-pull effect: surveys found that between 14 and 40 percent of passengers would either move closer to work or give up their jobs altogether if they could not use the shuttles—a fact that activists argued proved that too-convenient transportation was gentrifying the city.[45] A few weeks after the protests began, the city announced a pilot program to rein in shuttle misbehavior.

Still, most of the antipathy toward the shuttles grew out of their symbolism. The private buses, according to Solnit, contained "people too valuable even to use public transport or drive themselves" who were "undermining the financial basis for the commuter train."[46] But by riding vehicles paid for and operated by private companies, these employees actually helped out other San Franciscans. Public transit is subsidized by taxpayers; forcing tech employees onto Cal-train would only have added to that burden. If shuttle riders instead drove, they'd cause more traffic for other commuters. The shuttles also helped parking: Some 28 percent of shuttle riders didn't even own cars. San Franciscans, who have a suburban-like obsession with traffic and parking spaces, should have taken heart in that factoid: it meant more curb space for them.[47]

DIGITAL TOOLS

As the anti-tech movement grew, it paradoxically used the tools of Silicon Valley to turn against it. In 2013, Erin McElroy and some friends launched a website, the Anti-Eviction Mapping Project, that used publicly available data to analyze the depth of displacement around the Bay Area. One map showed the locations of all the eviction notices that had been registered in San Francisco since 1997: a sea of dots, of varying colors to signify different rationales for eviction. (The Mission District had the most of any neighborhood: nearly 6,000 by the end of 2016.) More significantly, the mapping project teamed up with Eviction Defense Collaborative, a legal aid clinic, to figure out where people go after they have been displaced by gentrification. They tracked down 500 former clients and found that a third of them had left San Francisco entirely, many for Oakland or Daly City, a working-class suburb to the south. About a sixth of the clients moved further away, to Los Angeles or Sacramento or out of state—moves that most likely also required them to get new jobs, new friends, and new social support networks. Of those who stayed in San Francisco, more than seventy ended up in Bayview or Ingleside, neighborhoods on the southern edge of the city where mass transit is hard to come by. Fourteen clients became homeless.

The research, while not peer-reviewed, was essentially the largest longitudinal study done by that point to trace where displaced individuals end up. (It was larger than the studies of Capitol Hill and Hayes Valley mentioned in chapter 5.) By contrast, scholarly research since 2000 has tended to downplay the seriousness of displacement. In a 2004 paper focused on New York City, for example, Lance Freeman and Frank Braconi suggested that gentrification helps just as many low-income people as it hurts, for the tenants who stay in gentrifying neighborhoods hang on because of better shopping opportunities, lower crime, and more responsive government services.[48] But the Freeman-Braconi paper and others like it had blind spots. For one thing, they relied on Census surveys, and could measure only whether people moved and not how far they moved. The Anti-Eviction Mapping Project found that less than one-quarter of the forty-eight clients evicted from the Mission and neighboring Bernal Heights were able to move into different apartments in the same neighborhood.[49] Extrapolating from the results of the 2015 study, one can conclude that at least 1,650 San Francisco households—and potentially many more—move out of the city each year due to gentrification.[50]

Beginning in about 2016, an anti-anti-gentrification movement took root, the Yes-in-my-backyard movement, or YIMBY. These adherents, like traditional economists, argue that the solution to high prices is to increase supply. But it is worthwhile to shed some skepticism on that solution, particularly as it pertains to San Francisco. A team of researchers at Berkeley has cautioned that building exclusively market-rate homes would be a painfully slow way of easing prices. In a robust housing market, most "market-rate" units are built for the high end of the price range, because they give developers the greatest profits. Supposedly, the new inventory "filters down" to lower-income residents, who occupy the apartments that the wealthy have moved out of. But in the Bay Area, researchers Miriam Zuk and Karen Chapple found it was a slow process. In the short term, the building boom in the 1990s led only to higher rents; it took more than a decade before they could detect a decline in rents. What's more, while increasing the supply of housing may temper prices at a regional scale, it does not affect the affordability of the neighborhoods where it is built. Instead, Zuk and Chapple argued for a healthy mix of market-rate and below-market-rate construction.[51]

Another study, this one performed by the California Legislative Analyst's Office, argued that San Francisco would need to double its population—from 800,000 to 1.7 million—in order to keep prices in check.[52] "You'd have to, like, build another city on top of the city," said David Campos, a former city supervisor who used to represent the Mission.[53] Even that wouldn't reduce prices significantly: instead of the city's median home price clocking in at twice the national figure, it would clock in at 1.8 times.

Increasing the density of a city—"upzoning" to allow developers to build higher and wider on certain parcels—in theory should make each apartment less expensive by increasing supply. But in the process, there are some "free riders"—economists' term for parties who benefit from a change in policy or practice without any sacrifice. In this case, the free riders are the landowners, who get to charge more for their property because they know the developer who builds upon it will make more money. In 2015, land costs in San Francisco were about $163,000 per unit, or about a third of an apartment's price. While each apartment's price might fall as supply increases, it will be offset to some degree by rising land costs. The corollary is also true: by making land *less* valuable, such as by requiring developers to include below-market-rate units, its price per acre drops.[54] In that sense, the YIMBY argument that inclusionary zoning requirements merely raise the cost of market-rate units is only partially true.

There was another issue that anti-gentrification activists were also sensitive to when confronted with proposals for taller buildings. Neighborhoods on the east and north sides, like Nob Hill, Russian Hill, and Chinatown, as well as the Mission, are about twice as densely populated as the west side. The city has largely left the west side to remain as it is—on the grounds that it does not have enough transit. Yet, whenever government has attempted to increase transit there, the communities have also objected to that. In the early 1960s, there was BART's proposal to add a line along Geary Boulevard. Then, in 1966, the Muni—the agency that runs buses and streetcars within the city limits—proposed building its own line down Geary. In the 1970s, Planning Director Allan Jacobs suggested laying a trolley track along an unneeded traffic lane on Sunset Boulevard.[55] In the 1990s, Deputy Mayor Jim Wunderman began to negotiate behind the scenes to increase housing density in Richmond. Shortly thereafter, Wunderman's boss, Mayor Frank Jordan, lost his bid for a second term.[56] A current proposal to put a bus rapid transit line along Geary and study new BART lines will put the neighborhoods' political resolve to the test.

Unable to build up due to zoning restrictions, and unable to build outward due to the city's tight boundaries, one would think San Francisco would put its limited space to best use. Yet, in many neighborhoods on the West Side as well as on the East—Glen Park, Ingleside, Cole Valley, Haight-Ashbury, and even side streets in the Mission—two-story homes have garages that take up half of the ground floor. That means that one-quarter of the city's precious built residential space is devoted not to housing more people, but to storing cars. In 1955, in an attempt to offer the same amenities as the suburbs did, San Francisco began to require that every new dwelling unit be equipped with at least one off-street parking space.[57] Older homes were often retrofitted with garages as well. For a city that prides itself on staging a famous "freeway revolt" in the late 1950s and early 1960s, San Francisco is strangely dependent on the automobile. Nearly one out of every two people own a car (counting adults *and* children); and 47 percent of residents drive to work. The percentage of people taking transit is actually dropping.[58]

Nor did garages do much to relieve the on-street parking shortage; a 2007 study of the Mission found that only about half of the garages in that neighborhood were used to store cars, yet all garages decreased the available on-street parking space by 41 percent. Each garage required a driveway, which requires a curb-cut, which monopolizes a 10-foot stretch of curb 24 hours a day, while several cars could pull in and out of the same horizontal space over that time.[59] Garage owners, after all, were not prohibited from parking on the street. In that sense, they got two gifts from the city: the curb-cuts, plus the same free curbside real estate every other car owner has access to.

Requiring a developer to include an off-street parking space in every building also raised housing costs—one study found by 11 percent.[60] Yet plenty of home builders would rather include more parking than required in their plans than risk having neighbors block their projects. City officials were slow to recognize the connection between off-street parking and housing affordability, and even slower to do something about it. The first residential rezoning plan to drop minimum parking requirements did not come until 2008—in the rezoning of the Eastern Districts. By mid-2018, that thinking had spread to seven other neighborhoods—all but one of them east of Van Ness. Undoing the harm caused by the garages already built will take longer, though the city in 2016 did authorize property owners to convert garages into in-law apartments.[61]

"MONSTER IN THE MISSION"

Following the Great Recession, developers returned to the Mission District, this time to take advantage of the 2008 zoning changes that had eliminated density limits in certain parts of the neighborhood. Several neighborhood organizations, under the umbrella group United to Save the Mission, had become disenchanted with the idea that increasing the supply of housing would make San Francisco more affordable. Even with the city's innovative inclusionary zoning policies, 89 percent of the new housing being built in the Mission post-2009 was market-rate, which meant the occupant had to earn twice the city's median income in order to afford it: by definition, new residents of the neighborhood were much higher-income than the ones living there previously.[62]

These housing groups also believed in the snowball effect: as more wealthy people moved into their neighborhood, the more attractive their neighborhood became to other wealthy people. In the weeks after a developer proposed a ten-story residential tower above the 16th Street BART Station, the Housing Rights Committee reported receiving a number of eviction cases in the immediate vicinity, which tenant advocates took to be a sign that landlords were anticipating that a sketchy corner of the Mission, known for its SROs and thrift stores, would be impacted by a large influx of individuals earning twice the neighborhood's median income.[63]

In about 2012, United to Save the Mission adopted a strategy of fighting every major development project proposed for the neighborhood. Once a week, seven representatives from the member organizations met to discuss the new applications that had been submitted to the city's Department of Buildings over the previous seven days. One of their tactics was to give nicknames to market-rate projects, based on the building's address: the Monster in the Mission, the Beast on Bryant, the Mess on Van Ness. "People on the planning commission make fun of us because they say, 'Why do you come up with these names?'" said Dairo Romero, one of the steering committee members. "Because it's fun. If you just said the address or the company name, it's not so catchy."[64]

In the press and at neighborhood meetings, the activists would use the names to smear the proposals; their goal was to get the developers to designate a larger percentage of the units as below-market rate. "We know the people on the other side of the negotiation can give us more inclusionary housing and more community benefits," Romero, a community organizer at the Mission Economic Development Authority, said. In 2013, the city began requiring that developers set aside 18 percent of a building's units as affordable; yet that just gave activists a new floor on which to operate. Thereafter, United to Save the Mission tried to push that percentage upwards, to 25 percent, and then to 30 or even 33 percent.

According to California state law, every new structure that goes up must go through an environmental assessment before it can get a building permit. Often, buildings are innocuous enough that the assessment determines the structure will cause no adverse impacts. But citizens, often the building's neighbors, are allowed to object and demand the planning commission—which is largely appointed by the mayor—review the determination. If it passes again, neighbors can appeal to the San Francisco Board of Supervisors. A well-organized group of neighbors can block a project even if it is within the scope of zoning laws for that parcel. The idea is to "democratize" the planning process, but developers and their pro-growth allies claim the extra burden only makes market-rate housing more expensive.

United to Save the Mission would end up, directly and indirectly, helping René Yañez and his wife, Cynthia, but not for a while. After receiving the Ellis Act eviction notice, the couple began looking for another apartment. But even that was hard: when Cynthia was recovering from chemotherapy, she was too weak to leave the house. They liked one apartment they saw in a converted warehouse in Oakland, but then learned that their next-door neighbor was a drummer. "She said, 'No way,'" Yañez recalled. They came back to their one-bedroom depressed. Yañez suspected the stress made her condition worse. In the back of his mind, he was hoping that he could at least forestall the eviction until after she passed away.

Yañez once again began to publicize his plight, with even greater force than in 2000. He gave interviews to pretty much anyone who asked: first to the *Bay Guardian*, and later to the *San Francisco Chronicle*, the *New York Times*, and Al-Jazeera America. "I kind of took it as an art project," he said later. "I didn't have money, but I could get publicity." The Anti-Eviction Mapping Project included Yañez's landlord, Sergio Iantorno, among its "Dirty Dozen"—landlords who had invoked the Ellis Act against tenants. Other activist groups used the list as a guide of whom to target. "We'd call them. We'd call their pastors. We'd call their financial and business partners. We'd protest their wife's business," said Sarah "Fred" Sherburn-Zimmer, executive director of the Housing Rights Committee. "A year of fifty people calling your cell phone every day. How long can you stand it?" Activists also took aim at Iantorno's son Paolo, a partner in his father's real estate business who also owned a shoe store. In Octo-

FIG. 10.1. René Yáñez photographed in the garden at the SOMARTS, an art center in the South of Market area, in 2014. (Photo by Marshal Weber)

ber 2014, protestors showed up at the shoe store, marching first on the sidewalk, and then into the store. Paulo responded by saying the family was losing $2,000 per unit by keeping Yáñez and the other rent-controlled tenants. "Paying $300 a month does not cover the mortgage," he shouted.[65]

Meanwhile, Yáñez's attorney, Raquel Fox, began looking for a solution that would allow both sides to save face. She learned from the city's housing office that it had finally put aside money to buy up endangered rent-controlled buildings like Yáñez's. (The Small Sites Program, a form of a community land trust, had first been discussed thirteen years earlier as a gentrification prevention measure to be included in the Eastern Districts rezoning.) Fox enlisted the Mission Economic Development Agency, one of the members of United to Save the Mission, to apply for some of that money to buy Yáñez's building and the others that Iantorno was threatening to de-control.

Iantorno began by asking for $2 million per building. In the end, the city paid $8.15 million for five buildings, or about $429,000 for each apartment. (Had the city purchased the buildings back during the dot-come bust, they would have cost about a third as much.)

Paolo Iantorno, the landlord's son and the shoe store owner, came to the press conference announcing the purchase. For him, the deal was a good one: it helped him avoid negative publicity and additional legal fees, while letting him unload underperforming assets at market rates. "Over the last nine months," he said, "we were able to iron out the terms for this transaction to the benefit of the tenants and future occupants of these buildings."[66] Mayor Ed Lee turned out as well to deliver an anti–Ellis Act message to landlords. "If you want to get out of the business of being a property owner, okay, no problem," he said. "But you don't have to evict long-term tenants to do so." The compromise, as appealing as it was, wasn't a very economical one. On top of the purchase price, the units each needed an average $77,000 in renovations, bringing the total price up to what it would cost to buy them new on the free market.[67]

For Yañez, it was a bittersweet victory. Three months later, Cynthia died. The service was at St. Peter's Church, in the heart of the Latino Mission, followed by a reception two blocks away at the Brava Theatre, an eclectic performing arts center. Her photographs—for she was a photographer as well as an actor—lined the lobby. José Cuellar, a Chicano studies professor and Latin musician, played "Danny Boy" on saxophone. Guillermo Gomez-Peña, San Francisco's poet laureate and an old friend of Yañez's, read a poem adapted for the occasion.

When Yañez left the Brava that day, he no longer had his partner of twenty-six years, nor the same community in which they had grown old. His son Rio had moved across the bay to Oakland. The muralists with whom Yañez had worked in the 1970s were disappearing. Mike Ríos, the Santana album cover artist, had been told by his landlord that he was going to more than double his rent, to $4,000 a month. Ríos' unit wasn't rent controlled, so he moved his family to Concord, a suburb 45 minutes away on the far side of the Berkeley Hills. The owner of the little bungalow on Balmy Alley that had sheltered numerous Latin American artists in exile decided to tear it down and erect a three-story condominium in its place. Ray Patlan, the so-called grandfather of American Muralismo, who had lived there since the mid-1980s, was told to get out. He moved into an old cookie factory in East Oakland that wasn't even zoned residential. He lived there anyway, making art in one end of the vast open-ended space, and sleeping in the other. Carlos "Cookie" Gonzalez, the former gang member whom Patlan had taken on as an apprentice, moved out of the Mission in 2009 to a two-bedroom house in San Bruno, a suburb south of the city.

During this time, the demographics in the Mission had drastically changed to become richer, whiter, and more transient. Between 1980 and 2013, the percentage of the population that was Latino dropped from 50 percent to 38 percent. The median household income rose from $46,749 to $76,762 (from 25 percent *below* the city's median income to 1.5 percent above it). The percentage of households that had moved within the previous five years rose from 55 percent to a stunning 80 percent.[68] A study commissioned by Supervisor Campos found that the neighborhood had lost nearly 7,000 Latinos between 2000 and 2011 and saw an increase of 2,900 non-Latinos. The number of wealthy households—those earning more than $150,000 annually—increased by 65 percent, compared to just 10 percent citywide.[69]

Every street, every block had its own memories and significance for Yañez. As he walked down 24th Street, he passed the Galería that he had helped found. On its wall was the billboard that he had helped transform into a public art space. Across the street was a playground built in memory of his late business partner Ralph Maradiaga. Next was Modern Times bookstore, a crossover space that he liked even though it was a magnet for hipsters. Further up, at Mission Street, was the former site of the donut shop where he and his son had lined up after the 1989 earthquake because it was the only place to get coffee. Nearby was a giant pit left when a residential hotel had burned down years earlier. It was about to be turned into condos. All in all, he still loved the Mission. He loved walking down the street and running into friends with whom he might share ten, twenty, or thirty years' worth of history. He loved walking into stores and knowing the owners' first names. He loved recruiting people to new projects, bringing them to fruition, celebrating, and then later on doing something completely different with the same people. He loved making things happen and watching the audience respond.

On May 29, 2018, after a long battle with bone and prostate cancer, René Yañez passed away. "Throughout the past two weeks my dad's spirit has defied every expectation of his mortality to talk, laugh, joke, and sing with us," his son Rio posted on Facebook that day. "Once my dad entered the hospital he was never alone, there was always a friend by his side."[70] La Galería held an open mic that night for friends to come by and reminisce. Mayor Mark Farrell issued a statement: "René dedicated decades of his life to uplifting the voices of Chicano artists and preserving the cultural heritage of the Mission District, while striving toward a more just, equitable, and sustainable future for all." That July, a community art center in SOMA hosted a memorial for him and adorned its walls with his artwork. Hundreds of people came.

ELEVEN

300 NASSAU AVENUE: NEW YORK CITY, 2004–2016

It is hard to say whether gentrification is more pronounced in San Francisco or in New York City, for it has different flavors in each place. San Francisco's rent laws are in some ways looser, which is perhaps why the backlash began earlier and reached a fevered pitch faster. In New York, gentrification entered citywide discourse only when, paradoxically, Mayor Bill de Blasio came into office in 2014 promising to do something about it. But, compared to San Francisco, gentrification had been simmering for much longer; the tactics of landlords were more nefarious, and the desire for profits more widely accepted in the place known for its embrace of capitalism.

New York City's brand of gentrification is all too evident in the story of Catalina Hildalgo, a Brooklyn native of Colombian extraction who, at the age of 22, wanted to move out of her mother's apartment and get a place of her own. This was in 2004, but even then she knew, because she was a savvy New Yorker, that she wanted a rent-regulated unit. Not only that, she wanted her name on the lease. She knew some people just took over the lease of the previous tenant and kept paying the rent, and that she probably could get away with that.

Getting a new lease in New York carried some risks—namely, the landlord can pop up the rent another 20 percent automatically. If he made renovations, he could also pass along a portion of those costs to her.[1] Or, he could simply refuse to rent it to her. But Catalina knew that having her own lease would give her more rights, down the line.

She got her place through word of mouth—Friedman and Stigler might say by "chance and favoritism." She had heard a friend's grandmother was moving into a nursing home and giving up her apartment, and it was rent stabilized. When Hidalgo asked the landlord, Joel Israel, for her own lease, she was pleasantly surprised. Even with the vacancy increase, the new rent came in at only $600 a month for a two-bedroom in Greenpoint, just two blocks away from where she grew up.[2] Both Greenpoint and its better-known neighbor Williamsburg were heavily industrial at that time, residential buildings cheek-by-jowl with factories. Domino Sugar was still being refined beside the Williamsburg Bridge, while Wonder Bread was baked across the street from Catalina's home. As she was growing up in the 1980s and '90s, Greenpoint was mixed ethnically. One of Catalina's best friends at P.S. 110 was Chinese. There were drug dealers on the streets, but her mom displayed a sense of vigilance, rather than of fear.

The building she moved into in 2004 was a three-story, yellow-brick walk-up with six apartments at 300 Nassau Avenue. It was one in a row of almost identical buildings built in the early 1930s in the Italianate style. Its ornate wooden eaves stuck over the top floor like a fedora. Concrete arches adorned the entranceway, and where the keystone would normally be placed—at the top of the arch—was instead a sculptured face. Each building's face was a little different. The one on the building to the right of Catalina's was a mustachioed man. The one to the left was a woman looking off to the side. Above the entrance of Catalina's, the face looked straight on. It was an androgynous figure, maybe 16 years old, with long wavy hair. The entrance was in the middle of the building, leading to a central staircase with one apartment on each side. Hidalgo's apartment was on the third floor, to the left. It had a living room and a dining room in front, then a kitchen, and then two bedrooms that led, railroad-style, one to the other, in the back. Across the street lay a low single-story warehouse, also made of brick, used by a company that fabricated picture frames. It stretched the entire block. Beyond it were another two blocks' worth of industry—junk yards, lumber yards, school bus parking lots—that lined Newtown Creek, one of the most polluted waterways in the United States.

Catalina was generally happy there. After a while, she tried to get her friends apartments in the building and asked the landlord in the same way that her friend had for her. But Israel was no longer helpful or friendly. He told her the vacant apartments were in horrible condition and needed to be renovated. By 2013, she realized that half of the units in her building had been vacant for three to four years and began to worry that he was intentionally keeping them vacant in order, at some point, to be able to charge much higher rents.

Israel was, like many other owners of small, marginal buildings in Brooklyn, a Hasidic Jew who wore black suits and white shirts and wide-brimmed hats. He was tall and slender; his cousin, Amron Israel (Catalina knew him as Aaron), who had taken over the day-to-day management of the building, was short and stout. Hidalgo had found both of them pleasant enough to deal with. It would sometimes take two or three days to receive a response to a text or email, but she didn't think much about that at first.

Then Aaron told Catalina that Joel was going to begin serious renovation work and that she would at some point have to move out. Their plan was to move the staircase from the front of the building to the rear in order to free up more space. She didn't know quite what to think. Her rent at that point was $754. Because it was rent-stabilized, she figured it would go up only about 2 to 4 percent a year, or however much the city's Rent Guidelines Board dictated. Rents in unregulated buildings in the neighborhood had shot up much faster, to about $2,000 to $2,500 a month. She had heard that some landlords had offered rent-regulated tenants lump sums of several thousand dollars in exchange for leaving the apartment. But she hadn't been offered anything so far and had just given birth to twin boys. She decided just to wait and see.

Catalina, a compact, thin woman with a staccato voice, was far better prepared to fight back than the average tenant. She knew something about how the vast bureaucracy at New York's Department of Buildings worked. Around the time she graduated from Long Island University, she started working at a construction company. Her boss let her shadow him as he went out to worksites and applied for permits for sidewalk containers and the like. Eventually, the two of them set up a small permit expediting company, meaning they filed paperwork to get permits from city agencies for demolition companies— a simple-sounding job that nonetheless required great skill and experience with bureaucracy.

Within a few months, however, the renovations were underway and conditions inside the building were growing intolerable, particularly for a single mother with two babies. Dust was coming up from the floor below into her unit, dust which she assumed contained lead and possibly asbestos. Yet the workers didn't seem to be using any wrapping to contain it.

Next, her bathroom floor sunk and her toilet stopped operating correctly. She suspected it was because a supporting beam was removed from the apartment below. The area around her bathtub sunk. Then it cracked. Waste water from the toilet began to leak out.[3] In May, Aaron Israel offered to find her an apartment where she and her kids could live for a year until the renovations were complete. She agreed, and they signed a contract. Aaron found her a place in another Greenpoint building that he was managing. But the rent, he said, was $2,500. And while he agreed to cover most of the additional rent, he expected her to chip in an extra $500 a month beyond the $754 she was already paying. She did not understand why she should bear any burden for their building project and refused. Catalina and Aaron voided the move-out agreement.

In September, Aaron came by to tell Catalina she was holding up the renovation project. His cousin had taken out another mortgage on the building to pay for it, and they had to get going so they could pay it back. He offered to buy her out of her rent-regulated lease for $50,000. She quickly did the math: if market rates in Greenpoint were roughly $1,750 a month more than what she was paying at the time, she would eat up that $50,000 within two and a half years' time. She could perhaps move further out into Brooklyn or Queens where rents were cheaper, but she liked Greenpoint. It was the center of her world: near her work, a few stops on the subway from Manhattan, and right up against the Brooklyn-Queens Expressway, which could take her, on a good day, to Staten Island within half an hour. Plus, her mother still lived there, two blocks away, and was taking care of the twins when Catalina was at work. Many of her old friends were still around. She told Aaron no. He said "Okay," and left.[4]

THE NEW BOHEMIANS

The gentrification of Greenpoint grew out of the gentrification of Williamsburg, which lies to the south. Williamsburg began changing in the 1980s in large part because the artists who had been pushed out of Dumbo moved further north up the Brooklyn waterfront. Williamsburg had good transportation. The Bedford Avenue stop on the L line, in the heart of the neighborhood, was less than a five-minute ride from what was then the punk-rock East Village. It was fringed by a series of warehouse buildings that could be turned into artist studios for cheap. The interior of the neighborhood was made up of small three- and four-story brick apartment buildings. These, populated at the time by Latinos (on the southern end) and Polish immigrants (on the northern end), made for convenient, cheap lodging for young adults in their 20s finding their way in New York City. In 1992, *New York* magazine photographed some of these transplants and put them on its cover under the headline, "The New Bohemia." The article's author, Brad Gooch, spoke of drag queens holding court at underground nightclubs, and a pre-Internet communication system in which artists set up a call-in number so others could find out about gallery openings. "A sort of *Blade Runner* Industrial Gothic is evident throughout the neighborhood—from the kicker boots of the clerk at EARWAX to the stage set of a recent production of Kafka's *The Penal Colony*," he wrote.[5] Along the river lay ghostly outlines of giant worn-out vacant factories—but, Gooch noted, at least parking was plentiful. The article hinted at signs of real estate speculation, but one local played down the neighborhood's future prospects: "[A]n authentic description of Williamsburg," J. Henry Williams wrote in a letter to the editor shortly after the article appeared, "could not be complete without mentioning the almost constant sounds of random gunfire, the sing-song sales pitch from crack-dealers, and the pounding bass from car stereos."[6]

City Hall's attitude toward this part of Brooklyn had been one of neglect. The legendary Robert Moses had built a massive swimming pool during the Great Depression in McCarren Park, on the border of Williamsburg and Greenpoint. It had fallen into disrepair and closed. The Poles and Puerto Ricans could not agree on how, or whether, to refurbish it. So it just remained closed. Streetlights didn't work; the schools declined; sidewalks crumbled.

What help Williamsburg got was largely from its own residents. When, in the 1970s, Mayor Abe Beame closed one of its firehouses in a version of "*un*planned shrinkage" (the city simply had run out of money to operate it), neighbors flocked to the scene and occupied it, and then began to respond to fire calls themselves. After the city, concluding the area was underutilized, began to locate waste processing facilities along its waterfront, the community organized against them.[7] On the south, and largely Latino, side of the neighborhood, one of the city's most effective community organizations, Los Sures, redeveloped rundown tenement buildings, sometimes through sweat equity programs. In the 1990s, as the neighborhood became more attractive and more and more landlords converted their spaces to legal and illegal residential lofts, the local community board created plans for the orderly development of the area. (The boards advise the city on land use and other issues but have limited power.) Community members did not oppose development along the waterfront—they thought they could get new parks built as part of the process—but wanted the buildings to be low-rise, in keeping with the rest of the neighborhood. Right at the beginning of Mayor Michael Bloomberg's first term, the City Planning Commission certified the plans, but, significantly, did not endorse them.[8]

Indeed, the Bloomberg administration had a very different vision for the neighborhood, as it did for the whole city. Though he took over four months after the Sept. 11th attacks, when many New Yorkers worried the city would never recover, Bloomberg wanted to make New York competitive with other world cities—principally London. His deputy mayor for economic development, Daniel Doctoroff, was largely responsible for enacting that vision. A graduate of Harvard College and the University of Chicago, Doctoroff was a newbie to politics, a hedge-fund manager who, like Bloomberg himself, was so wealthy that he was willing to work for one dollar a year. While often maligned as a modern-day Robert Moses, Doctoroff bore more resemblance to Alexander Hamilton. Both men were prolific, charismatic, and extremely self-assured. They believed in the necessity of public debt (Hamilton to raise an army, Doctoroff to make capital improvements) and also in the power of the private sector to do good—not through altruism, but rather through self-interest.

Doctoroff operated under a principle he called "the virtuous cycle of growth": basically, the more people that move to a city, the more they pay in taxes, and the more the government can reinvest that tax revenue in making the city appealing to the next person who might move there. Just as a smart business owner sinks her money into *capital*—the machines, factories, or, in the modern day, talent that can produce more money, which can in turn be reinvested—so Doctoroff believed that extending a subway line to Manhattan's West Side would reap long-term benefits. (Bloomberg and Doctoroff would refer to incentives and other perks given to real estate companies as "investments" rather than "subsidies" for the same reason.) Doctoroff also believed that city life was scalable in the same way that making a piece of software is scalable: the upfront costs of writing code or building a new subway line may be considerable, but the more customers/passengers one has, the smaller the incremental cost to serve them.[9] In order to make his model work, New York, just like a private company, had to make sure that its revenues continually increased in order to pay the debt service on its "investments." (As it happened, New York City's population did grow, though chiefly due to the 1965 immigration law: between 1980 and 2011, 1.3 million foreign-born residents moved to New York; the population of the city grew by 1.2 million.[10])

Higher population would mean higher housing costs—unless somehow, New York City's chronically low housing supply was able to keep up with demand. From virtually his first day at City Hall, Doctoroff recognized that the city had to launch a massive affordable housing plan in order to grow. He set a target of creating or preserving 65,000 units of affordable housing over ten years—later upped to 165,000 units—and employed several Hamiltonian techniques to achieve that.[11] For one, he helped turn the sleepy, even corrupt, New York City Housing Development Corporation into a major bank that would loan $100 million a year to developers to build affordable housing.[12] No longer would the city have to rely on the Chase's and Citibank's of the world; the Bloomberg administration could do it itself. He also advocated that the city take on more debt, and leverage tax and zoning incentives.

But creating affordable housing and controlling gentrification are not the same thing. Building new affordable housing at times even *encourages* gentrification, since a unit can be technically "affordable" by the city's definition but still too expensive for the typical neighborhood resident. In order to reach that 165,000 number, for example, the Bloomberg administration equally counted a $531/month three-bedroom apartment, where four or five people could live, or a $1,492/month studio, where one or two people could.[13] In fact, between fiscal year 2004 and 2011, two-thirds of the "affordable housing" built in New York City was unaffordable at the median household income of whatever neighborhood it was in.[14] A big part of the reason for this mismatch has to do with the definition of "affordable housing." In New York City, that term traditionally referred to apartments with rents that a family earning 80 percent of the "area median income" can afford. Since the 1980s, the federal government has considered a household able to "afford" its housing if it spends 30 percent of its income on rent. In other words, the yearly rent for city-built affordable housing should be no more than 24 percent of the "area median income." The trouble comes from the definition of "area." For complicated reasons, the "area" used to calculate the threshold for what's "affordable" includes the entire city and some suburban counties. Wealthier areas raise the median income, even when the apartment is built in a poor one. Hence, the "area median income" for a family of four living in metropolitan New York in 2010 was $79,200; the median income within the city limits was considerably lower, $62,799. In Brooklyn's Community Board 1, which includes Williamsburg and Greenpoint, the median household income was even lower: $41,540.[15] As a result, city, state, and federal funds went toward apartments that rented for $1,584 a month in Williamsburg and Greenpoint, while the typical four-person family in that neighborhood could afford to pay only two-thirds that amount. By definition, the subsidized units brought in higher-income residents and gentrified the neighborhood.

Doctoroff went one step further. Because market-rate rents were unaffordable even to upper-middle-income families (i.e., they would have to pay more than 30 percent of their income on housing), the Bloomberg administration began subsidizing units for people earning as much as 1.8 times the area median income (or 2.27 times the city's median) could afford them. Officials began to call this housing "workforce housing," and justified it on the grounds that teachers, police officers, and firefighters otherwise would not be able to afford to live in the city. San Francisco similarly subsidized workforce housing—that was what split the Mission Housing Development Corporation during the dot-com era—but the thresholds, and vocabulary, were different on the West Coast. No one earning more than 1.2 times the San Francisco median income would qualify for a subsidized unit, and such housing was called not "affordable," but rather "below market."

Doctoroff and Bloomberg were fairly unconcerned about gentrification. The mayor once said, "If you're worried about gentrification, don't improve the schools and don't bring down crime."[16] He took a hands-off approach to overseeing the city's one-million rent-regulated units and appointed a Goldman Sachs partner as his first chairman of the Rent Guidelines Board.[17] Bloomberg vetoed a city council bill that would have required landlords to accept federal Section 8 vouchers, even though Chicago, Seattle, Washington, DC, and the state of New Jersey already had such a law.[18] Between 2011 and 2014, harassment complaints filed in housing court nearly doubled, but neither he nor the city council took any comprehensive action.

In general, Bloomberg seemed reluctant to perpetuate a system that infringed on property owners' rights to charge whatever the market would bear.[19] His affordable housing program imposed rent regulations on landlords, but participation was by choice: if you wanted low-interest bonds to build your apartments, you had to agree to enroll them in the city's rent-regulation system. (You didn't need to keep them in the rent-regulated system permanently, however—only for the length of the bonds, which, his critics charged, was only setting up another affordable housing crisis thirty years into the future.)

To make room for population growth in an already crowded, expensive city, Doctoroff looked to rezone industrial or low-rise areas for residential, thereby allowing developers to knock down existing buildings and replace them with high-rise apartment towers. Fortunately for him, the Giuliani administration had already been studying Greenpoint and Williamsburg and was considering creating an esplanade along the river and new zoning that would permit the construction of 7,000 more apartments.[20] That idea also dovetailed nicely with Doctoroff's own personal dream: bringing the 2012 Summer Olympics to New York City. Planner Alex Garvin—who had been the city's deputy housing commissioner during the 1970s—had come up with a scheme in which the aquatic center for swimming, diving, and synchronized swimming would be located along the river there.[21] Doctoroff jumped on board and the plan was made public in June 2003.

While the planning department asserted that it was complying with the development plans the community board had come up with, neighborhood activists thought the claim was preposterous. The city's proposal *did* put parkland along the East River, but it also permitted towers of up to 350 feet high, far above anything in the two communities at the time.[22] In addition, affordable housing advocates feared that the addition of 8,257 new apartments (a slight increase from the Giuliani administration's version) would bring in a huge new population of wealthy professionals, destroying the Latino and Polish character of the neighborhood, while also forcing out the remaining light-industrial jobs on which many of those working class residents depended.[23]

In the years following, these fears have largely been realized. Some fifty industrial firms moved away or closed up shop.[24] Between 2000 and 2010, the Latino population in South Williamsburg fell by 5,293, while the white population grew; more than 9,000 new apartments have been built or are planned, many in condominium towers along the waterfront, yet only 16 percent are affordable.[25] Between 2000 and 2014, rents in Greenpoint-Williamsburg rose by 57.7 percent, far faster than any other area in the city.[26]

While the Bloomberg administration added provisions to protect industrial jobs and increase affordable housing, those community benefits lagged behind the displacement pressures of the private sector. On the eve of the city council vote on the plan in 2005, Doctoroff promised that 1,345 affordable units would be created on twenty sites owned by the city, MTA, and the Catholic Archdiocese.[27] After the city council's approval, it turned out those sites were not as readily available as Doctoroff had hoped. By 2013, only nineteen of those units had been built.[28]

Another Doctoroff promise—$2 million to legal aid clinics to represent tenants facing evictions—took two years to secure.[29] The waterfront parks also lagged. The Bushwick Inlet Park—the proposed Olympic site—was not fully completed even six years after the 2012 Olympics would have been held had New York won the games. The park's price tag, once a modest $20 million, ballooned to more than $400 million, largely because the property's value increased due to the rezoning.[30] It was said that even before the Greenpoint-Williamsburg rezoning took effect, the price of land along the water had doubled in anticipation of Mayor Bloomberg's rezoning.[31] The very public nature of planning changes, and the length of time it takes to enact them, gives speculators an advantage over the public interest.

TAKING STOCK

It is hard to know just how much the rezoning caused Greenpoint-Williamsburg's gentrification and led to the type of harassment that Catalina Hidalgo and her neighbors on Nassau Avenue experienced. The neighborhoods were changing anyway: rents had risen by 42.8 percent between 1990 and 2000. Before the rezoning was approved, a study for the city planning department estimated that the number of residents in the neighborhood would increase by 12 percent, most of whom would have higher incomes than the current population. The study even acknowledged that population increase would be high enough to displace existing residents, though it did not estimate how much.[32]

There is healthy academic debate about whether this sort of changing demographics, however, represents "displacement"—that is, long-time residents being forced to move out because of higher rents—or "succession"—people are always moving out for a variety of non-compulsory reasons (marriage, divorce, job, etc.) and the people who replace them can be of a different race or income level. A Furman Center report did not try to test this question, and the most famous study on this issue gives an inadequate answer.[33]

In 2005, Columbia University Professor Lance Freeman surveyed urban census tracts from across the country and calculated that about 1.4 percent of individuals were displaced from gentrifying neighborhoods annually during the 1990s because they could not pay the rent.[34] But, he notes, a good number of people have to move because they cannot pay the rent *in non-gentrifying neighborhoods*, so he puts the likelihood of an individual being displaced because of gentrification at 0.5 percent a year. He concludes: "Although displacement was significantly related to gentrification, the substantive size of this relationship is very small."[35]

Yet there are three important caveats that call this conclusion into question. For one, 0.5 percent is the estimated *annual* displacement rate. If the same pace of gentrification continued over thirty years, 15 percent of a neighborhood's residents would move specifically because gentrification.[36] That still doesn't sound like much, but here's the second caveat: that figure is the national average for more than 2,000 gentrifying tracts, which means that the displacement rate among the most rapidly gentrifying areas of the country would likely be significantly higher. Third, Freeman's study did not distinguish between households that move elsewhere in the same neighborhood and those that move further away. This last point is important because even in non-gentrifying communities, low-income people move quite often, independent of rising rents. It is very possible, however, that in non-gentrifying areas, these movers are able to move to other places in their neighborhoods, while in gentrifying neighborhoods, they end up far away from their jobs and support networks because they cannot afford anything closer. Freeman himself admitted that his conclusions are so counterintuitive that he feared he might be missing something.[37]

Of course, even if Greenpoint-Williamsburg saw significant displacement, it is still difficult to pin the blame on the 2005 rezoning. In fact, another, quieter trend during the Bloomberg administration may have been even more responsible. Bloomberg rezoned some 40 percent of the city during his twelve years in office, yet an overwhelming percentage of those actions produced not more housing, but less. These rezonings took place largely in white, middle-income communities on the fringes of the city, in Staten Island, the far reaches of Queens, etc. In other words, instead of *increasing* supply as a means to control housing prices, Bloomberg actually *decreased* the potential for growth. Ostensibly, the administration practiced a form of "smart growth" to increase population density in neighborhoods near job centers and transit. But since those inner-city areas had often turned majority-minority as whites migrated to the suburbs, this policy had a distinct racial tinge: the areas with downzonings or "contextual" rezonings (realignments that did not significantly affect the construction density), were majority white, while those that were upzoned had greater percentages of blacks and Latinos. Furthermore, another Furman Center study found that the principle of transit-oriented development was applied unequally: 59 percent of the downzoned areas were within half a mile of a subway or commuter rail station.[38]

This disparity of treatment—not unlike upzoning San Francisco's eastern neighborhoods but not the western ones—was an outgrowth of deep disagreements between Doctoroff and the chairwoman of the city planning commission, Amanda Burden. Burden was an avowed acolyte of Jane Jacobs and William H. Whyte. While she reported to Doctoroff, she was not his first choice for the job, but rather a social acquaintance of Bloomberg.[39] Doctoroff was a supply-sider who believed that increasing population density was paramount to the city's survival; Burden was a neighborhood preservationist. Doctoroff wrote: "Sometimes, our different philosophical approaches led to real tension—even one or two screaming fights—but ultimately, I think, the beauty of our relationship was that we pushed each other and came to compromises that brought us aspirational, sensitive, and feasible rezonings."[40]

To housing advocates on the outside looking in, however, the result was that Doctoroff and Burden divided the city into fiefdoms, with the industrial and poor neighborhoods slated for upzoning, while development was tightly controlled in established white middle-class neighborhoods. In 2009—shortly after Doctoroff had left city government and most of the major rezonings had been accomplished—the Furman Center determined Bloomberg had downzoned more neighborhoods than he had upzoned, and that in fact he had expanded residential capacity by only 1.7 percent.[41] Yet this countertrend got very little attention: who is going to rise up at a public hearing if the city is *not* allowing a developer to build a tall tower right next door to you?

While Doctoroff may have thought through the need to increase housing supply, Mayor Bloomberg's record on the matter is far less clear. In addition to putting a neighborhood advocate in charge of the planning department, Bloomberg put in place a very strong and active Landmarks Preservation Commission. This was in keeping with his admiration of London and its historical character, as well as with the values of the elite social circles in which he moved. (Bloomberg himself lived in a brownstone on the Upper East Side and kept another town home in the British capital.) The landmarks commission—an outgrowth of the drive half a century before to preserve Brooklyn Heights—designated forty-four neighborhoods as historic districts during Bloomberg's three terms, or an average of 3.67 districts per year, more than under any other mayor. Historic district status did not prohibit redevelopment, but it imposed such constraints on it that it would be very unlikely that anyone could increase housing density in a meaningful way. It is hard to measure just how much Bloomberg's downzonings and historic district designations contributed to gentrification or the affordability crisis, but according to economic logic, they would push prices up across the board by limiting supply, and force new construction into areas that did not have the same protections.

STREET LIFE

Catalina Hidalgo's neighborhood was protected neither by landmarking nor by downzoning, but she lived on the very far edge of Greenpoint, so far removed from the center of activity that she did not notice the neighborhood changing until 2008, three years after the rezoning was approved. She was working at a construction company at that point and saw a job come in to bring down a three-story building at 123 Kingsland Avenue, about a 10-minute walk from her house. Pretty soon, Catalina was seeing demolition plans for her corner of the neighborhood left and right. She also saw changes on the street. Genevieve's, her favorite variety store on Manhattan Avenue, closed, replaced by a succession of chain drug stores—all with higher prices. Her favorite Chinese restaurant also went out of business, two laundromats shut their doors, and her closest grocery store was sold.

But she adapted easily enough. In some ways, for a single mom climbing the economic ladder, gentrification was exciting: she saw around her more diversity of races, more young people, more bars and restaurants, different styles of dress. Her neighborhood, she thought, was becoming more and more like the East Village every day. She had enough spending money that she could afford the higher prices and take advantage of the new opportunities. As for her apartment, where a substantially higher rent could really do damage to her household budget, she thought it was safe because it was rent-regulated.

The trouble began in the fall of 2013. Each year, beginning October 1, New York City landlords are required to provide heat in apartments if temperatures dip below 55 degrees Fahrenheit during the day. The weather in the middle of October 2013 was brisk, but Catalina noticed that her radiators would never come on. She texted her landlord Aaron. When they did turn on the heat, the first floor was flooded because the radiators had been removed from the apartment that was under renovation. Then, because of all the construction work in adjacent apartments, mice started coming into her apartment and left droppings in her sons' clothing. She called up a tenant organizer, Martha Vargas at St. Nick's Alliance, a community organization in North Brooklyn, who had helped Catalina's mother years earlier in a dispute with her landlord.

Vargas already knew about Joel Israel, Catalina's landlord. St. Nick's had heard from tenants in other buildings he owned and had identified his modus operandi: first, he keeps some apartments vacant, and then, when the other tenants don't move out, he undertakes a series of measures to prod them to leave: troublesome renovations, no heat, etc. Once he gets the whole building vacant, he can sell it to a buyer at a premium; or he could pour enough money into renovating the units that New York state law would allow him to remove the building from the rent regulation system altogether. Instead of six households paying $700 or so a month, the landlord stood to have tenants paying three times that much, every month, and rising.

Catalina enlisted her neighbors. There were only two other apartments occupied at the time, both on the first floor. In one lived Gustavo and Rosita Navarro, a Peruvian couple who had met in 1988 when each of them moved into the building: Rosita to an apartment on the second floor with her sister; Gustavo on the first floor with a cousin. They had two children. In the other apartment lived another Peruvian family, the Palominos.

Hidalgo argued her case in mid-December in Brooklyn housing court and won. Joel Israel was ordered to fix her bathroom. Catalina thought her ordeal was over. She was looking forward to spending the next two weeks in a hotel with her twins while the repairs were taken care of. But earlier that morning, unbeknownst to her, someone had come into the basement with a sledge hammer and started swinging it around. He ruptured the plumbing, causing water to spurt out as if from a fire hose. The electric meters were smashed, the boiler that heated water for the building's radiators and bathrooms was ruined. When she arrived home from court, Catalina found all of her neighbors huddled on the street outside. It was dark and some had flashlights in their hands; others were crying. Officials from the gas company and the city's buildings department were shutting down the building's systems. Catalina took out her cell phone and called Aaron. She got his voice mail.

You gotta come to the building! she shouted.

They waited for two or three hours, until after dinner time, but still Aaron did not arrive.

A buildings department supervisor told the tenants they couldn't stay there that night—it was too dangerous when there was no power. Catalina also called Martha at St. Nick's, who got the city's housing department to come the next morning. Those inspectors determined 300 Nassau was in such bad shape that they had to evacuate it, even if it meant throwing about a dozen people out on the street. They gave Catalina and her neighbors 30 minutes to run inside and grab whatever they could, and could not guarantee when, if ever, they would see what was left behind. Catalina had driven back to her office the night before to pick up a roll of giant 50-gallon trash bags expressly for that purpose. They were demolition-grade bags, almost twice as big as the ones you would use to stuff leaves into—and thicker. Inside the cold eerie apartment, she filled up bag after bag with her pictures of her children, her children's clothing, her own clothing, and dragged them down the stairs to the street and left them there, then ran back upstairs to do more. In the 30 minutes she was given, she had filled six trash bags. She left the remainder inside, including a fully decorated Christmas tree she had brought home just a few days earlier.

A few days later, Catalina and her neighbors and their children—basically, everybody who still lived at 300 Nassau—showed up at the office of Brooklyn Legal Services in Williamsburg, where Martha Vargas brought some of her toughest cases. She got them assigned to Adam Meyers, a genial Midwesterner who had just graduated from Harvard Law School. Meyers had learned, by posting to a listserv shared by tenant lawyers, that two other buildings owned by Israel had been in housing court. In a building on Central Avenue, a judge had ruled that a female tenant had been illegally evicted and ordered Israel to reinstate her; the next day, the woman's lawyer told Meyers, Israel had apparently retaliated by ripping out the floors of her apartment. In a case on Linden Street, workmen entered several apartments to do renovations, but only knocked down walls and disconnected pipes. They never came back, leaving the occupants to borrow the kitchen and bathroom of the one neighbor who had not allowed the workmen to enter that day. Meyers suspected that Israel was intentionally triggering evacuations of his buildings in order to get rid of rent-stabilized tenants.

Rent-regulated housing used to be considered a poor investment. In the mid-2000s, however, a small number of property companies, using money from private equity firms and real estate investment trusts, began investing heavily in large rent-regulated buildings in parts of New York. They were betting that as many as 20 percent of their rent-regulated tenants would leave in a given year, allowing them to do renovations and jack up the rent. That was well above the average 5 percent turnover of years past, and when rent-stabilized tenants did not leave as quickly as investors had projected they would—after all, as housing prices rose, the incentives to remain in one's regulated apartment grew stronger—the landlords took action. One tactic was not to cash tenants' checks and then bring the renter to court for failing to pay rent. In 2010, Andrew Cuomo, who was then New York attorney general, settled with one company, Vantage Properties, which he accused of issuing one thousand faulty eviction notices. In 2011, after more than five years of fighting, another large property group, Pinnacle LLC, reached an agreement with its 22,000 tenants to settle accusations of similar behavior.

Israel was a much smaller landlord. For his handful of properties, it was not entirely clear whether he was the owner or merely the managing agent. A limited liability company called Salmor Realty had bought 300 Nassau Avenue in 1999 for $240,000. The company took out a $27,000 loan on the property in 2006. In 2012, just before Catalina started having trouble, the property was transferred to a spin-off LLC, Salmor Realty 2. LLCs do not have to disclose who their owners are, and Israel's name does not appear on any of the real estate transaction documents. It is likely, assuming Salmor Realty is no different than any other small rental owner in New York, that the LLC was a means of pooling money from a variety of individuals, while making it harder for the government, and the tenants, to determine who was responsible.

Meyers, the Legal Services lawyer, thought the tenants had a good case, couldn't lose really—unless the landlord succeeded in picking them off one by one or wearing them down.[42] The case in housing court was therefore a race against time: Could he convince a judge to wrest 300 Nassau out of the landlord's hands and give it, at least temporarily, to an independent manager? The whole process, he told the tenants, would take a few months. They would need to find other places to live in the meantime.

During the trial, Israel argued that he had tried multiple times to make repairs to Catalina's and other apartments, but that the tenants never let him in. He disputed the idea that Catalina's bathroom was sinking because of the structural work in the apartment below. He said the real problem was that Catalina had used the toilet after the Buildings Department declared her bathroom unsafe. His lawyer presented emails supporting Israel's claims. As for the vandalism in the basement, he said it was perpetrated directly or indirectly by the tenants themselves as part of a scheme to seize control of the building.

Those few months that the case was supposed to take turned into a few more months, then into something more like a year. Catalina's resolve was waning. She had first moved with her twins into a city-run shelter, but she was forced to move because she had only partial custody of her kids and ended up renting a much more expensive apartment in Bushwick, the next neighborhood over. The rent was $2,600 a month, or more than three times what she had been paying, and she had to cut expenses and make other sacrifices. But she was relatively well-off compared to her neighbors. The Navarros stayed for much longer in a shelter. They had their own apartment there, but it felt like a prison. They had to sign themselves in and out when they came and went, and there was a curfew they had to observe to avoid being locked out all night.[43] The Palominos split up: the mother, sister and daughter moved into a relative's home nearby, while the grown son, Juan Carlos, lived with an uncle, because no family member had an apartment large enough to take everyone in.

During the course of the trial, Israel tripled the buy-out amount he had offered Catalina the previous year, to $150,000. At one point, the judge, Marina Cora Mundy, asked Catalina if she wanted a settlement plan. "I can get you more [than that even] because it's a high-profile case," she said. Later that day, Catalina took Meyers aside in the hallway outside the courtroom and asked him to take up the judge's offer.

Something's got to give, she said. *I'm paying all this money on rent, and I need to take care of my family.*

Are you sure you want to settle? Meyers asked.

Yes, she pleaded. *Settle, settle, settle. My family and I are struggling right now. I don't expect to pay all this rent forever, but at the end of the day, I'm stuck.*

You have to stick with this, Meyers told her. *We have an extremely strong case. This is your home and we are going to be able to keep it affordable for you in the foreseeable future.*

By this point, Catalina was crying. Meyers went on, in a gentle but chiding voice.

If you give up, they will get exactly what they were looking for when they destroyed the building last December. Is that what you want?

There were the other tenants to think of also. She wasn't exactly the leader of the group, but she was the center of the case, the one with the worst complaints, the one whose case most clearly showed a pattern of retribution. And unlike the other two families involved, she was fluent in English, which helped both in court and in the media. Meyers told her if she settled, she would screw up the chances the others had to retain their apartments. They might get settlements too, but once those units left the city's rent regulation system, they would never come back. Catalina changed her mind. She resolved to stick out the case. It would only be a little while longer, she thought.

But the case dragged on for another four or five months. In the fall, as testimony wrapped up and the lawyers were asked to file their post-trial briefs, Catalina got a phone call.

Hello, Catalina. This is Aaron Israel. How are you?

I'm okay. What are you doing calling me?

I'm calling to see how you are.

I'm okay, Catalina repeated, and waited, suspicious.

I would like to meet with you in person and talk to you about the case, he said.

I don't think we should be talking like this.

It's okay that we do this, Aaron said. *It's good that we do this.*

I think I should talk to my lawyer, Catalina responded.

No, it is okay, Catalina, Aaron went on. *I have a proposal I want to outline to you. But I want to do it in person.*

The two of them met after work on the second Thursday in November at Chagall, a restaurant in Park Slope. Chagall was at once kosher and gentrified, lined with large mirrors and wood carvings as if from the Paris of the late nineteenth century. Catalina hadn't told Meyers she was going. When she arrived, Aaron was already there, in his black suit and wearing his black wide-brimmed hat, with a plate of appetizers and a bottle of wine laid out on the table in front of him.

He offered her some food and drink but she refused.

What is it that you want to talk to me about? Catalina asked.

I want to talk to you about the building, he said.

What is it?

You know that we are planning on renovating it. We have taken out a mortgage on it and need to pay it back.

You took out the mortgage, not me, she shot back.

And in order to do the renovations, we need to get access to your apartment. Then Aaron paused. *So I want you to make me an offer. How much do you want to move out of the apartment?*

Catalina waited a moment. She had thought about this question once or twice before and had a number in her head.

500, she said.

500? Aaron asked.

500,000 dollars, she repeated.

500,000 dollars? he asked. *Half a million dollars? No, no, that's too much.*

You asked me how much I wanted.

I can give you 150, maybe 200.

With half a million dollars, she would almost be able to pay cash for one of the new condominiums in her old neighborhood. She would still be liable for monthly charges, but they would probably not amount to more than her old rent at 300 Nassau. Owning a place, she figured, was the only way to withstand gentrification, the only way she could directly benefit from the changes in her old neighborhood rather than being victimized by them. But anything less than that, she would be back in the same place at some point in the future. Today, she'd get pushed out of Greenpoint. Later, out of Bushwick, then further and further out into the extremities of Brooklyn.

That won't get me very far, she told Aaron. And then, without touching anything to eat, she got up and left.

On January 26, 2015, Judge Mundy found in the tenants' favor. She wrote in her decision that Joel Israel made no attempt to make any repairs to the building and was "unpersuasive" in proving that he was not able to gain access to Catalina's apartment.[44] Mundy took control of the apartment from Israel and gave it to an independent administrator, who went on to make the repairs at the landlord's expense. The work would take more than another year and a half to complete. Catalina and the other tenants returned home to Nassau Avenue in August 2016. Because of some of the renovations, Hidalgo's apartment was a bit smaller, but in general, everything was in far better shape than it had been: their leaks had been fixed, their plaster repaired, the mice and asbestos gone. It had been a long fight, but they had won.

CONCLUSION

Stories about 300 Nassau Avenue and the four other buildings owned by Joel Israel appeared on local news shows and in blogs, community newspapers, and even the *New York Times*. "Through the entire winter, we had no heat, the mice infestation," Catalina Hidalgo told the local CBS affiliate. "I had mice droppings in my kid's crib, all over my kid's clothes."[1] The media coverage attracted the attention of Brooklyn District Attorney Kenneth P. Thompson. In April 2015, three months after the tenants won their housing court case, Thompson secured a fifteen-count indictment alleging that Israel had illegally evicted tenants in five buildings and defrauded them of their property.[2] While investigating the case, the district attorney found that Israel had filed plans with the buildings department stating that the building would not be occupied during the gut renovation—when, of course, it was. Had the landlord admitted the truth—or if city inspectors had bothered to check—he would have been required to secure a tenant protection plan to keep the renovation work from disturbing the remaining occupants.

About a year and a half later, before the case went to trial, Joel and Aaron Israel pleaded guilty. In the plea agreement, the Israels admitted to all sorts of strategies in order to force tenants to leave. The Israels had hired people to walk around their buildings with pit bulls, hold loud parties in vacant apartments, and invite strangers in to use drugs in the hallways. They convinced city marshals to evict three tenants for nonpayment of rent, even though they had paid on time. At Catalina Hidalgo's building, the plea agreement stated, the Israels "paid a sum of money to an individual for information on how to vacate a building and to cause damage to the building . . . so that the remaining tenants would leave." At 98 Linden Street, they had workers demolish the apartments' kitchens and bathrooms under the guise of making renovations, who then never came back. At 15 Humboldt Street, they pushed out every rent-stabilized tenant, renovated the building, and installed all new market-rate tenants paying more than $4,000 a month each. Yet the Israels' pièce de résistance was what they did at 386 Woodbine Street: when a rent-stabilized tenant insisted on staying until the end of his lease, the Israels went into his apartment under the guise of making some repairs. Once inside, the Israels built a wall in the middle of his kitchen, and then another in front of his door, preventing him from getting into and out of the apartment. The Israels admitted to all of these actions in order to avoid going to trial; as part of the agreement, any jail time was suspended so long as they paid eight tenants a total of $248,097.62 as compensation for their crimes, plus another $100,000 to offset other expenses should they arise. They also had to perform 500 hours of community service and pay to repair the damage they did. As for 300 Nassau, the Israels agreed the building would be managed in perpetuity by a third party, even after they sold it, thereby drastically reducing the value of the property.[3]

The case against the Israels was a rare criminal prosecution of landlords for harassment. The prosecutors behind the case were astounded at the depth of the chicanery, though they figured there were probably numerous such landlords over the years; it was just that no one had ever bothered to bring them to justice. Finally, people were bothering. About a year after the Israels were indicted, Attorney General Eric Schneiderman filed a civil lawsuit against Stephen Croman, a much larger landlord with more than one hundred properties. One of Croman's top employees, Anthony Falconite, allegedly cultivated a culture of harassment among building managers, referring to the process of securing buyouts as a "team sport" and tenants as "targets." Croman, who served a year in prison for separate charges related to refinancing loans and tax fraud, eventually agreed to pay $8 million in restitution and to hire an independent management company to operate his buildings for five years.[4]

Once government officials bothered to look, they discovered the extent to which New York City's rent laws were being regularly flaunted. Rent regulations depended on landlords to self-report a whole host of information that was not in their self-interest to report truthfully: they reported how many rent-regulated apartments they had in their buildings, whether any remained occupied when a renovation was being undertaken, whether there was asbestos in the insulation or lead in the paint, and what the legal rent should be for each apartment. Over the course of three years, the state's Tenant Protection Unit found that 37,000 units had illegally exited the rent regulation system.[5] State officials had also begun to notice just how poorly they had enforced the 421-a program, in which landlords get deep tax breaks for building new apartment buildings, but also cannot hike rents more than what is allowed for rent-regulated buildings. They created an enforcement program and discovered that nearly 2,000 landlords in the J-51 program were regularly ignoring the requirement that they keep their apartments in the rent regulation system as long as they receive tax exemptions and abatements.[6] But state officials may have vastly underestimated the problem: an investigation by the nonprofit media organization ProPublica determined that a total of 50,000 units receiving J-51 or 421-a tax breaks did not show up in the registry.

In March 2018, the federal prosecutor's office in Brooklyn reportedly subpoenaed records from the Kushner Companies, the real-estate firm partly owned by President Donald Trump's son-in-law. The subpoena was apparently in response to a report by the Associated Press that claimed the company had incorrectly filled out applications for building permits. The situation resembled the one that the Israels perpetrated at 300 Nassau Avenue: the Kushner Companies certified the buildings they wanted to renovate had no rent-stabilized tenants in them, though they in fact were occupied. The misleading paperwork allowed the firm to avoid undertaking tenant protection plans and subjecting their buildings to regular inspections by the New York City Department of Buildings—both measures that would have slowed down renovations. (The Kushner Companies passed the blame on to a third-party that filled out the paperwork, though the AP reported nearly all the eighty applications for construction permits had been signed by a Kushner employee.)[7]

Mayor Bill de Blasio took many steps to tame the excesses of gentrification. He increased funding for legal aid lawyers by $2 million, enabling outfits like Brooklyn Legal Services to take on many more cases, and required that every tenant in housing court be guaranteed a lawyer. He appointed members to the Rent Guidelines Board who imposed rent freezes for two consecutive years. When choosing re-zoning targets, de Blasio at first intentionally leap-frogged the next hot neighborhoods (Bushwick, Inwood) and instead focused on the neighborhoods beyond that (East New York, Kingsbridge), so that subsidized housing could be built before market developers moved in. His staff believed that even though they could not stop gentrification, there were many ways to enforce the laws on the books. De Blasio also, unlike his predecessor, made sure that any new affordable unit the city financed was permanently affordable, and would not revert to market rents in fifteen or twenty or thirty years.

Similar types of measures were also adopted in San Francisco. At the beginning of his mayoralty in 2011, Edwin M. Lee was a pro-business politician with close ties to Silicon Valley entrepreneur Ron Conway. Mayor Lee continued the tech-friendly policies of outgoing mayor Gavin Newsom, undertaken in the midst of the Great Recession, and secured a payroll tax break for companies, such as Twitter, that located in the South of Market area. Yet even before the tax break was enacted, San Francisco's job engine had already been roaring back, rendering the incentives largely unnecessary. The next year, 2012, the number of jobs rose to 475,600, an all-time record for the city; meanwhile, the median home price had risen more than 20 percent over the previous year to more than $800,000.[8] In 2013, after considerable public pressure, Mayor Lee turned his attention from economic growth to housing. He formed a task force that called for a continuation of the rent control program and an increase in the housing supply. In January 2014, Lee announced a goal of producing 30,000 units over the following six years and backed a $310 million affordable housing bond issue. The goal was less than a third of the estimated 100,000 new units needed to gets costs under control, and contained significant caveats, among them the fact that nearly half of the 10,000 affordable units wouldn't be new at all. Instead, the city was planning to count nearly 5,000 rehabilitated and recapitalized public housing apartments toward its affordable housing goal.[9] Lee died unexpectedly at age 65 in December 2017, but his successor, London Breed, pledged to continue to pursue those housing goals.[10]

Meanwhile, the Chicago Housing Authority continued to correct some of the early mistakes of the Plan for Transformation. It took steps to improve the quality of the privately owned housing where its voucher recipients lived, including giving incentives to those who pass inspections quickly and suspending landlords who repeatedly violate building standards. The authority also expanded its mission to include job training and placement and made a more concerted effort to place retailers and other employers where residents can work in the mixed-income developments. According to the CHA, 11,500 residents had found employment through the two programs as of 2016.[11]

KEEPING PEOPLE IN PLACE

The examples above show that cities eventually take measures to reduce the negative effects of gentrification. But along the way, thousands of lives have been disrupted in incalculable ways: people have moved further away from their neighbors and jobs; they have had to spend time and energy fighting their landlords or looking for new apartments; and they have had to endure the stress of not knowing what will happen to their homes. Indeed, one of the major lessons to emerge from the past sixty years of urban revitalization is how policy makers have consistently failed to accurately estimate the threats of the back-to-the-city movement and have addressed gentrification only when it reaches a crisis point—at which point the solutions are much costlier. That half a million dollars that San Francisco paid for Rene Yanez's apartment in 2016? It would have covered the cost of his entire building had the city thought ahead and bought when the real estate market slumped after the dot-com bust.

As far back as 1965, BART consultants warned that the rapid transit line would push out low- and moderate-income residents along its route, including in the Mission District.[12] In 1977, Bob Schur asked the Senate, "What role can government play in maximizing the benefits and minimizing, if not eliminating, the harm for the greatest numbers of people?"[13] A year later, Conrad Weiler warned HUD: "The more successful cities are in attracting middle-income residents, the more displacement will become the dominant issue of housing policy."[14] In 1996, tenant leader Cora Moore warned about mixed-income redevelopment of Cabrini-Green: "The CHA plans to leave us out in the cold."[15]

Admittedly, it is unfair to judge past decisions too harshly. There are many voices in the wilderness, and as gentrification was first emerging, it was hard to know just how big the phenomenon would become. At the same time that Cassandras like Bob Schur and Conrad Weiler issued their warnings, some pundits predicted gentrification would not proceed to the extent it has. In 1979, the New York academic Peter Salins predicted that "Bedford-Stuyvesant, and virtually the entire Bronx outside of Riverdale, will resist all but the most limited gentrification."[16] How could a policy maker know whom to believe? More frequently, however, those in power embraced gentrification because it was a welcome relief to urban decline and promised stronger tax receipts. After all, to urban-philes, the story of gentrification is a powerful tale about good (cities) over evil (suburbs), and one whose benefits should not be undersold.

New York City's experience in particular should be instructive to places like Newark, New Jersey, and Detroit, both of which are already undergoing the early stages of their renaissances and are poised to embrace "the creative economy." During the 1970s, New York embarked on two tax incentive programs designed to spur new building and renovation of existing structures: 421a and J-51. Once these initiatives proved popular, they became harder to change and impossible to police—especially because no policing mechanism was established at their inception. As a result, developers were able to get tax breaks for building in neighborhoods long after those neighborhoods could be considered investment risks, and frequently failed to comply with the programs' requirements.

As a city's development apparatus becomes more complex—a network of intersecting tax incentives, density bonuses, community benefits agreements, etc.—it becomes easier and easier for a bad actor to manipulate. These "bad actors" are not fringe. Approximately 100,000 units—a good 10 percent of New York City's rent-regulated stock—have been implicated in enforcement actions since 2014. Perhaps the worst example of manipulation, however, is how landlords can make their buildings unlivable and prompt the Department of Buildings to do their bidding and evict rent-stabilized tenants in the name of safety. The most recent example was at 83–85 Bowery, where the housing department as early as 2015 ordered the landlord to fix a deteriorating stairwell immediately. He didn't, but instead of making the repairs itself and putting a lien on the building, the Department of Buildings evicted more than two dozen families—a repeat of what happened at 300 Nassau Avenue in Greenpoint—though they were eventually compensated after the media and local lawmakers intervened.[17] In the name of efficiency and economy, New York City puts an unusual amount of trust in its property owners, allowing them to self-certify building plans, self-report the number of rent-regulated units in each building, and self-patrol their violations. Such an approach penalizes law-abiding developers and rewards scofflaws. The city would be better off having fewer rules but enforcing them better.

In both New York City and San Francisco, the gap between supply and demand arises from the fact that jobs can grow at a much faster pace than houses can be built to accommodate them. This discrepancy is partially attributable to housing's long gestation period: it can take easily three to four years between a developer's acquiring land to signing his first lease. The number of jobs in the city may have increased 16 percent in that time—as it did in San Francisco between 2009 and 2013, or it may have fallen by almost that much, as it did between 2000 and 2004. But accelerating development timelines can only do so much. A job by its nature is very ephemeral; it can appear or disappear, move overseas or across the country, overnight. A home by contrast is far more permanent.

The proliferation of legislation that preserves historic buildings constrains housing supply, as does zoning that limits the height of buildings or density of housing units. It is tempting to advocate fewer regulations as a means to lower prices—Houston is the widely cited example. But such comparisons deserve some words of warning. First, density limits and preservation legislation in New York and San Francisco came about partly in *response* to fears of overdevelopment; they did not cause the housing shortage so much as the housing shortage caused them (though they later exacerbated the shortage). In other words, high demand existed before such regulations were adopted. Also, is it fair to criticize certain cities for adopting growth controls, when Houston is one-fifth as densely populated as San Francisco, and one-seventh as densely populated as New York? How sure can we be that the reason home prices are lower there is because supply is greater—rather than simply that demand is lower? And will Houstonians demand the same type of zoning controls once high-rises and tear-downs proliferate? We should also recognize the ways in which Houston's sprawl has externalized the cost of housing: Houston has twice the car ownership rate as New York City, and its metro region has a 50 percent larger per capita carbon footprint.[18]

While it is important for growing cities to produce more housing to keep down prices, increasing supply is an imperfect solution to gentrification. For one thing, more supply can reduce prices throughout a metro area, but not necessarily in the neighborhood that is most threatened by gentrification. For another, developers generally build for the upper end of the market, and it takes decades for that new supply to filter down and make apartments affordable for low- and middle-income tiers. In the meantime, an infusion of high-end housing in a neighborhood can theoretically accelerate the appreciation of prices overall. Building more housing may also require knocking down smaller residential buildings, displacing their residents in the name of higher supply and lower prices in the long run.

Supply-siders are also selective in where they want supply to be increased, which leads to an inequitable distribution of density. The Bloomberg administration rezoned more than 40 percent of New York City, ostensibly to plan for another million people, yet taken as a whole, the mayor increased capacity by only 1.7 percent. That's because downzonings—which took place in largely white neighborhoods— far outnumbered upzonings—which took place generally in minority neighborhoods. He could have avoided such a dubious legacy had he crafted a citywide plan to distribute the increased density fairly and logically, rather than approaching each neighborhood individually. A similar pattern has emerged in San Francisco, where population density is much higher on the city's east than west side.

When it comes to balancing supply and demand, San Francisco poses a number of other challenges. For one, all California cities have been hobbled by Proposition 13, the 1978 ballot measure that restricts both the growth of the tax rate and the degree to which municipalities can depend on residential property taxes. As a result, even though San Francisco's real estate values doubled between January 2012 and May 2018, the city has reaped limited additional tax revenues that it could apply toward building affordable housing.[19] For another, the power of the referendum in California can hobble the mayor and force the city to head in two opposite directions at once. A pro-growth mayor, who had the public's interest at heart, might borrow to build affordable housing, but in California he or she would be forced to get voters to approve any expenditures at a referendum. (Expenditure bonds require a two-thirds majority. Yet it only took a simple majority to pass Proposition M in 1986 to curtail the amount of office space—and therefore new tax revenue.) As it happened, between 1996 and 2011, advocates put three referendums on the ballot to raise money for affordable housing, but none of them passed. That's what makes Mayor Ed Lee's effort in 2014 all the more remarkable—by forging an agenda that would appeal to both middle-class and low-income voters, the business community as well as advocates, he was able to get a $310 million bond act passed.

There has been intense interest recently in the California State Legislature on reforming the state's land-use laws, but very little about the need to modernize the 2.5 percent tax cap legislation or the referendum system. Meanwhile, New York City's lesser known 6 percent tax cap also reinforces the inequity of gentrification: those who bought a brownstone early in a neighborhood's rejuvenation get to benefit from their property's appreciation without paying their fair share of taxes.

The Chicago Housing Authority's Plan for Transformation elucidates some of the same paradoxes, though its details are far different than what occurred in brownstone Brooklyn or San Francisco's Mission District. Chicago officials used gentrification as a tool to dismantle public housing rather than as an end in itself. But an overoptimistic timeline led the city to demolish the high-rises faster than they could be replaced. Chicago officials also underestimated the difficulty residents would face finding housing they could afford with their vouchers except in poor neighborhoods. There were plenty of people on the inside of Mayor Daley's administration who were aware of what could go wrong. Setting more realistic expectations would have instilled greater confidence in the Plan for Transformation and stranded fewer people in Section 8 housing, waiting to return.

SAVING WHICH CITY

The history of gentrification is full of deception, including self-deception: Young marrieds in Brooklyn Heights claimed they were looking out for public housing residents when they blocked a 173-unit building. The Mission Coalition Organization members thought it was safeguarding the neighborhood when they derailed a redevelopment plan—and all the affordable housing that came with it. David Walentas convinced the public he was reviving Dumbo, when the neighborhood was already alive with small manufacturers and renegade artists.

Another deception is believing that gentrification helps a neighborhood because it is better than the alternative. Gentrification doesn't so much help people living in a neighborhood as it replaces them with new ones with higher incomes. At times, the physical condition of a neighborhood's buildings can become so detrimental, and the concentration of poverty so intense, that replacing buildings does have some logic. And to some extent, the prosperity of a neighborhood *does* benefit longtime residents—but only if they are able to stay in their homes, and only in a limited fashion. Community benefits agreements—pacts between developers and neighborhood groups—provide little more in the way of jobs to local residents than what would have been offered without such pacts, and the new boutiques and restaurants that appear in gentrified neighborhoods have limited use for individuals with spotty work histories and truncated educations.

During the course of writing this book, many of the people whom I've interviewed have asked me: "So what do you think? How do we 'fix' gentrification? Less restrictive zoning? More affordable housing? Rent regulation? Community land trusts? Sweat equity?" The answer, I think, is "all of the above." The creative class that seeks city living is growing, but market-rate housing alone will not ease affordability. Rent control is the single most effective strategy to prevent displacement—though it should be income-restricted and accompanied by strong enforcement. Entrusting buildings to nonprofit housing organizations reduces the risk of tenant harassment. Encouraging low-income tenants to buy their buildings grants them stability, but only if they are steadily employed and can manage their household expenses. All of these strategies have been around for decades. It is not that we have not known about them; rather, it's that we have not implemented them widely or early enough.

At the outset of this book, I mentioned that history is better at teaching us what *not* to do, rather than what we should do. The reason policy makers did not heed the warnings of Conrad Weiler and others was by and large because they could never fathom that cities would once again become desirable, that wealth would move toward the centers of metropolitan areas rather than to their fringes, that accessories such as cars or backyards would lose their cachet, or that people would leave the brick walls in their living rooms exposed even when they had the means to cover them. But of course, they did. So even as public policy makers must catch up to this trend sixty years in the making, they must also anticipate the next great change in living and working patterns, and what challenges and threats it will pose.

Gentrification will not last forever. The creative economy that so upended Americans' assumptions about the inevitable decline of cities will at some point morph into something else. Advances in communication have made it easier to work from home; the gig economy has meant that more people than ever are working without set office locations; computers are eliminating whole job categories. All of these trends could have profound effects on where we live and work. The future is hard to predict, but we should know by now it will be different.

ACKNOWLEDGMENTS

I always thought writing a book would be a solitary experience, but this one has tested my social skills. I have relied upon old friends, friends of friends, friends of the family, Facebook friends, high school and college classmates, and numerous strangers in order to get the information, and the interviews, I needed. Among those who helped me make connections, and to whom I am deeply grateful, are Scott Sherman, Gary Rivlin, Malcolm Bush, Bryan Greene, Natasha Holbert, Bill Brazell, Loren Marsh, Adam Marsh, Andrea Cohen, Ethan Michaeli, Robert J. Phillips, Anna Maria Mayda, Andi Rosen, Claudia Hirsch, Kate Grossman, Robert Cherny, Bill Issel, Philip Tegeler, Judy Nemzoff, Robyn Takayama, and Samira Nazem.

As a journalist, though, my biggest debt is no doubt to the interview sources who gave me their time and trusted me to treat what they said fairly. Most of them are cited in the endnotes, and to repeat their names here would take up too much space; but it is worth calling out those who gave generous amounts of their time and trust to this project, plus a few whose names are not listed elsewhere: Richard LeGates, Martin L. Schneider, Julia Stasch, Daniel Doctoroff, Alexander Polikoff, Bill Wilen, Conrad Weiler, Latrice Hudson, Vanzelia

Young, LaFaye Garth, George Sweeting, Alex Garvin, Vicki Been, Brad Lander, Rudolph Hirsch, Blanche Hirsch, David Campos, Dean Macris, Randy Shaw, James Hong, Michael Freedman-Schnapp, Susan Popkin, Don Lindey, the Rev. Randall K. Blakey, Doug Farr, Roberta Feldman, Craig Newmark, Marc Janowitz, Sam Moss, Adrian Covert, Michael Cunningham, Jim Wunderman, Egon Terplan, Mike Ríos, Tom Angotti, Andrew Zacks, Steven L. Vettel, Daniel Bornstein, Kate Rosenberger, Amie Fishman, Fernando Martí, Leslie Dreyer, Deepa Varma, Sarah Weil, Raganuth K. Dindial, Roberto Hernandez, Tommi Avicolla Mecca, George Triano, and Charles Laven. During the many years it has taken me to write this book, a number of my most important interview subjects passed away, including the Rev. Donald McKinney, Everett Ortner, and René Yañez. May they rest in peace.

Wayne Brasler, my high school journalism teacher, taught me pretty much everything I know about reporting and writing, and what he didn't, I picked up along the way working for or alongside Tom Robbins, David Collins, Scott Timberg, Karen Frillmann, Andrea Bernstein, Steve Slosberg, Lance Johnson, Tom McGeveran, and the late Peter Kaplan.

The Furthermore Foundation gave me a generous grant to complete the research and travel for this book. Many people at New York Public Radio—in particular Jim Schachter, Sean Bowditch, and Dean Cappello—showed me incredible flexibility and support during the research and writing process. The pages and interlibrary loan staff at the New York Public Library found just about any document I was looking for, which I was able to collect, store, and pore over thanks to Melanie Locay and my appointment as a scholar in the Frederick Lewis Allen Room. I am also indebted to Julie I. May, Tess Cowell, and Cecily Dyer at the Brooklyn Historical Society for their extraordinary attentiveness, and Kate Blackmer for working with me so diligently on the elegant maps. D. Bradford Hunt, Marshall Weber, and Louis Dematteis graciously lent me their photos.

Tim Mennel was my patient, astute editor whose expertise in the subject matter has made the work that much stronger. My agent,

Elizabeth Kaplan, believed in this project and stuck with me through thick and thin. John P. Williams read every page and gave me much-needed constructive criticism and enthusiastic encouragement. Mark Schapiro, Rob Perris, Natasha Shapiro, and Joseph Capriglione also provided valuable feedback. Alyssa Katz and David Margolick read early versions of my book proposal. My faithful research assistants, Gilda di Carli, Grace Stanton, and Gwynne Hogan, organized my disorganization and made sense of my notes and sources.

The subject matter of this book has a lot to do with my parents, John and Charlotte Schuerman, who raised me in the exceptionally integrated and socially aware Hyde Park of the 1970s and '80s, and around whose kitchen table I first learned about *Gautreaux*, Section 8 housing, and the consequences of concentrated poverty. My sister Gabrielle Schuerman has always been a huge booster and sharp interlocutor. My wife, Meredith Phillips, has been my unsung hero throughout this long process, and our two children, Henry and Ivy, have patiently (and impatiently) endured my absences. Now that this book is finished, I am looking forward, as they say in politics, to spending more time with my family.

NOTES

ABBREVIATIONS

B.H. Press = Brooklyn Heights Press
NYT = New York Times
S.F. Chronicle = San Francisco Chronicle
Tribune = Chicago Tribune

INTRODUCTION

1. Mike Maciag, "Gentrification in America Report," *Governing* (Feb. 2015), http://www.governing.com/gov-data/gentrification-in-cities-governing-report.html.

2. See the interpretation in Daniel Stokols, *Sociology in the Digital Age: Solving Complex Problems in a Globalized World* (London: Academic Press, 2017), p. 28.

3. Joe Cortwright and Dillon Mahmoudi make a compelling case that the threat of gentrification has been exaggerated. They found very few census tracts gentrified between 1970 and 2010; however, they examined only high-poverty tracts—those with at least 30 percent of the population living below the poverty line—and defined as "rebounding areas" those that reached less than 15 percent poverty. Many gentrifying tracts may have been poorer than an area's median income and yet not so poor as to qualify for their definition. See Cortwright and Mahmoudi, *Lost in Place: Why the Persistence and Spread of Concentrated Poverty—Not Gentrification—Is Our Biggest Urban Challenge* (Portland, Ore.: City Observatory, 2014), http://cityobservatory.org. In addition, the NYU Furman Center has

shown that a neighborhood can gentrify while still retaining a high poverty rate. See *State of New York City's Housing and Neighborhoods in 2015* (New York: NYU Furman Center, June 9, 2016), pp. 14, 18, http://furmancenter.org.

4. HUD has a slightly different classification system, using "very low," "low," "moderate," and "middle" to refer not to quintiles, but to how much a household makes in comparison to the area's median income (AMI)—i.e., "very low-income housing" is priced to be affordable to those making 50 percent of the AMI. Some of my discussions of affordable housing follow HUD's definitions—i.e., in chapter 8, when relating how a study determined that rent regulations helped "low-income" households. However, the differences between my quintile-based definition and HUD's percentage-based categories are generally minor and insignificant.

5. Ruth Glass, "Introduction," in *London: Aspects of Change*, ed. Centre for Urban Studies (London: MacGibbon and Kee, 1964), pp. xviii, xx.

6. William H. Whyte, *The Organization Man* (New York: Simon and Schuster, 1956), p. 267.

CHAPTER ONE

1. Unless otherwise cited, biographical information about the Schneiders is from author's interviews with Martin L. Schneider, June 26, 2009; July 29, 2010; and Aug. 2, 2016.

2. Pete Hamill, *A Drinking Life* (Boston: Back Bay Books, 1994), p. 209.

3. Harrison Salisbury, *The Shook-up Generation* (New York: Harper, 1958), p. 13.

4. Sue Corbett, "Norton Juster and Jules Feiffer: Once Upon a Half Century," *Publishers Weekly*, Oct. 5, 2009 (online edition), https://www.publishersweekly.com.

5. *B.H. Press*, Nov. 7, 1957, p. 1.

6. Truman Capote, *A House on the Heights* (New York: Little Bookroom, 2001), p. 19. Also see Sherrill Tippins, *February House: The Story of W. H. Auden, Carson McCullers, Jane and Paul Bowles, Benjamin Britten, and Gypsy Rose Lee, under One Roof in Brooklyn* (Boston: Houghton Mifflin, 2005).

7. Norman Mailer, *Barbary Shore* (New York: Vintage International, 1997), p. 8.

8. R. John Walton, "Arts Colony Is Flourishing on Hicks," *B.H. Press*, Nov. 13, 1958, p. 1.

9. "Two Beat Poets," *B.H. Press*, June 16, 1959, p. 5.

10. Author interviews with Diane Margolis, May 23, 2010, and Oct. 16, 2010.

11. See *B.H. Press*, Oct. 17, 1957, p. 2; Feb. 12, 1959, p. 1.

12. See "Trouble in Paradise," *B.H. Press*, May 25, 1957, p. 2.

13. Maryalicia Crowell, "Family Life on the Heights: They've Had Enough of Both India and Suburbia," *B.H. Press*, Sept. 5, 1957, p.1.

14. "Home Is the Hunted," *B.H. Press*, Dec. 18, 1958, p. 4.

15. Suleiman Osman, *The Invention of Brownstone Brooklyn: Gentrification and the Search for Authenticity in Postwar New York* (New York: Oxford University Press, 2011), p. 89.

16. Author interview with Otis Pratt Pearsall, Aug. 14, 2009.

17. Edmund Wilson, "On This Site Will Be Erected," *New Republic*, May 20, 1925, p. 342. Quoted in Capote, p. 6.

18. *The Regional Plan of New York and Its Environs* (Philadelphia: William F. Fell Co., 1931), vol. 2, p. 476.

19. Robert Moses, *Cadman Plaza: Report to Mayor Wagner and the Board of Estimate by the Committee on Slum Clearance* (New York: April 20, 1959), p. 20.

20. Martin L. Schneider, *Battling for Brooklyn* (New York: Brooklyn Heights Association, 2010), p. 5.

21. Martin Tucker, "'Blue Book' Lists Nobility," *B.H. Press*, March 21, 1957, p.1; "1957 Blue Book's Directory of Society on the Heights," *B.H. Press*, March 21, 1957, p. 5.

22. Suleiman Yusuf Osman, "The Birth of Post-modern New York: Gentrification, Post-industrialization, and Race in South Brooklyn, 1950–1980" (PhD diss., Harvard University, 2006), pp. 65–66.

23. Lois F. Childs to Brooklyn Heights Association, Oct. 8, 1959. In Brooklyn Heights Association Records, Box 13, "Housing Violations Committee—1959–61," Brooklyn Collection, Brooklyn Public Library.

24. Helen P. Coburn to Brooklyn Heights Association, May 23, 1960. In Brooklyn Heights Association Records, Box 13, "Housing Violations Committee 1959–61," Brooklyn Collection.

25. Arthur B. Hooker, chairman, Brooklyn Heights Association Housing Violations Committee, to Buildings Commissioner Harold Birns, Nov. 2, 1959. In Brooklyn Heights Association Records, "Housing Violation Committee—1959–61," Brooklyn Collection.

26. Fitzhugh White, "Echo from Beacon Hill," Letter to the Editor, *B.H. Press*, Jan. 31, 1957, p. 2; Mrs. William R. Willets, "Keep Village Out," Letter to the Editor, *B.H. Press*, Jan. 24, 1957, p. 2.

27. In 1949, the median income of the New York-New Jersey Statistical Metropolitan Area was $3,241. Brooklyn Census Tracts 1, 7, and 9, which covered the southern, northern, and eastern sections of the Heights, had median household incomes $2,348; $2,392; and $1,989, respectively. The wealthiest part of the Heights was Census Tract 3, which corresponded to the prime real estate along the Promenade along the East River; the median income there was $3,661. Census Tract 5, the central part of the Heights, had a median income just about on par with the region as a whole: $3,278. The median annual income for the five census tracts (weighted for population) was $2,875, or about 12 percent below the metropolitan statistical area (MSA). US Department of Commerce, Bureau of the Census, *1950 United States Census of Population: Selected Population and Housing Characteristics: New York, NY, Census Tracts* (Washington, DC: GPO, 1952), Table I: Characteristics of the Population by Census Tract, 1950.

28. Schneider, author interviews.

29. Schneider, *Battling for Brooklyn*, p. 13.

30. Schneider, *Battling for Brooklyn*, p. 14.

31. A list of some of the positions Moses held is reproduced in Hilary Ballon and Kenneth T. Jackson, eds., *Robert Moses and the Modern City: The Transformation of New York* (New York: W.W. Norton, 2007), p. 134. That list omits several others of which he was in charge until 1962, including the chairman of the New York State Council of Parks, the Long Island State Parks Commission, the Bethpage and Jones Beach authorities, and the New York Power Authority. See Robert A. Caro, *The Power Broker: Robert Moses and the Fall of New York* (New York: Vintage Books, 1975), pp. 1074–1075.

32. Some 456 of the 722 units were to be studios or one-bedrooms. Moses, p. 23.

33. Moses, p. 15.

34. "One hundred and sixty-one (161) of the families and all of the single persons are apparently eligible for public housing. Twenty-three (23) of the families will require private housing." Moses, p. 44. Moses was well known for double-counting the number of public housing units available to take in those displaced by his urban renewal projects. See the discussion on Manhattantown in Caro, pp. 962–963.

35. Ballon and Jackson include a catalog of Moses' works in New York City, pp. 134–313.

36. Ballon and Jackson, pp. 94, 106.

37. Caro, pp. 19–20.

38. Caro, p. 19.

39. Caro, pp. 984–1003.

40. Rev. Donald W. McKinney letter to Robert Moses, Jan. 17, 1957; Robert Moses letter to the Rev. Donald W. McKenney [sic], Jan. 28, 1957. Robert Moses Papers, New York Public Library, Archives, Manuscripts, and Rare Books Division. Box 116, Folder: "Committee on Slum Clearance, 1/1/57–12/31/57."

41. Author interview with Otis Pratt Pearsall, April 18, 2010; "The Reminiscences of Otis Pratt Pearsall" (New York: New York Preservation Society, 2004), p. 1–22, http://www.nypap.org/oral-history/otis-pratt-pearsall/.

42. Robert Moses letter to John Cashmore, April 29, 1959. Robert Moses Papers, New York Public Library, Box 118, Folder: "Committee on Slum Clearance 1959."

43. Conversation recounted in John Cashmore letter to Robert Moses, June 9, 1959. Robert Moses Papers, Box 118, Folder: "Committee on Slum Clearance 1959."

44. "Heights Is Not for Families—Cashmore," *B.H. Press*, June 4, 1959, p. 1. A copy of this article was included in Cashmore's June 9 letter to Moses without any corrections, indicating the accuracy of the *B.H. Press'* account.

45. Schneider, *Battling for Brooklyn*, p. 21; Schneider email to author, Sept. 20, 2018.

46. "BHA Calls Rents Unreal," *B.H. Press*, Feb. 26, 1959, p. 8; "Republican Leader Urges Higher Rents for Cadman Plaza," *B. H. Press*, April 30, 1959, p. 1.

47. "Slum Plan Opposed," *NYT*, April 22, 1959. Via Times Machine.

48. Peter Braestrup, "Civic Units Decry Luxury Project," *NYT*, June 30, 1960. Via Times Machine.

49. Author interview with Eric and Lorna Salzman, Nov. 20, 2010.

50. Martin S. James, ed., *Cadman Plaza in Brooklyn Heights: A Study of the Misuse of Public Power and Funds in Urban Renewal* (New York: North Brooklyn Heights Community Group, 1961), pp. 13–15. In Brooklyn Heights Association Records, Box 13, "Housing Cadman Plaza–1961."

51. Eric Salzman and Jane Jacobs, "Urban Renewal in New York," Press Release, May 15, 1961. In Brooklyn Heights Association Records, Box 13, "Housing Cadman Plaza—1961."

52. James, unpaginated addendum.

53. "Minister Opposes Cadman Renewal," *NYT*, Nov. 6, 1961. Via Times Machine.

54. For details on the Goodman Plan, see flyer headlined, "Learn More about the Goodman Proposal" (October 1961). In Brooklyn Heights Association Records, Box 13, "Housing Cadman Plaza—1961."

55. At an emergency meeting of governors of the association, President William R. Fisher said he had met with the Housing and Redevelopment Board and that "the board indicated that if the community switched its support to the Goodman Plan, the city will probably refuse to develop the controversial site at all because it does not believe the plan could achieve its stated objectives." Press Release, Brooklyn Heights Association, Nov. 16, 1961, p. 3. In Brooklyn Heights Association Records, Box 13, "Housing Cadman Plaza—1961."

56. Brooklyn Heights Association, p. 3.

57. Robert T. H. Davidson letter to William R. Fisher, Nov. 16, 1961. In Brooklyn Heights Association Records, Box 13, "Housing Cadman Plaza—1961."

58. "The Facts? Who Cares? A Statement about Cadman Plaza by the Brooklyn Heights Association," advertisement [*B.H. Press*, Nov. 16, 1961]. In Brooklyn Heights Association Records, Box 13, "Housing Cadman Plaza—1961."

59. Sherman O. Schachter to Brooklyn Heights Association, Nov. 17, 1961. Brooklyn Heights Association Records, Box 13, "Housing Cadman Plaza—1961."

60. Brooklyn Heights Association, Letter to R. E. Peattie, Jan. 3, 1962. Brooklyn Heights Association Records, Box 13, "Housing Cadman Plaza—1962."

61. City of New York Housing and Redevelopment Board, Press Release, March 20, 1962.

62. "The Cadman Plaza Project," *NYT*, April 16, 1962. Via Times Machine.

63. Brooklyn Heights Community Council et al., "We Are Afraid *for* Virginia," flyer. Brooklyn Heights Association Records, Box 13, "Cadman Plaza—1963."

64. Brooklyn Heights Community Council and Brooklyn Heights Association, "Are You for the Heights?," June 16, 1963, flyer. Brooklyn Heights Association Records, Box 13, "Cadman Plaza—1963."

65. The Brooklyn Heights Community Council and the Brooklyn Heights Association, "Board of Estimate Hearing on Housing Proposal," undated flyer; for distribution numbers, see Brooklyn Heights Association, Press Release [undated]: "The attached flyer was distributed to five thousand Heights residents. . . ." A Brooklyn Heights Community Council press release, April 16, 1963, recounts an extensive recruitment and petition drive. That document also mentions Dr. Weeks, who had been co-organizer of the anti-Cadman North Heights Community Group, as a supporter of the Brooklyn Heights Community Council, which organized against the public housing proposal. Brooklyn Heights Association Records, Box 13, "Cadman Plaza—1963."

66. The Independent Budget Office, a municipally funded, nonpartisan think tank, found that properties within historic districts saw faster price appreciation and were more valuable overall than similar houses outside district boundaries. Alan Treffeisen, "The Impact of Historic Districts on Residential Property Values" (New York: Independent Budget Office, 2003), http://www.ibo.nyc.ny.us.

67. Cadman Plaza South, at Clark and Henry streets, was the last of the towers to be constructed, in 1973. See Norval White and Elliot Willensky, *AIA Guide to New York City: The Classic Guide to New York's Architecture* (New York: Three Rivers Press, 2000), pp. 664–665, 667–668.

68. Alexander Garvin, *The American City: What Works, What Doesn't*, 2nd ed. (New York: McGraw Hill, 2002), pp. 170–171.

69. "Building: 54 Garden Place," Street Easy, https://streeteasy.com.

70. "88 Joralemon Street," Trulia, https://www.trulia.com.

CHAPTER TWO

1. "The Reminiscences of Evelyn and Everett Ortner," New York Preservation Archive Project. Interview conducted by Florence Daniels, Dec. 19, 2003, http://www.nypap.org.

2. Author interview with Everett Ortner, Oct. 13, 2008.

3. New York Preservation Project, p. 63. Evelyn G. Ortner, Resume (hand-dated June 1998). Evelyn G. and Everett F. Ortner Papers, Box 11, Folder 3. Brooklyn Historical Society.

4. Samantha Lindenauer, "Everett Ortner's World War Two Experiences," unpublished manuscript, circa 2003, p. 4. Ortner Papers, Box 7, Folder 5.

5. See, for example, "Grandad Read the Bible," unpublished manuscript. Ortner Papers, Box 12, Folder 2.

6. Lindenauer, p. 4.

7. Lindenauer, pp. 4, 6.

8. Lindenauer, pp. 7, 9–12.

9. "Performance Appraisal for Exempt Employees: Everett Ortner," April 27, 1983 [author's name is illegible]. Ortner Papers, Box 16, Folder 5.

10. US Censuses of Population and Housing : 1960 : New York, NY (Washington, DC: GPO, 1962), Table P-1, Brooklyn Tract 0159, p. 64.

11. New York Preservation Project, p. 9.

12. Williamsburgh Savings Bank, "Analysis of Escrow and Revision of Monthly Payment," Dec. 1, 1963. Ortner Papers, Box 24, Folder 1.

13. New York Preservation Archive Project, pp. 8, 56.

14. Notes for a lecture at Home Expo in Brooklyn. Ortner Papers, Box 11, Folder 3.

15. New York Preservation Project, p. 55.

16. New York Preservation Project, p. 54.

17. New York Preservation Project, p. 30.

18. Suleiman Osman, *The Invention of Brownstone Brooklyn: Gentrification and the Search for Authenticity in Postwar New York* (New York: Oxford University Press, 2011), p. 203.

19. New York Preservation Project, pp. 32–33.

20. New York Preservation Project, pp. 30–34.

21. Author interview with Everett Ortner, Oct. 13, 2008.

22. Suleiman, 2006, pp. 353–354.

23. New York Preservation Project, pp. 39, 70.

24. Everett H. Ortner, "Goodbye Old Friend: Brooklyn Union Gas Company . . . Keyspan Energy, Keyspan, Will it Be National Grid?" unpublished manuscript, not dated. Ortner Papers, Box 16, Folder 5. "Old Brownstone to Be Gas Showcase," in *Sendout* [Brooklyn Union Gas newsletter], Feb. 24, 1967, pp. 1, 3.

25. *Brooklyn Union Gas: A Centennial History* (New York: Brooklyn Union Gas, 1975), p. 109.

26. Author interview; New York Preservation Project, p. 44.

27. *Brooklyn Union Gas*, pp. 110–111.

28. New York Preservation Project, pp. 47–48.

29. Letter from Champion to Ortners, Jan. 21, 1972. Ortner Papers, Box 9, Folder 2.

30. Letter from Executive Mansion to Ortners, October 1974. Ortner Papers, Box 9, Folder 2; Letter from Conklin to Ortners, Oct. 21, 1974. Ortner Papers, Box 9, Folder 2.

31. New York Preservation Project, p. 42.

32. Assemblyman Melvin Miller and State Senator Joseph Montalto, "Park Slope Anti-crime Network Receives $20,000 in State Budget," Press Release, circa 1983. Author's collection.

33. New York Preservation Project, pp. 66–67.

34. Back to the City program, *Brownstoner*, September 1974, pp. 7–8.

35. List of registrants, Ortner Papers, Box 32, Folder 1.

36. New York Preservation Project, pp. 61–62.

37. New York Preservation Project, p. 60.

38. Dana Crawford and Nellie Longsworth, Letter to Everett Ortner, June 2, 1983. Ortner Papers.

39. Deborah Weser, "Conference Eyes Back to the City Move," *San Antonio Express*, Oct. 29, 1977, p. A4. In reality, however, there were very few financial benefits for middle-class preservationists. The federal Historic Rehabilitation Tax Credit applied only to "investment properties"—renovations of old buildings into offices, retail, or residential rental units. See *Federal Tax Incentives for Rehabilitating Historic Buildings: 35th Anniversary* (National Park Service, US Department of the Interior, March 2013), pp. 4–5, https://www.nps.gov.

40. "The Brownstone," Editorial, *NYT*, June 21, 1974, p. 36.

41. Everett H. Ortner, "The Brownstone Is Not Lost," Letter to the Editor, *NYT*, July 19, 1974, p. 34.

42. Clem Labine, "Displacement," Letter to the Editor, *Preservation News*, January 1979, p. 4.

43. Susan Draper, *A House Is on the Outside, a Home Is on the Inside: Gentrification as a Social Movement*, (PhD diss., New York University, 1991), pp. 104–105.

44. Tamar Rothenberg, "'And She Told Two Friends': Lesbians Creating Urban Social Space," in *Mapping Desire: Geographies of Sexualities*, ed. David Bell and Gill Valentine (London: Routledge, 1995), pp. 168–169.

45. *Line Waiter's Gazette*, Sept. 22, 1973. [The name of the newsletter was later changed to *Linewaiter's Gazette* and then *Linewaiters' Gazette*.] Linewaiter's Gazette, Box 1. Brooklyn Collection, Brooklyn Public Library.

46. "The Mongoose Food Co-op Will Be Closed," flyer [October or November 1973]. Linewaiter's Gazette, Box 1.

47. *Line Waiter's Gazette*, Dec. 8, 1973. Linewaiter's Gazette, Box 1.

48. *Line Waiter's Gazette*, July 11, 1974. Linewaiter's Gazette, Box 1.

49. Max Falkowitz, "Birth of the Kale," Grubstreet.com, April 19, 2018, http://www.grubstreet.com/2018/04/history-of-the-park-slope-food-coop.html.

50. Anemona Hartcollis and Juliet Linderman, "At a Food Co-op, a Discordant Thought: Nannies Covering Shifts," *NYT*, Feb. 17, 2011, p. A24, https://www.nytimes.com/2011/02/18/nyregion/18coop.html.

51. Jane Peterson, "Anguish and Joy in a Changing Neighborhood," *Historic Preservation*, July–August 1983, p. 22.

52. Draper, pp. 114, 142.

53. Gail Collins, "'Post-Pioneer' Arrivals Keep Park Slope in Flux," *NYT*, Nov. 1, 1981, Sect. 8, p. 1.

54. Author interview with Clem Labine, Dec. 7, 2008.

55. Kenneth Jackson, *Crabgrass Frontier: The Suburbanization of the United States* (New York: Oxford University Press, 1985), p. 302.

56. Draper, p. 71.

57. David K. Shipler, "Experts Attribute Housing Decay Here to Landlords' Fears and Fantasies," March 22, 1970, *NYT*, p. 69. Via TimesMachine.

58. Luc Sante, "My Lost City," in *Kill All Your Darlings: Pieces 1980–2005* (New York: Yeti, 2007), p. 22.

59. Peter Marcuse, *Rental Housing in the City of New York: Supply and Condition, 1975–1978* (New York City Department of Housing Preservation and Development, January 1979), pp. 5–6.

60. Marcuse, *Rental Housing in the City of New York*, p. 9. In 1969, Congress codified the 25 percent figure as the threshold for "affordability." In the 1980s, because of federal budget cuts, the threshold increased to 30 percent.

61. Marcuse, *Rental Housing in the City of New York*, pp. 6, 8.

62. Peter Marcuse, "Gentrification, Abandonment, and Displacement: Connections, Causes, and Policy Responses in New York City," in *Journal of Urban and Contemporary Law* (St. Louis: Washington University) 28, no. 195 (1985), pp. 197, 200.

63. Ron Lawson, *"Owners of Last Resort": An Assessment of the Track Records of New York City's Early Low Income Cooperative Conversions* (New York City Department of Housing Preservation and Development, Office of Program and Management Analysis, June 1984), pp. 11–12. New York City Municipal Archives.

64. "Some Friends Remember Bob Schur," *City Limits*, April 1982, pp. 33–34; Andrew Reichler, "Philip St. Georges, 1951–1998," *City Limits*, February 1999, http://citylimits.org.

65. Lawson, p. 14.

66. Lawson, pp. 14–15.

67. Lawson, p. 31.

68. Lawson, pp. 25–27, 31.

69. Anthony J. Blackburn et al., *Evaluation of the Urban Homesteading Demonstration Program: Final Report: Vol. 1: Summary Assessment* (US Housing and Urban Development, 1981), p. 4.

70. Lawson, pp. 115–117; Urban Homesteading Assistance Board, *2017 UHAB Annual Report*, p. 4, http://uhab.org.

71. Joseph P. Fried, "Starr Resigning as Chief of New York City Housing," *NYT*, July 9, 1976, p. 30. Via Times Machine.

72. Lawson, pp. 17–19.

73. Joseph P. Fried, "Brownstone Renewal Creates Dispute," *NYT*, July 16, 1976, p. 23.

74. Lawson, p. 17.

75. Blake Fleetwood, "The New Elite and an Urban Renaissance," *New York Times Magazine*, Jan. 14, 1979, pp. 17–18. Via Times Machine.

76. Author interview with Alex Garvin, Feb. 19, 2018. For particulars of the program, see Deloitte Haskins and Sells, *Review of the J-51 Program* (New York City Department of Housing Preservation and Development, 1984), pp. B1–2. New York City Municipal Library.

77. Peter Marcuse, *Rental Housing*, pp. 65, 68.

78. "While most apartments become vacant through normal turnover, there

have been documented cases of owners harassing tenants to encourage their departure. . . . To the extent the J-51 program encourages owners to create vacant buildings suitable for conversions, it has contributed to the use of these techniques." See Deloitte Haskins and Sells, p. H9.

79. Garvin interview.

80. Roger Starr, "Making New York Smaller," *New York Times Magazine*, Nov. 14, 1976, p. 32.

81. Starr, p. 31.

82. Gordon J. Davis, "On 'Shrinking' Our Poor Communities," Letter to the Editor, *NYT*, Feb. 11, 1976; Alan S. Oser, "Starr's Exit from Beame Administration Marks the End of a Hectic Era," *NYT*, Sept. 16, 1976; "Minority Caucus Bids Starr Quit," *NYT*, March 5, 1976.

83. Fried, "Starr Resigning as Chief of New York City Housing."

84. Joseph P. Fried, "City's Housing Administrator Proposes 'Planned Shrinkage' of Some Slums," *NYT*, Feb. 3, 1976.

85. Roger Starr, *The Rise and Fall of New York City* (New York: Basic Books, 1985).

86. Jonathan Soffer, *Ed Koch and the Rebuilding of New York City* (New York: Columbia University Press, 2016), pp. 278–279.

87. "Text of Address Delivered by Koch at His Inauguration as Mayor of New York City," *NYT*, Jan. 2, 1978, p. 13.

CHAPTER THREE

1. Mel Scott, *The San Francisco Bay Area: A Metropolis in Perspective*, 2nd ed. (Berkeley: University of California Press, 1985), pp. 143–148, 183–201. Newspaper quotation is from *Sacramento Union*, cited in Oakland Chamber of Commerce *Bulletin* 3, no. 8 (August 1912), p. 1, and reproduced in Scott, p. 145.

2. Michael Storper, "Why San Francisco's Way of Doing Business Beat Los Angeles'," *Los Angeles Times*, Oct. 23, 2015, http://www.latimes.com/opinion/op-ed/la-oe-storper-how-sf-beat-la-20151025-story.html.

3. Randy Shaw paints an intriguing picture of the way in which "loose morals" led to the fight for women's rights. See pp. 33–46 in his *The Tenderloin: Sex, Crime and Resistance in the Heart of San Francisco* (San Francisco: Urban Reality Press, 2015).

4. Chester Hartman with Sarah Carnoche, *City for Sale: The Transformation of San Francisco*, rev. ed. (Berkeley: University of California Press, 2002), p. 3.

5. *Final Environmental Impact Report for the Proposed Amendments to the Text of the City Planning Code and to the Zoning Map Relating to the Residential Districts and Development* (San Francisco Department of City Planning, June 27, 1978), pp. 5, 8.

6. Quoted in Gary Kamiya, *Cool Gray City of Love: 49 Views of San Francisco* (New York: Bloomsbury USA), p. 262.

7. Allan Temko, "Environmental Design: A Plan to Let the Sunshine into S.F.," *S.F. Chronicle*, July 18, 1983, p. 6.

8. The details of Yañez's life not otherwise cited come from the author's multiple interviews with him from 2015 to 2017.

9. Gruen Gruen and Associates, *Analysis of the Economic Impacts of the Proposed Change in San Francisco Zoning* (San Francisco: Gruen Gruen, Dec. 17, 1976).

10. See José Vasconcelos, *The Cosmic Race: A Bilingual Edition*, trans. Didier T. Jaén (Los Angeles: California State University, 1979), pp. 34–39.

11. Alejandro Murguía, *The Medicine of Memory* (Austin: University of Texas Press, 2001), p. 120.

12. Patlan in "Murals and Their Power to Change: A Real Earl Documentary Production," https://vimeo.com.

13. Stone and Youngberg, *Rapid Transit for the Bay Area: The Four-County System* (1961), p. 26.

14. Stone and Youngberg, p. 32.

15. See map in Stone and Youngberg, p. 15.

16. Richard Grefe and Richard Smart, *A History of the Key Decisions in the Development of Bay Area Rapid Transit* (prepared for the US Department of Transportation and the US Department of Housing and Urban Development, 1975), p. 110.

17. Wolfgang S. Homburger, "Mass Transit Planning and Development in the San Francisco Bay Area," Urban Mass Transit Planning, held in New York, Sept. 12–16, 1966 and Asilomar, Pacific Grove, Ca., presented by the Polytechnic Institute of Brooklyn and by the Institute of Transportation and Traffic Engineering and U of California Extension. Cited in Grefe and Smart, p. 39.

18. Mike Healy, the longtime press secretary for the BART, wrote in a March 4, 2017, email to author: "While I did not come to BART until long after this, it is my recollection that this change in design was done for both equity in terms of San Francisco's share of bond money . . . and for social reasons. It was always believed BART would be a catalyst for development." For the changes in routes, see maps at Stone and Youngberg, p. 15, and Parsons, Brinckerhoff, Quade, and Douglas, *The Composite Report: Bay Area Rapid Transit* (Oakland: Bay Area Rapid Transit District, May 1962).

19. "BART & Redevelopment & Reconstruction," *Basta Ya*, August 1970, p. 7.

20. San Francisco Department of City Planning and San Francisco Redevelopment Agency, *Rapid Transit Corridor Study* (1965), p. 1. Cited in Ocean Howell, *Making the Mission: Planning and Ethnicity in San Francisco* (Chicago: University of Chicago Press, 2015), p. 253; San Francisco Redevelopment Agency, "Rapid Transit Corridor Study: Summary and Background of the Study to Be Undertaken by the Redevelopment Agency and the Department of City Planning" (Oct. 29, 1963) [p. 1].

21. Howell, p. 260.

22. Howell, pp. 260–264.

23. Howell, p. 265.

24. Howell, p. 211.

25. Author interview with Mike Miller, Dec. 19, 2016.

26. Mike Miller, *A Community Organizer's Tale: People and Power in San Francisco* (Berkeley, California: Heyday Press, 2009), p. 215.

27. Howell, pp. 293, 295.

28. Miller, p. 225.

29. Howell, p. 294.

30. George and Eunice Grier, "Urban Displacement: A Reconnaissance," in *Back to the City: Issues in Neighborhood Renovation*, ed. Shirley Bradway Laska and Daphne Spain (New York: Pergamon Press, 1980), p. 256.

31. Grier and Grier, p. 263.

32. National Urban Coalition, *Displacement: City Neighborhoods in Transition* (Washington, DC, 1978), p. 15.

33. Mission Housing Development Corporation, *A Plan for the Inner Mission* (San Francisco, 1974), book 2, p. 10. At the time, rent that equaled 25 percent of a household's income was considered "affordable"; today the percentage is 30 percent.

34. Mission Housing Development Corporation, book 2, p. 2.

35. Mission Housing Development Corporation, book 1, p. 31. San Francisco's zoning governs the size of the apartments that can be built at any one site. Mission Housing opposed R-4, which permitted 200-square foot studios, while favoring R-3, which required 800-square-foot apartments.

36. For 800-unit goal, see Mission Housing Development Corporation, book 1, p. 17. Completion count is based on MHDC's website and includes single-room occupancy units and units built in partnership with organizations, but it excludes apartments built outside of the Mission neighborhood. See missionhousing.org /mhdc_project_type/mission-housing-portfolio/.

37. Allan B. Jacobs, *Making City Planning Work* (Chicago: American Society of Planning Officials, 1978), p. 261.

38. Jacobs, p. 25.

39. For the following 46 years, La Galería rented the storefront on a month-to-month basis, although it would repeatedly ask the landlord for a lease. In October 2018, the gallery announced it would have to move because its rent was being doubled.

40. For the allure of murals, see Angela Frucci, "In San Francisco's Mission District, Touring Clarion Alley Murals," *Los Angeles Times*, May 13, 2012, http:// articles.latimes.com/2012/may/13/travel/la-tr-sanfrancisco-20120513.

41. Interview with Liliana Wilson by Cary Cordova for the Archives of American Art (Washington: Smithsonian Institution), July 13–27, 2004, https://www .aaa.si.edu.

42. Author interview with Lou Dematteis, Nov. 16, 2016.

43. Irma D. Herrera, "Vamos Cruisin'," in *Lowriders*, photographs by Lou De-

matteis, texts by Irma D. Herrera and René Yañez (San Francisco: Malulu Editions, 2016), no pagination.

CHAPTER FOUR

1. George Murray, "Old Town: The Pickle and the Wobs," from the Old Town Art Fair program, 1958, reprinted in Shirley Baugher, *Our Old Town: The History of a Neighborhood* (Chicago: Old Town Triangle Association, 2001), pp. 83–85.

2. "Old Town Art Group to Show Its True Color," *Tribune*, May 28, 1950, p. N4.

3. Elizabeth Rannells, "Chicago's Sleepy 'Old Town' Awakens," *Tribune*, May 30, 1954, p. G23. Via ProQuest.

4. Robert Cross, "Big Noise from Lincoln Park," *Tribune*, Nov. 2, 1969, p. I30. Via ProQuest.

5. Carl W. Condit, *Chicago: 1930–70: Building, Planning, and Urban Technology* (Chicago: University of Chicago Press, 1974), pp. 215–219.

6. "Group in Old Town Will Oppose Urban Renewal High Rises," *Tribune*, April 19, 1964, p. N1; Buck Thomas, "2 Groups Approve Lincoln Park Plan," *Tribune*, June 23, 1965, p. B11. Via ProQuest.

7. Lynn Taylor, "Renewal Priority Plan Told: Lincoln Park Association Drops Housing Provision," *Tribune*, Sept. 29, 1966, p. 11; Barbara Amazaki, "Renewal Change Urged: Lincoln Park Group Sets Hearing," *Tribune*, Jan. 14, 1968, p. A1; Amazaki, "Lincoln Park Project Gets Approval," *Tribune*, June 27, 1968, p. N1. Via ProQuest. For summary numbers of displacement and relocation, see Cross.

8. Amanda Seligman, "Lincoln Park," in *Encyclopedia of Chicago*, ed. Janice L. Rieff, Ann Durkin Keating, and James B. Grossman (Chicago: University of Chicago Press, 2004), https://encyclopedia.chicagohistory.org (online edition).

9. Larry Vale, "Housing Chicago: Cabrini-Green to Parkside of Old Town," *Places Journal*, February 2012.

10. Harvey Warren Zorbaugh, *The Gold Coast and the Slum: A Sociological Study of Chicago's Near North Side* (Chicago: University of Chicago Press, 1929), p. 10.

11. Zorbaugh, p. 16.

12. D. Bradford Hunt, *Blueprint for Disaster: The Unraveling of Chicago Public Housing* (Chicago: University of Chicago Press, 2009), pp. 130–131.

13. Julian Whittlesey, "New Dimensions in Housing Design," *Progressive Architecture*, April 1951, pp. 57–68. Cited in Hunt, p. 124.

14. Amanda Seligman, "Cabrini-Green," in *The Encyclopedia of Chicago* (online edition).

15. Hunt, pp. 112–113.

16. Harold Baron, "Public Housing: Chicago Builds a Ghetto" (speech delivered at Center for Continuing Education, University of Chicago, March 10, 1967), p. 6. Available at Chicago History Museum.

17. Harold M. Baron, "Building Babylon: A Case of Racial Controls in Public

Housing" (1971), p. 73. Unpublished manuscript available at Chicago History Museum.

18. Baron, "Babylon," p. 73.

19. Alexander Polikoff, *Waiting for Gautreaux* (Evanston: Northwestern University Press, 2006), p. 34.

20. Polikoff, p. 81.

21. Author interview with Polikoff.

22. Polikoff, p. 47.

23. Author interview with Milton Shadur, Nov. 13, 2017.

24. This analysis is drawn from Shamoon Zamir, *Dark Voices: W. E. B. Du Bois and American Thought, 1888–1903* (Chicago: University of Chicago Press, 1995), pp. 200–201.

25. Polikoff, *Gautreaux*, p. 21; Kenneth B. Clark, *Dark Ghetto* (New York: Harper & Row, 1965), p. xxiii.

26. Clark, p. 25.

27. Clark, p. 23.

28. Polikoff, p. 74.

29. Polikoff, p. 212.

30. Polikoff, pp. 226–227.

31. Hunt, pp. 155–156, quoting Robert H. Murphy letter to Harry J. Schneider, "Taylor (37): Comments on Magazine Article," Oct. 21, 1963. Manager's Folder, Robert Taylor Homes, CHA Files.

32. Hunt, p. 148.

33. Hunt, pp. 152–153.

34. Hunt, p. 204.

35. "Defensible space theory" holds that the less attachment a resident has towards common property, the less willing he or she is to take care of it. It is the basis for most public housing design today, which favors row houses or small buildings, where front yards are privately owned or shared among a small group of neighbors, instead of large high-rises, where common spaces are ignored or neglected.

36. Institute for Community Design, "Review and Analysis of the Chicago Housing Authority and Implementation of Recommended Changes: Final Report of Phase 1: Recommended Changes and Resulting Savings" (New York: March 31, 1982), pp. 4, 6.

37. Jane Byrne, *My Chicago* (New York: W.W. Norton, 1992), p. 320.

38. Edward Marciniak, *Reclaiming the Inner City* (Washington, DC: National Center for Urban Ethnic Affairs, 1986), pp. 156–157.

39. Larry Bennett and Adolph Reed Jr., "The New Face of Urban Renewal: The Near North Redevelopment Initiative and the Cabrini-Green Neighborhood," in *Without Justice for All: The New Liberalism and Our Retreat from Racial Equality*, ed. Adolph Reed Jr. (Boulder, Colo.: Westview Press, 1999), p. 178.

40. Marciniak, p. 158.

41. Marciniak, p. 103.

42. Advisory Council on the Chicago Housing Authority, *New Strategies, New Standards for New Times in Public Housing* (June 29, 1988), p. 22. Available at Chicago History Museum.

43. Advisory Council, p. 23.

44. Robert A. Slayton, *Chicago's Public Housing Crisis: Causes and Solutions* (Chicago: Chicago Urban League, June 1988), p. 13.

45. Slayton, p. 66.

46. Patrick Reardon and Jorge Casuso, "CHA Draws Fire from Urban League," *Tribune*, July 21, 1988.

CHAPTER FIVE

1. Alexander Garvin, *The American City: What Works, What Doesn't*, 2nd ed. (New York: McGraw Hill, 2002), pp. 170–171.

2. Paul Levy, *Queen Village: The Eclipse of Community* (Philadelphia: Institute for the Study of Civil Values, 1978), p. 24.

3. Author interview with David Auspitz, April 23, 2017.

4. The biographical details of Weiler are based on the author's interviews with him on April 23, May 26, and July 6, 2017.

5. Conrad Weiler, "Neighborhood's Role in Optimizing Reinvestment: Philadelphia," in *Back to the City: Issues in Neighborhood Renovation*, ed. Shirley Bradway Laska and Daphne Spain (New York: Pergamon Press, 1980), pp. 226–227.

6. *Neighborhood Diversity: Hearings before the Committee on Banking, Housing and Urban Affairs, United States Senate, Ninety-Fifth Congress, July 7–8, 1977* (Washington, DC: GPO, 1977), p. 99.

7. Levy, p. 26.

8. Conrad Weiler, "Property Assessment: Tax Penalizes Homeowners," Letter to the Editor, *Philadelphia Inquirer*, Oct. 1, 1976, p. 8A.

9. Gregory L. Heller, *Ed Bacon: Planning, Politics and the Rebuilding of Modern Philadelphia* (Philadelphia: University of Pennsylvania Press, 2013), p. 124.

10. Dempsey J. Travis, "How Whites Are Taking Back Black Neighborhoods," *Ebony*, September 1978, p. 74.

11. Quoted in Heller, p. 133.

12. Author interview with Weiler.

13. Author interview with Weiler.

14. Weiler, 1980, p. 225.

15. Weiler, 1980, pp. 228–229.

16. Benjamin Looker, *A Nation of Neighborhoods: Imagining Cities, Communities, and Democracy in Postwar America* (Chicago: University of Chicago Press, 2015), pp. 235–236.

17. For more details on how Kotler differed from Alinsky, see "Interview Milton

Kotler," *Historic Chevy Chase DC* (website), Aug. 25, 2012, http://www.historic chevychasedc.org.

18. Looker, pp. 248–259.

19. Looker, p. 249.

20. Franklin J. James, "Private Reinvestment in Older Housing and Older Neighborhoods: Recent Trends and Forces," printed in *Neighborhood Diversity*, pp.162–163.

21. Carla Hills, speech given at 43rd Annual Conference of Mayors, Boston, July 8, 1975, cited by J. Thomas Blake, "Private Market Housing Renovation in Central Cities: An Urban Land Institute Survey," in Laska and Spain, p. 4.

22. Specifically, 73 percent of 19 surveyed cities with 500,000 people or more; 63 percent of 19 cities with populations between 250,000 and 500,000. See Blake, p. 4.

23. National Urban Coalition, *Displacement: City Neighborhoods in Transition* (Washington, DC, 1978).

24. *Community Credit Needs: Hearings Before the Committee on Banking, Housing and Urban Affairs, United States Senate, Ninety-Fifth Congress, First Session*, March 23–25, 1977 (Washington, DC: GPO, 1977), p. 90.

25. *Community Credit Needs*, p. 95.

26. *Community Credit Needs*, p. 76.

27. *Neighborhood Diversity*, p. 40.

28. *Neighborhood Diversity*, p. 151.

29. *Community Credit Needs*, p. 91.

30. "Take the Money and Run: Redlining in Brooklyn" (Albany: New York Public Interest Research Group, 1978), reprinted in *Community Credit Needs*, p. 348.

31. *Community Credit Needs*, pp. 217, 221.

32. *Community Credit Needs*, p. 140.

33. Robert Kuttner email to author, July 16, 2017.

34. Conrad Weiler, letter to Robert Kuttner, April 4, 1977. Weiler's private papers.

35. Very little research has been done on whether the CRA encouraged gentrification. Experts caution that for the first 20 years of its life, the CRA was poorly enforced, suggesting that banks had little reason to further gentrification by making loans to gentrifiers. Samuel P. Vitello and John Fitzgerald found incomes rose in CRA-eligible census tracts between 1990 and 2000, but there was no significant change in the number of residents with college degrees nor a sizeable decrease in long-term residents. See Vitello and Fitzgerald, "Impacts of the Community Reinvestment Act on Neighborhood Change and Gentrification," *Housing Policy Debate* 24, no. 2 (2014), pp. 446–466.

36. Proxmire did not take campaign contributions for his 1976 and 1982 campaigns. See Douglas Waller, "Senator William Proxmire: A Personal Appreciation," *Time*, Dec. 15, 2005, http://content.time.com/time/nation/article/0,8599 ,1141494,00.html.

37. *Neighborhood Diversity*, p. 2.

38. *Neighborhood Diversity*, pp. 49–50.

39. *Neighborhood Diversity*, pp. 15–17.

40. Author interview with Robert Embry, May 19, 2017.

41. Alexander Polikoff, *Waiting for Gautreaux* (Evanston: Northwestern University Press, 2006), pp. 261–262.

42. Conrad Weiler, *NAN Handbook on Reinvestment Displacement: HUD's Role in a New Housing Issue*, (Washington, DC: National Association of Neighborhoods, May 1978), p. 57.

43. Weiler, 1978, p. 58.

44. Weiler, 1978, p. 4.

45. Weiler, 1978, pp. 34–36, 48, 102–103.

46. Community land trusts are entities run by cities or nonprofit organizations to buy apartment buildings and rent them at affordable rates in perpetuity.

47. Weiler, 1978, p. 5.

48. Robert Embry letter to Conrad Weiler, April 8, 1978. Weiler's private papers.

49. Robert Cassidy, "Can Success Kill a Neighborhood?" *Planning*, July 1978, p. 6.

50. Cassidy, p. 7.

51. National Urban Coalition, pp. 6–7.

52. National Urban Coalition, p. 23.

53. Alice Bonner, "Urban Revitalization Is Displacing the Poor, Study Confirms," *Washington Post*, Aug. 1, 1978, p. A3.

54. "The Re-invasion," *Afro American* (Baltimore), Feb. 4, 1978.

55. Dempsey, "How Whites Are Taking Back Black Neighborhoods," pp. 73–74.

56. Dempsey, p. 82.

57. Dempsey, p. 76.

58. Sharon Kornegay, "Hold Off on Moving to the Suburbs, Blacks Advised," *Chicago Sun-Times*, Nov. 7, 1977.

59. Section 902 of the Housing and Community Development Amendments of 1978, cited in *Displacement Report: Interim*, Feb. 1979, p. i. Jimmy Carter Presidential Library, Domestic Policy Staff—Banking & Housing Resource Publication Files, Box 75.

60. *Residential Displacement in the U.S., 1970–77* (Survey Research Center, University of Michigan, 1981), p. 25.

61. Upon the author's request, Conrad Weiler analyzed the final report in 2017, and noted, among other shortcomings, that the researchers counted displacement in outlying suburban and rural areas—as well as non-gentrifying neighborhoods within city cores—as "urban displacement;" and that their definition of displacement included move-outs instigated by governmental, as well as private, actions. Weiler email to author, July 2, 2017.

62. *Residential Displacement—an Update: Report to Congress* (Department of Housing and Urban Development, October 1981), p. 26.

63. *Residential Displacement—an Update*, pp. 36, 40–41, 43, 56–57. Economist Jacob Vigdor suggests this study indicates that displacement is beneficial. "Those displaced were less cost-burdened than voluntary movers, experienced a decrease in crowding, and only a minority reported decreased satisfaction with neighborhood quality, public services, or housing characteristics." However, it should not be surprising that people forced out of an area because they were paying too much would have found an apartment that was cheaper; they moved in the first place because their apartment was too expensive. See Vigdor, "Does Gentrification Harm the Poor?" Brookings-Wharton Papers on Urban Affairs, 2002, p. 150. The HUD study drew a bleaker portrait of those who were displaced: "Older displacees and those that are poorer than average prior to displacement experience greater increases in crowding than do similar households that are not displaced. Displaced minority households are more likely to become welfare dependent than are non-displaced minorities." See *Residential Displacement—an Update*, p. 57.

64. The guests included Rolf Goetze from the Massachusetts Institute of Technology and Franklin James from the Urban Institute. Karen Kollias, "Agenda for September 28th Meeting (Memorandum)," US Department of Housing and Urban Development, Sept. 19, 1977. Conrad Weiler's private papers.

65. George and Eunice Grier, in Laska and Spain, p. 268.

66. See, for example, Jen Kinney, "New Map Tool Can Serve as Gentrification Early Warning System," Next City, Aug. 25, 2015, https://nextcity.org.

67. Karen Kollias, "Revitalization without Displacement," *HUD Challenge*, March 1978, p. 7.

68. Author interview with Feather O'Connor Houstoun, July 20, 2017.

69. Author interview with Karen Kollias, July 16, 2017.

70. Author interview with Kollias.

71. *Residential Displacement—an Update*, p. vi. It is admittedly crude to assume that a 1 percent annual rate of displacement translates into a 33 percent rate over 33 years, but it is important to recognize that gentrification is a cumulative phenomenon, and that the displacement that a researcher may measure in a single year does not adequately express the proportion of a neighborhood's population that is forced to move.

72. *Residential Displacement—an Update*, pp. iii, vi.

73. Weiler email to author, Nov. 18, 2018; Looker, p. 256.

CHAPTER SIX

1. Donna E. Shalala and Carol Bellamy, "A State Saves the City: The New York Case," *Duke Law Journal* (1976), pp. 1128–1131.

2. Joshua B. Freeman, *Working Class New York: Life and Labor since World War II* (New York: New Press, 2000), p. 8.

3. Bureau of Labor Statistics figures show a drop of 607,000 jobs in manufac-

turing, wholesale trade, and transportation from 1969 to 1989. See Matthew P. Drennan, "The Decline and Rise of the New York Economy," in *Dual City: Restructuring New York*, ed. John H. Mollenkopf and Manuel Castells (New York: Russell Sage Foundation, 1992), Table 1.5, p. 32.

4. Drennan, p. 31.

5. Shalala and Bellamy, pp. 1124–1125; Ken Auletta, *The Streets Were Paved with Gold* (New York: Random House, 1975), p. 56.

6. Drennan, p. 33. See also Mark Willis, "New York's Economic Renaissance," in *New York Unbound*, ed. Peter Salins (New York: Basil Blackwell, 1988), pp. 40–43.

7. Drennan, p. 36.

8. Deregulation of the banking industry also played a part. See Willis, p. 43.

9. Drennan, pp. 33–35.

10. William H. Whyte, *The Organization Man* (New York: Simon and Schuster, 1956), pp. 10, 267.

11. Whyte, p. 4.

12. David Ley, *The New Middle Class and the Remaking of the Central City* (New York: Oxford University Press, 1996), p. 206.

13. Ley, pp. 199–200.

14. US Census of Population and Housing, 1970 and 1980. Quoted in Paul Knox, "Capital, Material Culture, and Socio-Spatial Definition," in *The Restless Urban Landscape*, ed. Knox (Englewood Cliffs, N.J.: Prentice-Hall, 1993), p. 25.

15. Louis Menand, "Thirteen Crucial Years for Art in Downtown New York," *New Yorker*, March 28, 2017, https://www.newyorker.com/.

16. *The Arts as an Industry: Their Economic Importance to the New York–New Jersey Metropolitan Region* (New York: The Port Authority of New York and New Jersey and the Cultural Assistance Center, 1983), p. 5.

17. Neil Smith, *The New Urban Frontier: Gentrification and the Revanchist City* (London: Routledge, 1996), pp. 67–68.

18. Smith, pp. 23, 26.

19. Smith, p. 22.

20. Smith, pp. 68, 97.

21. Smith, p. 14.

22. See, for example, Tamar Rothenberg, "'And She Told Two Friends': Lesbians Creating Urban Social Space," in *Mapping Desire: Geographies of Desire*, ed. David Bell and Gill Valentine (London: Routledge, 1995), pp. 165–181.

23. Aaron Shkuda, *The Lofts of Soho: Gentrification, Art, and Industry in New York 1950–1980* (Chicago: University of Chicago Press, 2016), p. 25.

24. Shkuda, pp. 27, 37.

25. Shkuda, p. 44.

26. Shkuda, pp. 211–213.

27. Sandy Hornick and Suzanne O'Keefe, "Reusing Industrial Loft Buildings for Housing: Experiences of New York City in Revitalization and Misuse," *Journal*

of Urban and Contemporary Law 27 (January 1984), p. 168, http://openscholarship .wustl.edu.

28. Caleb Melby, "Brooklyn's Billionaire," *Forbes*, Feb. 10, 2014, p. 86. Via Nexis. Marcia Greenwood, "David Walentas: From Nowhere to Billionaire," *Rochester Magazine*, March 2013. Reprinted in DemocratandChronicle.com, Oct. 14, 2014, https://www.democratandchronicle.com. Two Trees Management Co. spokesmen declined repeated interview requests by the author for Walentas and also did not respond to written questions for this book.

29. Penelope Green, "The Duke of Dumbo Rides Tall in Horse Country," *NYT*, Aug. 15, 2004, Sect. 11, p. 1. Via Nexis.

30. Melby.

31. Green.

32. Dena Kleiman, "J. Frederic Byers, 38, Real Estate Executive, Is Killed in Plunge," *NYT*, Jan. 1, 1978; David Dunlap, "SoHo, Tribeca, and Now Dumbo?," *NYT*, Oct. 25, 1998, Sect. 11, p. 1. Via Nexis.

33. Archives of American Art, "Oral History Interview with Chuck Close, 1987 May 14–September 30," interviewed by Judd Tully, https://www.aaa.si.edu.

34. Melby.

35. Green.

36. Melby.

37. Max Abelson, "The Walentas Family," *New York Observer*, Dec. 18, 2006, http://observer.com; Gabriel Sherman, "The Flying Walentases," *New York*, June 23, 2014, http://nymag.com/.

38. Peter Hellman, "Over the River, No Longer Fringe," *NYT*, Sect. F, p. 1; Alan Finder, "Long View from the Waterfront: Developer Has Pursued a Brooklyn Dream for 20 Years," *NYT*, June 24, 1999, Sect. B, p. 1. Via Nexis.

39. Melby; Dunlap.

40. Norval White and Elliot Willensky, *AIA Guide to New York City*, 4th ed. (New York: Three Rivers Press, 2000), p. 669.

41. Elizabeth Reich Rawson, "Fulton Ferry [Fulton Landing]," in Kenneth T. Jackson, ed., *The Encyclopedia of New York City* (New Haven: Yale University Press, 1995), pp. 443–444.

42. Author interviews with Crane Davis, Feb. 19 and March 5, 2018.

43. Shkuda, p. 104.

44. Author interview with Davis.

45. Author interview with Davis.

46. Author interview with Davis.

47. Crane Davis, "How Dumbo Got Its Name," unpublished manuscript quoted in "How Dumbo Got Its Name and What It Was Almost Called," dumbonyc.com, May 21, 2007, http://dumbonyc.com/blog/2007/05/21/how-dumbo-got-its-name/.

48. Joe Brancatelli, "The Story behind the Fulton Landing Fiasco," *New York City Business*, March 26–April 6, 1984, p. 1.

49. The Department of Planning study was never released, but its findings were quoted in a letter from Joseph Ferris et al., to Herbert Sturz, July 2, 1982, and in a memorandum from Ira N. Brophy to Robert A. Kandel and Herbert Sturz, "Fulton Ferry Marketable Space," Jan. 25, 1982. Author's collection.

50. Melby.

51. "Summary of Job Losses," March 12, 1984. Author's collection.

52. Author interview with Crane Davis, Feb. 19, 2018.

53. The author made repeated attempts to interview David Walentas or have him answer written questions through his representatives at Two Trees Management Co. and its outside public relations company BerlinRosen on Jan. 17, Feb. 2, Feb. 6, Feb. 26, March 13, and March 15, 2018.

54. Mario M. Cuomo, Press Release, Dec. 18, 1984. Author's collection.

55. Many media characterizations of Walentas' holdings suggest he controlled a much larger proportion, which is true if one confines one's definition to the area between the two bridges. But the city's Office of Economic Development counted five million square feet within the broader Fulton Ferry/Two Bridges/Vinegar Hill area. See Brophy memo.

56. Jane Jacobs, *The Death and Life of Great American Cities* (New York: Vintage Books, 1989), pp. 50–53.

57. Hellman.

58. Matthew Schuerman, "Dumbo King Wants a Piece of New Brooklyn Waterfront," *New York Observer*, Oct. 17, 2005, http://observer.com; for Jane Jacobs' views on population density see Jacobs, pp. 200–204; for her distrust of parks, see pp. 89–95.

59. Ruth Cutler, who lived in a building owned by Walentas in the 1980s, was one such tenant who was bought out after a lengthy fight. Author interview with Cutler, May 25, 2018.

60. Hellman.

61. Robin Finn, "One Name He Can Remember: It Was an Elephant's," *NYT*, July 16, 2003, Sect. B, p. 2.

62. Based on New York City's Department of Finance J-51 calculator for 1998 to 2018 for the following properties: 25 Washington Street, 65 Washington Street, 66 Water Street, 1 Main Street No. 15. His other properties were converted to office space or condominiums, which also likely received tax benefits. The J-51 tax incentive accords two benefits: an exemption from the additional value to the building from alterations, and an abatement of the remaining taxes of 90 percent of the certified costs of the alteration. These exempted amounts were adjusted for the property tax rates in effect for each year and converted, according to the consumer price index in January of the tax year, to 2018 dollars. For the J-51 look-up tool, go to http://webapps.nyc.gov:8084/cics/cwba/dfhwbtta/abhq.

63. "Recycled Homes: Renovation Best Hope for Future," *Tribune*, Jan. 28, 1978, p. A2. Via ProQuest.

64. Catherine Collins, "Printers Row: Historic Street Writes New Chapter in Urban Progress," *Tribune*, Oct. 27, 1985, p. K1. Via ProQuest.

65. Ann Marie Lipinski, "Controversial 'Dinner Party' Planned for Exhibit," June 23, 1981, *Tribune*, p. A6. Via ProQuest.

66. Elizabeth Brenner, "Condo Conversion List Now Includes a Giant Icebox," *Tribune*, Sept. 30, 1979, p. B1. Via ProQuest.

67. Collins, "Historic Street Writes New Chapter in Urban Progress," pp. K1–2.

68. Felicia Eisenberg Molnar, *Lofts: New Designs for Urban Living* (Gloucester, MA: Rockport Publishers, 1999), p. i.

69. Alex Marshall, "Suburbs in Disguise," *Metropolis*, July 1996, p. 70.

70. See Andres Duany, "Three Cheers for Gentrification," *American Enterprise* 12, no. 3 (April/May 2001), p. 36.

71. In the late 1990s dot-com boom, the city somehow lost track of between $12 million and $22 million of these revenues. Chester Hartman with Sarah Carnochan, *City for Sale: The Transformation of San Francisco* (Berkeley: University of California Press, 2002), pp. 320–321.

72. Theresa Devine, *Twenty-Five Years after S7000A: How Property Tax Burdens Have Shifted in New York City* (New York: Independent Budget Office, 2006), p. 18.

73. Devine, 2006, p. 31.

74. Jillian Jorgenson, "Malliotakis Rips de Blasio for Benefitting from Property Tax System that Favors Those in Hot Neighborhoods," *New York Daily News*, Oct. 26, 2017 (online edition), http://www.nydailynews.com/. The 6 percent property appreciation limit was one complaint that a New York City property tax reform commission was examining in 2018–2019. See Christopher Robbins, "Fixing NYC's Unfair Property Tax System: How Hard Could It Be?," Oct. 16, 2018, Gothamist, http://gothamist.com.

75. James Parrott, *New York City Taxes—Trends, Impact and Priorities for Reform* (New York: Fiscal Policy Institute, 2015), p. 51, http://fiscalpolicy.org. What makes the shifting burdens of property versus income tax even more dramatic is that the property tax rate has risen during this period while the top income tax rate has fallen. Parrott, p. 53; Devine, p. 18.

76. For a comparison of property taxes and other costs, see, for example, Tara Siegel Bernard, "High Rise, or House with a Yard," *NYT*, July 2, 2010, p. B1, https://www.nytimes.com/.

77. The 1997 Tax Reform and Relief Act allowed couples to avoid capital gains taxes on the first $500,000 in profit from selling a primary residence; previously, homeowners could also avoid taxes by putting that capital gain towards the purchase of a new house within two years.

CHAPTER SEVEN

1. Calvin Welch, "The Fight to Stay: The Creation of the Community Housing Movement in San Francisco, 1968–1978," in *Ten Years that Shook the City: San Francisco 1968–1978*, ed. Chris Carlsson (San Francisco: City Lights Books, 2011), p. 160.

2. Welch, p. 161.

3. Author interview with Calvin Welch, Jan. 18, 2017.

4. San Francisco Planning Commission, "Minutes of the Special Meeting," Jan. 19, 1978, p. 12.

5. S.F. Planning Commission, p. 5.

6. S.F. Planning Commission, p. 11.

7. S.F. Planning Commission, p. 10.

8. S.F. Planning Commission, "Minutes of the Special Meeting," Feb. 14, 1978, p. 2.

9. Jerry Roberts, "Lower Density: S.F. Board OKs Zoning Changes," *San Francisco Chronicle*, Sept. 19, 1978, p. 12.

10. San Francisco City Department of Planning, *Final Environmental Impact Report*, June 27, 1978, p. 122.

11. See Karl Beitel, "Did Overzealous Activists Destroy Housing Affordability in San Francisco?" *Urban Affairs Review* 42, no. 5 (May 2007), pp. 741–756, http://citeseerx.ist.psu.edu/viewdoc/download?doi=10.1.1.912.2519&rep=rep1&type=pdf.

12. Bureau of the Census, *1970 Census of Population*, vol. 1, (Washington, DC: US GPO, 1973), Table 16: Summary of General Characteristics.

13. Author interview.

14. See San Francisco Planning Office, "Office Development Annual Limitation Program," http://sf-planning.org/office-development-annual-limitation-program.

15. Richard DeLeon, *Left Coast City* (Lawrence: University Press of Kansas, 1992), p. 56.

16. Adam Lashinsky, "Netscape IPO 20-Year Anniversary: Read *Fortune*'s 2005 History of the Birth of the Web," *Fortune*, Aug. 9, 2015, http://fortune.com/2015/08/09/remembering-netscape/.

17. "Industry Employment Data: San Francisco County, 1990–2015 (Annual Average)," State of California Employment Development Department, http://www.labormarketinfo.ca.gov/file/indhist/sanfrhaw.xls.

18. Chester Hartman with Sarah Carnochan, *City for Sale: The Transformation of San Francisco* (Berkeley: University of California Press, 2002), pp. 306–321.

19. Adam Feuerstein, "Tech Firms Line Up for a Spot in 'Multimedia Gulch,'" *San Francisco Business Times*, July 14, 1996, http://www.bizjournals.com.

20. Bay Area Economics, *San Francisco Tenant Survey: Summary Report* (San Francisco: Board of Supervisors, 2002), p. 14.

21. Alejandro Murguia, *The Medicine of Memory: A Mexican Clan in California* (Austin: University of Texas Press, 2002), p. 126.

22. Jesse Hamlin, "Money Crunch Threatens Festival 2000," *S.F. Chronicle*, Oct. 18, 1990, p. E1. Via Nexis.

23. Steve Winn and Susan Sward, "What Went Wrong with SF's Festival 2000," *S.F. Chronicle*, Oct. 26, 1990, p. A1. Via Nexis.

24. Tony Bizjak, "San Francisco's New Bohemia," *SF Chronicle*, Dec. 28, 1988, p. B4; Ryan Kim, "Different as Day, Night: Is the Colorful Mission District Big Enough to Play Host to Both the Working-Class Residents and the Upscale Revelers Who Occupy It?," *San Francisco Examiner*, Aug. 29, 2000, p. A1. Accessed via Infotrac Newsstand.

25. Rebecca Solnit, *The Hollow City: The Siege of San Francisco and the Crisis of American Urbanism* (New York: Verso, 2001), pp. 125–128. Keating authored a noteworthy critique of his activities: https://www.indybay.org/newsitems/2013/12/11/18747606.php.

26. Laurel Rosen, "Yuppies Are Always 'Them'; Responsibility for Urban Problems Lies with Us," *S.F. Chronicle*, Nov. 12, 1999, p. A25. Accessed via Nexis.

27. Dan Rottenberg, "About that Urban Renaissance . . . There Will be a Slight Delay," *Chicago Magazine*, May 1, 1980, http://www.chicagomag.com/Chicago-Magazine/May-1980/Yuppie/. Though *Tribune* columnist Bob Greene is often credited with popularizing the term, he first used it three years after Rottenberg.

28. Anatole Broyard, "A Portrait of the Hipster," *Partisan Review*, June 1948.

29. Sam Whiting, "Neo-Hipsters Keep the Beat in the Mission," *S.F. Chronicle*, Nov. 6, 1995, p. 30. Via Nexis.

30. David Brooks, *Bobos in Paradise: The New Upper Class and How They Got There* (New York: Simon and Schuster, 2000), p. 41.

31. Brooks, pp. 93, 95.

32. Brooks, p. 125.

33. Kim.

34. Kim.

35. "State of the Cities" report, US Department of Housing and Urban Development, 2000. Cited in Hartman, p. 325. The federal government defines "affordable rent" as 30 percent of a household's gross income.

36. Rent increases were set at 60 percent of the consumer price index instead of 100 percent because it was thought a large portion of a landlord's expense went to mortgage payments, which were generally fixed and would not rise with inflation. See Hartman, pp. 354–356.

37. Hartman, p. 357.

38. Hartman, p. 357.

39. Daniel Zoll, "The Economic Cleansing of San Francisco: Is San Francisco Becoming the First Fully Gentrified City in America?" *San Francisco Bay Guard-*

ian, Oct. 7, 1998. Cited in Nancy Raquel Mirabel, "Geographies of Displacement: Latina/os, Oral History, and the Politics of Gentrification in San Francisco's Mission District," *Public Historian* 3, no. 2 (Spring 2009), p. 13, https://wp.nyu.edu/displacedurbanhistories/wp-content/uploads/sites/3081/2016/01/Mirabal-Geographies-of-Displacement-2009.pdf.

40. Quoted in J. Grodin, Opinion, Nash v. City of Santa Monica (1984) 37 Cal. 3d 97, 207; http://scocal.stanford.edu/opinion/nash-v-city-santa-monica-28399.

41. Dean Preston, *The Speculator Loophole: Ellis Act Evictions in San Francisco* (Tenants Together and the Anti-Eviction Mapping Project), April 2, 2014, p. 1, http://antievictionmappingproject.net/speculatorloophole.html.

42. Rebecca Graff and Lisa Gray-Garcia, "Ellis Act Hits Home: Tenants Victims of Loopholes," *S.F. Chronicle*, Dec. 13, 1999, p. A25. Accessed via Nexis.

43. Author interview with Andrew Zacks, Dec. 13, 2016.

44. Author interview with Daniel Bornstein, Nov. 18, 2016.

CHAPTER EIGHT

1. Richard Arnott, "Time for Revisionism on Rent Control?" *Journal of Economic Perspectives* 9, no. 1 (Winter 1995), p. 99.

2. F. A. Hayek, "The Repercussions of Rent Restrictions," in *Rent Control: A Popular Paradox* (Vancouver: The Fraser Institute, 1970), p. 69.

3. Mara Verlič, "Emerging Housing Commons: Vienna's Housing Crisis Then and Now," draft submitted for Research Committee 21 Conference, "The Ideal City" (Aug. 27–29, 2015), p 5.

4. Hayek's book, *The Road to Serfdom* (1944), argued strenuously against socialism, which at the time was gaining support among war-weary Europeans. However, Hayek did allow that free-market competition could coexist with the government provision of social services. That qualification was omitted in a comic version of the book printed by *Look* magazine in the 1940s. In 2010, conservative broadcast host Glenn Beck spent an entire hour praising the book—also glossing over Hayek's equivocations—and propelled the book onto the *New York Times* bestsellers list. See Jennifer Schuessler, "Hayek: The Back Story," *New York Times Book Review*, July 9, 2010, p. 27. Hayek uses the term "Old Whig" in his essay "Why I Am Not a Conservative," in *The Constitution of Liberty* (Chicago: University of Chicago Press, 1960), p. 409.

5. Hayek, "Repercussions," p. 71.

6. See "Vienna's Unique Social Housing Program," PD&R EDGE, Jan. 13, 2014, https://www.huduser.gov/portal/pdredge/pdr_edge_featd_article_011314.html; Denise Hruby, "Why Rich People in Austria Want to Live in Housing Projects," *GlobalPost*, Oct. 26, 2015, https://www.pri.org/stories/2015-10-26/why-rich-people-austria-want-live-housing-projects.

7. Milton Friedman and George J. Stigler, "Roofs or Ceilings? The Current Housing Problem," in *Rent Control: A Popular Paradox* (Vancouver: The Fraser Institute, 1970), p. 86.

8. "Relief Work in Oakland," *S.F. Chronicle*, April 25, 1906, p. 6. Via ProQuest.

9. "Prefer Tents to the Houses," *S.F. Chronicle*, April 25, 1906, p. 2. Via ProQuest.

10. "Rapid Progress in Relief Work," *S.F. Chronicle*, April 21, 1906, p. 3. Via ProQuest.

11. "Realty Market and Building News," *S.F. Chronicle*, Aug. 4, 1906, p. 5.

12. Classified Ad, "Houses and Flats Wanted," *S.F. Chronicle*, April 27, 1906, p. 6. Via ProQuest.

13. "Mayor Outlines Plan for Housing Twenty Thousand," *S.F. Chronicle*, June 30, 1906, p. 14. "The Housing Problem," *S.F. Chronicle*, Aug. 30, 1906, p. 6. Via ProQuest. Mel Scott, *The San Francisco Bay Area: A Metropolis in Perspective*, 2nd ed. (Berkeley: University of California Press, 1985), pp. 133–134.

14. Friedman and Stigler, p. 90.

15. Friedman and Stigler, pp. 90, 93–94, 98.

16. New York City Rent Guidelines Board, *2016 Housing Supply Report*, May 26, 2016, p. 18.

17. "Rent Stabilization," Editorial, *NYT*, July 15, 1969, p. 38. Via Times Machine.

18. Arnott, p. 101.

19. For the role of political radicalism in rent control policies, see Arnott, p. 101, and David P. Sims, "Out of Control: What Can We Learn from the End of Massachusetts Rent Control?" *Journal of Urban Economics* 61 (2007), p. 130.

20. Arthur Downs, *A Reevlauation of Residential Rent Controls* (Washington, DC: Urban Land Institute, Dec. 1, 1988), p. 4.

21. Charles W. de Seve, *The Effect of Deregulation on Rents and Economic Activity in New York City* (New York: Rent Stabilization Association, August 1997), Figure II-2, p. 9.

22. Advertisement, *NYT*, Dec. 23, 1985. Reprinted in Neil Smith, *The New Urban Frontier: Gentrification and the Revanchist City* (Routledge: London, 1996), p. 31.

23. Nick Ravo, "Is It Time to End Rent Regulation?" *NYT*, March 22, 1992, Sect. 10, p. 1. Via Nexis.

24. The commission's report suggested that developers did not build new units because they were afraid rent regulations would be expanded to cover newer buildings as well; however, the writers remarked, "Several studies attempted to measure the impacts of regulation on investment in new and existing housing in New York and elsewhere . . . but this work does not give strong support to the theoretical predictions." See Citizens Budget Commission, *Reforming Residential Rent Regulations*, February 1991, p. 24, n. 12.

25. Since rent regulations are not imposed on new construction, all buyers of multi-family properties are fully aware of profit limitations when they purchase a

rent-regulated building, and the purchase price should reflect the limited income potential; New York City property taxes are calculated on the basis of a building's rent revenues, such that the less money a rent-regulated building pulls in, the less it pays.

26. The Citizens Budget Commission found in 1991 that households with annual incomes under $20,000 received less than a $55 monthly discount off of market rents for similar apartments on average, while households earning more than $50,000 received discounts of $138 or more. However, most tenants in regulated housing were of low or moderate income. See Citizens Budget Commission, p. 18. Another study, completed in 1997, estimated that higher income households in rent-stabilized apartments saved $2,175 a year off of market rates in similar neighborhoods, while lower income households received just $515 a year in savings. Charles W. de Seve, *The Effects of Deregulation on Rents and Economic Activity in New York City* (New York: American Economics Group, 1997), p. ES-5. For details on the income status of rent-regulated households and their respective rent burdens, see Arthur D. Little, *Final Report for Rent Stabilization Association of New York City, Inc.*, May 1986, pp. B19–B26, B53.

27. Joel Schwartz, "Rent Regulation."

28. Citizens Budget Commission, p. 11.

29. Ravo.

30. James Dao, "Rent Law Extension Stays Unofficial as Albany Legislators Argue," *NYT*, June 19, 1967, p. B5. Via Nexis.

31. Kevin Sack, "A Test of Wills: In Albany Rent Stabilization Battle, G.O.P. Is Standing Firm on Changes," *NYT*, June 17, 1993, section B, p. 1.

32. Dao. Luxury decontrol only applied to units whose leases ended before Dec. 31, 1993. However, the city council made the provision permanent the following year.

33. Margaret Ramirez, "Taking the Lid Off: Plan to Abolish Rent Controls Stirs Protests; Tracing City History of Rent Regulations," *Newsday (New York)*, Dec. 6, 1996, p. A3. Via Nexis.

34. Tara George et al., "Tenants Fear End of Regs: Bruno Vow Spells Disaster, They Say," *Daily News (New York)*, Dec. 7, 1996, p. 7. Via Nexis.

35. Jim Dwyer, "As Money Talks, Albany Listens," *Daily News (New York)*, Dec. 8, 1996, p. 3. Via Nexis.

36. "A Sensible Plan for Rent Control," Editorial, *NYT*, Dec. 8, 1996, Section 4, p. 14. Via Nexis.

37. The argument that rent regulations discourage investment is a common misperception, but the law permitted landlords to raise their rents up to 6 percent in order to compensate for qualified repair and renovation costs. The CBC researchers found property owners would often take advantage of that provision to increase their revenues. See Citizens Budget Commission, p. 11. Equally perplexing is the argument that rent regulations depress investment in new build-

ings, given that the rules only apply to units built before 1974. The CBC study states: "Economists generally agree that rent regulations have adverse effects on new construction, but the consensus is based more on theory than empirical investigation." See p. 24, n. 12.

38. "This Is Your City . . . This Is Your City on Rent Control," Editorial, *Newsday*, April 13, 1997, p. G1. Via Nexis.

39. Elizabeth Kolbert, "The Rent Debate: The Overview; Studies Suggest Tenants in Upscale Neighborhoods Would Be Hit the Hardest," *NYT*, April 6, 1997, Section 1, p. 38. Relatively few—only 1,350—apartments had left the rent regulation system between 1993 and 1997 due to luxury decontrol. See Randy Kennedy, "Some Gains for Landlords Emerge in the Fine Print," *NYT*, June 20, 1997, Section B, p. 7.

40. Kolbert.

41. Dennis Hevesi, "Deregulation: A Seismic Shift, Intensity Unknown," *NYT*, Jan. 19, 1997, Section 5, p. 5. Via Nexis.

42. Raymond Hernandez, "Bruno, Threatened, Attacks Rent Groups," *NYT*, April 12, 1997, Section 1, p. 24.

43. Richard Perez-Pena, "Legislature Approves Bill to Keep Rent Rules for Six Years," *NYT*, June 19, 1997, Section B, p. 1. Kimberly Schaye et al., "Landlords' New Lease on Strife: Tenants Get Unfair Advantage, They Say," *Daily News (New York)*, June 17, 1997, p. 7; Fred Kaplan, "New York Preserves Controlled Rents; Compromise Is Reached at Last Minute," *Boston Globe*, June 17, 1997, p. A3.

44. "A Molehill of Rent Reform," Editorial, *NYT*, June 17, 1997, Section A, p. 20.

45. New York City Rent Guidelines Board, "Changes to the Rent Stabilized Housing Stock in New York City in 2017," May 24, 2018, pp. 5–9.

46. Arthur D. Little, Table B-14.

47. In 1993, Steven B. Caudill predicted that deregulating rents in New York City would cause market rents to fall 22–25 percent. However, he used data from 1968, which preceded rent stabilization. Hence, his sample was likely made up of "rent-controlled units," a strict regimen that kept prices close to their 1947 levels. The median market-rate units in his sample were 46 percent higher than his rent-regulated sample. The rent stabilization system, an example of what Downs called "temperate" controls, was introduced the following year and gave landlords freedom to impose much higher annual increases; most of the rent-controlled units have now converted to stabilization, which has allowed them to climb closer to market rates. As a result, in 2017, the Housing Vacancy Survey determined that the median non-regulated rent was "just" 33 percent higher than the median rent for stabilized units—still a bargain, but not as much of a bargain as rent control was half a century earlier. As a result, Caudill's estimate of falling rents may well be high under today's conditions. Steven B. Caudill, "Estimating the Costs of Partial Coverage Rent Controls: A Stochastic Frontier Approach," *Review of Economics and Statistics* 75, no. 4 (November 1994), pp. 730–731; E. Gaumer, "Selected Initial Find-

ings of the 2017 New York City Housing and Vacancy Survey" (New York: New York City Department of Housing Preservation and Development, 2018), p. 5, https://www1.nyc.gov/assets/hpd/downloads/pdf/about/2017-hvs-initial-findings.pdf.

48. De Seve, pp. 5–6.

49. Gaumer, p. 7.

50. Matt Carroll, "Showtime for Rent Control," *Boston Globe*, Oct. 23, 1994, p. A15. Via ProQuest.

51. Matthew Brelis, "Landlords, Tenants Clash on Rent Control," *Boston Globe*, Oct. 12, 1994, p. 19. Via ProQuest.

52. Pamela Ferdinand and Howard Manly, "Both Camps Silent on Rent Control Issue," *Boston Globe*, Oct. 16, 1994, p. 1. Via ProQuest..

53. Andrew Estes, "Out on the Street: Evictions Skyrocket with Demise of Rent Control," *Boston Herald*, Aug. 8, 1997, p. 1.

54. David H. Autor, Christopher J. Palmer, and Parag A. Pathak, "Housing Market Spillovers: Evidence from the End of Rent Control in Cambridge, Massachusetts," *Journal of Political Economy* 122, no. 3 (June 2014), pp. 661–717.

55. Rachel Dovey, "Tenant Rights Advocates Score Victory in Portland," Next City, Feb. 9, 2018, https://nextcity.org/daily/entry/tenants-rights-advocates-score-victory-in-portland.

56. Jacqueline Serrato, "Chicagoans Have Spoken: They Want Rent Control, Legal Weed, and Gun Restrictions," *Tribune*, March 21, 2018, https://www.chicagotribune.com/voiceit/ct-chicagoans-have-spoken-they-want-rent-control-legal-weed-and-gun-restrictions-20180321-story.html. Fred Mogul, "N.Y.'s Rent Reform Battle Has Just Begun," Gothamist, Feb. 12, 2019, http://gothamist.com.

57. Dominoe Ibarra, "Initiative to Overturn Rent Control in Mountain View Fails to Qualify for November Ballot," July 17, 2018, https://www.sanjoseinside.com/2018/07/17/initiative-to-overturn-rent-control-ordinance-in-mountain-view-fails-to-qualify-for-november-ballot/.

58. Hayat Norimine, "State Will Uphold Its Ban on Rent Control," SeattleMet, Feb. 5, 2018, https://www.seattlemet.com/articles/2018/2/5/state-will-uphold-its-ban-on-rent-control.

CHAPTER NINE

1. Robert Blau and John Kass, "Dantrell's Death Tied to Revenge," *Tribune*, Oct. 27, 1992, pp. 1, 7. Via ProQuest.

2. Blau and Kass, p. 7.

3. Terry Wilson, "Guard Testifies Defendant Admitted Killing Dantrell," *Tribune*, Feb. 2, 1994, p. 1. Via ProQuest.

4. John O'Brien, "Accused Sniper: I Didn't Kill Dantrell," *Tribune*, Jan. 27, 1993, p. 10. Via ProQuest. Garrett was found guilty of murder in the first degree and sentenced to 100 years; he maintained his innocence throughout his trial.

5. Matthew Nickerson, "Sniper Kills Cabrini Kid Steps from School," *Tribune*, Oct. 14, 1992, p. 1. Via Nexis.

6. "Tear Down the CHA High-Rises," *Tribune*, Nov. 15, 1992, Editorial Section, p. 2.

7. Lawrence J. Vale, *Purging the Poorest: Public Housing and the Design Politics of Twice-Cleared Communities* (Chicago: University of Chicago Press, 2013), p. 254.

8. Patrick T. Reardon and Paul Sloan, "CHA Aim: Make Cabrini 'a Normal Neighborhood,'" *Tribune*, Feb. 6, 1993, p. L1.

9. Quoted in Joel Kaplan, "Lane's 'Vision' for Cabrini Made HUD Blink: Questions Are Raised about Who Benefits," *Tribune*, June 9, 1995, p. 1. Via ProQuest.

10. David Jackson and William Gaines, "HUD Probing Nation of Islam Firms, CHA Boss," *Tribune*, May 17, 1995, http://articles.chicagotribune.com/1995-05-17/news/9505170232_1_federal-contracts-security-contracts-federal-investigation.

11. Vale, p. 262. Author interview with Shuldiner.

12. Cora Moore, "Residents Need Voice in Cabrini Fate," Letter to the Editor, *Tribune*, Nov. 13, 1996, p. 20.

13. Reardon and Sloan, p. 12.

14. Author interview with Julia Stasch, March 30, 2017.

15. "We were going to take a period of six to nine months to say, what do we have, what can we negotiate for—waivers, cash commitments—so that when we take it back, we have at least a running chance to do something different with it." Author interview with Stasch.

16. Janet L. Smith, "Community Resistance to CHA Transformation," in *Where Are Poor People to Live? Transforming Public Housing Communities*, ed. Larry Bennett, Janet L. Smith, and Patricia Wright (Armonk, NY: M. E. Sharpe, 2006), p. 158.

17. Richard J. Daley was mayor for 21 years, from 1955 to 1976, the years during which CHA housing significantly deteriorated. Nonetheless, historians are at odds about how much to blame him. D. Bradford Hunt does not place direct responsibility for public housing's failures on the mayor, instead saying the senior Daley was content with a "defanged CHA." See Hunt, *Blueprint for Disaster* (Chicago: University of Chicago Press, 2009), p. 118. In 2013, Daley told an interviewer, "One side of the city was radiant; the other side was public housing." See Susan J. Popkin, *No Simple Solutions: Transforming Public Housing in Chicago* (Lanham, Md.: Rowman and Littlefield and Urban Institute Press, 2016), p. 39.

18. Author interview with Stasch.

19. Vale, p. 284.

20. Author interview with Jack Markowski, March 31, 2017.

21. For waivers, see William P. Wilen and Wendy L. Stasell, "*Gautreaux* and Chicago's Public Housing Crisis: The Conflict between Achieving Integration and Providing Decent Housing for Very Low-Income African-Americans," *Clearinghouse Review* 34, nos. 3–4 (July–August 2000), p. 122. "Moving to Work" was a

misnomer and had nothing to do with employing public housing residents. (For that, HUD had already invented the "Moving to Opportunity" program.) "Moving to Work" was a regulatory regime, according to which well-run public housing authorities were given greater latitude in how they spent federal funds.

22. Daley maintained that federal support for the initiative had "nothing to do with politics," but also admitted he had to go around then-HUD Secretary Andrew Cuomo and got support directly from the White House. Vale, p. 286.

23. *Plan for Transformation: Improving Public Housing in Chicago and the Quality of Life* (Chicago: Chicago Housing Authority, Jan. 6, 2000), p. 2, http://www.thecha .org/file.aspx?DocumentId=1111.

24. *Plan for Transformation*, pp. 2, 47.

25. Author interview with Tim Veenstra, April 7, 2017.

26. "I am sure I felt strongly that a process without a deadline, even if circumstances might require that deadline to be modified, would fail to galvanize the action needed to stay on course. Specifically with respect to the CHA, after many years of false starts and false promises, it was important to propose a time certain, knowing full well that as no one had ever undertaken such a massive project, our timing might not be right and that external factors, like the Great Recession and its long-term effects on the real estate market, could not be predicted at the outset." Julia Stasch, email to author, March 9, 2018.

27. Smith, p. 129.

28. Popkin, p. 32.

29. Alexander Polikoff, *Waiting for Gautreaux* (Evanston: Northwestern University Press, 2006), p. 271.

30. Wilen and Stasell, p. 127.

31. "Statement of *Gautreaux* Plaintiffs on CHA Draft Transformation Plan," Nov. 9, 1999.

32. Wilen and Stasell, pp. 131, 134–135, 138–139.

33. Wilen and Stasell, p. 131.

34. Author interview with LAF Director of Advocacy Richard Wheelock, March 29, 2017.

35. Cora Moore, "Residents Need Voice in Cabrini Fate," Letter to the Editor, *Tribune*, Nov. 13, 1996. Via ChicagoTribune.com, http://articles.chicagotribune .com/1996-11-13/news/9611130270_1_cha-public-housing-chicago-housing -authority.

36. The redevelopment configurations of Horner and Cabrini were established by litigation started before the Plan for Transformation began. See Hunt, pp. 274–275; Vale, pp. 265–267.

37. Popkin, p. 39.

38. Popkin, p. 57.

39. Patricia Smith, "Community Resistance to CHA Transformation," in Bennett et al., p. 152.

40. Julie Elena Brown, Adam Gross, and Alex Polikoff, "Why Does BPI Support CHA's Plan for Transformation Plans," *BPI Perspectives*, August 2000, p. 5.

41. Popkin, pp. 81, 84.

42. Popkin, p. 51.

43. Polikoff, p. 332.

44. The details regarding the Holsten Company's bid process came from the author's interview with Peter Holsten, March 27, 2017.

45. Larry Vale, "Housing Chicago: Cabrini-Green to Parkside of Old Town," *Places Journal*, Feb. 2012, p. 15, https://placesjournal.org/article/housingchicago cabrinigreentoparksideofoldtown/#.

46. Hunt writes that the US Housing Authority, the precursor to HUD, "put costs first in a self-defeating effort that produced a stripped-down aesthetic easily legible to outsiders in terms of class and, later, of race." Hunt, p. 47.

47. Author interview with Holsten.

48. Robert J. Chaskin and Mark L. Joseph, *Integrating the Inner City: The Promise and Perils of Mixed-Income Public Housing Transformation* (Chicago: University of Chicago Press, 2015), p. xi.

49. Chaskin and Joseph, p. xiii.

50. "We thought isolation was the problem, and the antidote was connection." Author interview with Stasch.

51. Chaskin and Joseph, p. xiv.

52. Zach Mortice, "When Public Housing Goes Private: Can Chicago's Architects and Developers Work with Public Housing Residents to Change a Broken System?" Curbed Chicago, Sept. 28, 2016, https://chicago.curbed.com/2016/9/28/13063710/chicago-public-housing-cha.

53. The details of Latrice Hudson's life are drawn largely from the author's interviews on Sept. 17 and 28, 2017.

54. Author interview with Stasch.

55. The Minimum Tenant Selection Plan put in place at the start of the CHA's Plan for Transformation required almost all heads of household to work at least 30 hours a week. Yet, one November 2001 study of public aid recipients in Illinois found that only 39 percent were employed, and only 30 percent were employed more than 30 hours a week. See William P. Wilen and Rajesh D. Nayak, "Relocated Public Housing Residents Have Little Hope of Returning: Work Requirements for Mixed-Income Public Housing Developments," in Bennett et al., p. 222. Also pp. 225–227, for description of CHA and Horner-specific selection criteria.

56. William P. Wilen and Wendy L. Stasell, "*Gautreaux* and Chicago's Public Housing Crisis: The Conflict Between Achieving Integration and Providing Decent Housing for Very Low-Income African Americans," in Bennett et al., p. 240.

57. Alexander Polikoff, "Comment," *Clearinghouse Review* 34, nos. 3–4 (July–August 2000), p. 146.

58. Wilen and Nayak, p. 226.

59. Westhaven Park Apartments vs. Latrice Hudson, "Plaintiffs Motion to Reinstate," Feb. 2, 2012. Circuit Court of Cook County, Illinois, Municipal Park, First District. Index No. 09 M1 350659.

60. Author interview with Samira Nazem, Dec. 27, 2017.

61. Sun-Times Media Wire, "Man Killed in West Side Shooting," Homicide Watch Chicago, Oct. 11, 2013, http://chicago.homicidewatch.org/2013/10/11/man-killed-in-west-side-shooting-3/index.html.

62. 2018 completion numbers from *CHA Quarterly Report, 2nd Quarter 2018*, pp. 2, 5, https://www.thecha.org/sites/default/files/CHA%20Q2%202018%20Quarterly%20Report.pdf. For original target of more than 10,000 units in mixed-income locations, see *Plan for Transformation*, p. 17.

63. *CHA Quarterly Report*, pp. 9, 16.

64. Popkin, p. 84.

65. Chaskin and Joseph, p. 223.

66. Popkin, p. 90.

67. Popkin, pp. 100, 102.

68. Popkin, p. 106.

69. Popkin, p. 99.

CHAPTER TEN

1. The shorthand for the Mission Housing Development Corporation was formerly "MHDC," but since a recent rebranding effort, the organization prefers "Mission Housing." I use the latter throughout.

2. Aime Fishman, "Community Development Corporations' Strategies against Gentrification and Displacement: Leading Community Movements in Park Slope, Brooklyn, and the Mission District, San Francisco" (master's thesis, New York University, 2006), p. 60.

3. Ryan Kim, "Echoes in the Mission: Dot-Com Invasion, Gentrification Spurs a Raucous Community Activism Not Witnessed for Decades," *San Francisco Examiner*, July 10, 2000, p. A1. Via Infotrac Newsstand.

4. Ryan Kim, "15 Arrested in Mission Sit-In: Protestors Demand the Dot-Com Find Space for Nonprofits Forced from Building," *San Francisco Examiner*, Sept. 22, 2000, p. A26. Via Infotrac Newsstand.

5. Quoted in Fishman, p. 40.

6. Author interview with Larry Del Carlo, April 6, 2017.

7. Larry Del Carlo to Comptroller Ed Harrington, Nov. 30, 2005. Included in "Mission Housing Development Corporation," Audit No. 04043 (San Francisco: Office of the Controller, 2005), Appendix, pp. X–2.

8. A columnist for the contrarian *SF Weekly* argued that city supervisors were trying to punish Del Carlo for getting rid of politically beneficial employees. Matt Smith, "Doublespeak with Forked Tongue," *SF Weekly*, May 3, 2006,

http://archives.sfweekly.com/sanfrancisco/doublespeak-with-forked-tongue
/Content?oid=2159799.

9. Author interview with Sam Moss, executive director of Mission Housing
Development Corporation, Jan. 27, 2014.

10. Author interview with Moss.

11. The Apollo Hotel, a renovated residential hotel, opened in 1999. Bayview
Commons, Rich Sorro Commons, and Croker Amazon Senior Apartments are
all located outside the neighborhood. Valencia Gardens opened in 2006, but it
was a rehab of existing affordable housing. See http://missionhousing.org/mhdc
_project_type/mission-housing-portfolio/.

12. Author interview with Moss.

13. Randy Shaw, *The Tenderloin: Sex, Crime and Resistance in the Heart of San
Francisco* (San Francisco: Urban Reality Press, 2015), p. 228.

14. "San Francisco Affordable Housing: A Historical Analysis Mapping Project"
(San Francisco: Asian Neighborhood Design Community Planning Program, January 2008).

15. Shaw, p. 14

16. San Francisco Board of Supervisors Budget and Legislative Analyst's Office, *Performance Audit of San Francisco's Affordable Housing Policies and Programs*
(San Francisco: Board of Supervisors, Jan. 18, 2012), pp. iii, vii, x, http://sfbos.org
/sites/default/files/FileCenter/Documents/40671–011812_FINAL_SF_Affordable
_HousingPol%26Prog_NEW.pdf.

17. For background on what was known as the 421-a certificate program, see
C. J. Hughes, "Developer of Affordable Housing Faces New Challenge," *NYT*,
May 21, 2008, p. C6, https://www.nytimes.com/2008/05/21/realestate/commercial
/21atlantic.html.

18. The redevelopment agency had the advantage of having complete control
over property tax revenues (which were technically payments in lieu of taxes),
meaning that none of those revenues would go the city's general fund to support
public schools, fire protection, etc. Tax revenues from other San Francisco residents and businesses would pay for those services consumed by redevelopment
agency residents. So while this arrangement benefited affordable housing production, it put a burden on the city's other properties.

19. Marcia Rosen and Wendy Sullivan, "From Urban Renewal and Displacement to Economic Inclusion: San Francisco Affordable Housing Policy 1978–
2012" (Washington, DC: Poverty and Race Research Action Council and National
Housing Law Project), p. 9, http://www.prrac.org/pdf/SanFranAffHsing.pdf.

20. Margaret Pugh O'Mara, *Cities of Knowledge: Cold War Science and the Search
for the Next Silicon Valley* (Princeton: Princeton University Press, 2005), p. 68.

21. O'Mara, pp. 119, 126.

22. O'Mara, p. 126.

23. Goodwin Steinberg with Susan Wolfe, *From the Ground Up: Building Silicon
Valley* (Stanford: Stanford University Press, 2002), p. 75.

24. Vu-Bang Nguyen and Evelyn Stivers, "Moving Silicon Valley Forward: Housing, Transit & Traffic at a Crossroads" (Non-Profit Housing Association of Northern California and Urban Habitat, 2012), http://nonprofithousing.org /moving-silicon-valley-forward/. Some towns began to reverse these trends. Santa Clara County produced more low-income units between 1999 and 2010 than San Francisco did.

25. Quoted in Walter Isaacson, *Steve Jobs* (New York: Simon and Schuster, 2011), p. 58. See pp. 42–69 for Apple's early history and the influence of *The Whole Earth Catalog*.

26. Richard Florida, *The Rise of the Creative Class and How It's Transforming Work, Leisure, Community, and Everyday Life* (New York: Basic Books, 2002), p. 12.

27. Millennials, born between 1982 and 2000, were more populous than any previous generation—and more educated. In 2015, nearly two million Americans graduated from post-secondary institutions, twice as many as twenty years earlier. They were more likely to shun cars, less likely to value home ownership, and more interested in a casual work environment than previous generations.

28. Owen Thomas, "Google's First Shuttle Bus Made Just Two Stops," *Business Insider*, Oct. 12, 2012, http://www.businessinsider.com/google-employee-shuttle -route-2012–10.

29. City and County of San Francisco Board of Supervisors, Office of Budget and Legislative Analyst, "Policy Analysis Report RE: Impact of Private Shuttles," March 31, 2014, p. 1, http://sfbos.org/sites/default/files/FileCenter/Documents /48498-BLA.RegionalShuttles.033114.pdf.

30. "Commuter Shuttle Program Mid-Term Status Report, April-September 2016" (San Francisco Municipal Transportation Agency), p. 15.

31. Chris O'Brien and Jessica Guynn, "How the Other Half Commutes in Silicon Valley," *Los Angeles Times*, March 30, 2014, http://articles.latimes.com/2014 /mar/30/business/la-fi-google-bus-20140330.

32. Jeff McMahon, "Google CFO: Bus Your Employees to Work," *Forbes*, July 20, 2011, https://www.yahoo.com/news/google-cfo-bus-employees-180637127.html.

33. Sydney Cespedes et al., "Community Organizing and Resistance in SF's Mission" (Berkeley: Center for Community Innovation, 2015), p. 10, http://iurd .berkeley.edu/uploads/Mission_District_Final.pdf.

34. Author interview with René Yañez, Nov. 11, 2016.

35. Information about tenants is from author interview with attorney Raquel Fox of the Tenderloin Housing Clinic, Dec. 13, 2016. Sale price of home is from Office of the Assessor, San Francisco.

36. Author interview with Zacks, Dec. 13, 2016.

37. Lauren Smiley, "The Downtrodden Landlord," *New Yorker*, March 12, 2014.

38. Rebecca Solnit, "Diary," *London Review of Books*, Feb. 7, 2013, http://www .lrb.co.uk/v35/n03/rebecca-solnit/diary.

39. Leslie Dreyer, "Google Bus Blockades for a Right to the City," Heart of the City website, http://www.heart-of-the-city.org/history.html.

40. Alexandra Goldman, "The 'Google Shuttle Effect': Gentrification and San Francisco's Dot-Com Boom 2.0," unpublished professional report submitted in partial satisfaction of the requirements for the degree of Master of City Planning, University of California, Berkeley, p. 30.

41. Author interview with Leslie Dreyer, Nov. 30, 2016.

42. Tim Redmond, "You Want Scary? We've Got an Eviction Map," *San Francisco Bay Guardian* (online), April 30, 2013, http://48hills.org/sfbgarchive/2013/04/30 /you-want-scary-weve-got-eviction-map/?_sf_s=Evictions&_sft_writer=tim -redmond&post_date=04152013+05012013.

43. Sarah McBride, "Google Bus Blocked in San Francisco Protest vs Gentrifi- cation," Reuters, Dec. 9, 2013, http://www.reuters.com/article/us-google-protest -idUSBRE9B818J20131209.

44. Jessica Guynn and Chris O'Brien, "Tech Industry in San Francisco Ad- dresses Backlash," *Los Angeles Times*, Jan. 24, 2014, http://articles.latimes.com /2014/jan/24/business/la-fi-tech-image-reboot-20140124.

45. The 2011 survey by the San Francisco County Transportation Authority found that 14 percent of shuttle commuters would leave their jobs if the shuttles were not available (San Francisco County Transportation Authority, "Strategic Analysis Report: The Role of Shuttles in San Francisco's Transportation System," approved by the Authority Board June 28, 2011, p. 7, http://www.sfcta.org/sites /default/files/content/Programming/TWG/2011June/9-shuttle%20powerpoint .pdf, p. 8). A survey by the San Francisco Board of Supervisors three years later asked if passengers would move closer to work, not whether they would move out of San Francisco; 40 percent said they would (SF Board of Supervisors, p. 23). Even if 40 percent of shuttle riders chose to live in the city only because they had a free, convenient ride to work, it's difficult to believe they are causing the af- fordable housing crisis: 40 percent translates into about 2,000 people, or about a quarter of one percent of the city's population.

46. Solnit.

47. SFCTA, p. 7.

48. Lance Freeman and Frank Braconi, "Gentrification and Displacement: New York City in the 1990s," *Journal of the American Planning Association* (January 2004), pp. 39–52.

49. Anti-Eviction Mapping Project, "Mapping Relocation," 2015, https://anti- evictionmapd.maps.arcgis.com/apps/MapJournal/index.html?appid=e9d1638e c7724e899325e88ad62d4089. Also see Eviction Defense Collaborative, "Eviction Report 2015" (San Francisco, 2015), p. 5, http://antievictionmappingproject.net /EDC_2015.pdf.

50. The Mapping Relocation study began with researchers reaching out to 703 randomly selected clients, of which 500 were successfully located. The 500 clients represent about a tenth of the Eviction Defense Collaborative's annual caseload, which is about 5,000. The collaborative is the principal legal defense organization

for tenants, but not the only one, suggesting that the 1,650 number could be significantly higher. See the About Us section on the Collaborative's website: http://evictiondefense.org/about/.

51. Miriam Zuk and Karen Chappelle, "Housing Production, Filtering, and Displacement: Untangling the Relationships," *IGS Research Brief*, March 2016, pp. 7–10. https://urbandisplacement.org.

52. Mac Taylor, "California's High Housing Costs: Causes and Consequences," Legislative Analyst's Office, March 17, 2015, p. 24, http://www.lao.ca.gov/reports /2015/finance/housing-costs/housing-costs.pdf.

53. Conor Dougherty, "In Cramped and Costly Bay Area, Cries to 'Build, Baby, Build,'" *NYT*, April 16, 2016, https://www.nytimes.com/2016/04/17/business /economy/san-francisco-housing-tech-boom-sf-barf.html.

54. "In general, the impact of a higher inclusionary requirement on housing production depends on the extent to which developers can pass on the added costs of the policy to land owners, in the form of lower offers for the land on which housing developments can be constructed." *Inclusionary Housing Working Group: Final Report* (County and City of San Francisco: Office of the Comptroller, 2016), p. 3. For land costs, see p. 7, http://sfcontroller.org/sites/default/files/Documents /Economic%20Analysis/Final%20Inclusionary%20Housing%20Report%20Feb ruary%202017.pdf.

55. Allan B. Jacobs, *Making City Planning Work* (Chicago: American Society of Planning Officials, 1978), p. 262.

56. Author interview with Jim Wunderman, Feb. 9, 2017.

57. *Final Environmental Impact Report for the Proposed Amendments to the Text of the City Planning Code and to the Zoning Map Relating to the Residential Districts and Development* (San Francisco: Department of City Planning, June 27, 1978), p. 7.

58. San Francisco Planning Department, "San Francisco Neighborhoods: Socio-Economic Profiles," May 2011, p. 7.

59. Mary Brown, *Landscapes of Mobility* (master's thesis, San Francisco State University, 2007), pp. 133, 137, https://marybrown.files.wordpress.com/2008/01 /findingspart3.pdf. Another study of middle-class Los Angeles homes found only 25 percent of garages are used to store cars.

60. Luke H. Kipp, "The Real Costs of San Francisco's Off-Street Residential Parking Requirements," unpublished study submitted in partial fulfillment of course requirements for a Master's of Public Policy Degree at the Goldman School of Public Policy, University of California, Berkeley, May 2004. Conducted for Transportation for a Livable City, https://livablecity.org/wpcontent/upload s/2013/08/Parking_Housing_Affordability_Final.pdf. San Francisco Planning Department, "What Is the Problem with Parking," SF.gov website, http://sf -planning.org/what-problem-parking.

61. Livable City, "A Brief History of Parking in San Francisco," June 15, 2015, https://www.livablecity.org/parking-history-sf/.

62. "Mission Area Plan Monitoring Report 2011–2015" (San Francisco Department of Planning, September 2016), p. 28. The median household income in the Mission District was nearly 30 percent below the median for the city in 1980 but was on par in 2009–2013 American Community Survey. Cespedes et al., p. 3.

63. Author interview with Fred Sherburn-Zimmer, executive director of the Housing Rights Committee, Nov. 15, 2016.

64. Author interview with Dairo Romero, Nov. 10, 2016.

65. Anna Duckworth, "Protestors Storm SF Hayes Valley Shoe Store; Claim Property Owner Is Ellis Act Evicting Several Tenants," CBSLocal.com, Oct. 14, 2014, http://sanfrancisco.cbslocal.com/2014/10/17/protesters-storm-hayes-valley -shoe-store-claim-property-owner-is-ellis-act-evicting-several-tenants-san -francisco/.

66. Mission Economic Development Agency and San Francisco Community Land Trust, "MEDA and SFCLT Save Five At-Risk Properties Using City's Small Sites Program," Press Release, Feb. 10, 2016, https://medasf.org/15568/.

67. Laura Wenus, "SF Nonprofits Seal Deal to Keep Tenants in Place," Mission Local, Feb. 10, 2016, https://missionlocal.org/2016/02/nonprofits-secure-five-sf -buildings-keep-tenants-in-place/comment-page-1/.

68. Cespedes, p. 6.

69. Budget and Legislative Analyst, "Memo to Supervisor David Campos: Displacement in the Mission District" (City and County of San Francisco Board of Supervisors, Oct. 27, 2015), pp. 3, 9.

70. Rio Yañez, Facebook Post, May 29, 2018, at 12:44.

CHAPTER ELEVEN

1. New York City Rent Guidelines Board, www.nyc.gov.

2. These and other biographical details come from the author's interview with Catalina Hidalgo, February 2015, unless otherwise specified.

3. The apartment's housing and building violation records substantiates Hidalgo's complaints regarding mice, defective, or broken waste line connection and a broken concrete floor. See Housing Preservation and Development building information violation numbers 10033227, 10025292, 10025293, and 10025294 contained in Hidalgo et al., Petition, Civil Court of the City of New York, County of Kings, Part B, Index No. 060563, March 7, 2014. A buildings inspector cited the building for failing to safeguard inhabitants and property and noted that "full gut renovation at 2nd floor . . . has affected Apt 3L of which floor located at bathroom." See Environmental Control Board violation 35065566Y.

4. Joel and Amron Israel declined through their lawyer, Kevin Keating, to be interviewed for this book, April 26, 2018.

5. Brad Gooch, "The New Bohemia," New York, June 22, 1992, p. 29.

6. J. Henry Williams, Letter to the Editor, New York, July 13, 1992, p. 8.

7. Philip De Paolo and Sylvia Morse, "Williamsburg: Zoning Out Latinos," in Tom Angotti and Sylvia Morse, *Zoned Out: Race, Displacement, and City Planning in New York City* (New York: Urban Research, 2016), p. 75.

8. DePaolo and Morse, p. 77.

9. See Daniel L. Doctoroff, *Greater than Ever: New York's Big Comeback* (New York: Public Affairs, 2017), pp. 69–70.

10. *The Newest New Yorkers* (New York City: Department of City Planning, 2013), p. 10, https://www1.nyc.gov/assets/planning/download/pdf/data-maps /nyc-population/nny2013/chapter2.pdf.

11. Doctoroff, pp. 79–81.

12. Doctoroff, p. 79.

13. Association for Neighborhood and Housing Development (ANHD), *Real Affordability: An Evaluation of the Bloomberg Housing Plan, and Recommendations to Strengthen Affordable Housing Policy*, p. 5.

14. ANHD, p. 24.

15. ANHD, p. 56.

16. Quoted in Jonathan Mahler, "The Bloomberg Vista," *New York Times Magazine*, pp. 66+. Via Nexis.

17. Jennifer Steinhauer, "Bloomberg Says Rent Board Can Make Its Own Decisions," *NYT*, April 25, 2002, https://www.nytimes.com/2002/04/25/nyregion /bloomberg-says-rent-board-can-make-its-own-decisions.html. Eliot Brown, "Marvin Marcus Resigns as Rent Guidelines Board Chairman," *New York Observer*, Jan. 13, 2010, http://observer.com/2010/01/marvin-markus-resigns-as -rent-guidelines-board-chair/.

18. Manny Fernandez, "Mayor Vetoes Bill Protecting Section 8 Tenants from Landlord Bias," *NYT*, March 8, 2008, p. B4.

19. Doctoroff, pp. 82–87

20. Doctoroff, p. 190.

21. *How New York Won the Olympics* (New York: Rudin Center for Transportation Policy and Management, Robert F. Wagner Graduate School of Public Service, New York University, November 2011), p. 41.

22. See "Planning Framework" and "Waterfront Development: Proposed Zoning" in the online presentation of the 2005 Greenpoint-Williamsburg plan at the Department of City Planning's website, http://www1.nyc.gov/assets/planning /download/pdf/plans/greenpoint-williamsburg/greenpointwill.pdf.

23. Unit count is from Department of City Planning, *Greenpoint Williamsburg Waterfront Plan, Final Environmental Impact Statement*, pp. 1–28. For summary of opposition, see De Paolo, pp. 78, 80.

24. Matthew Schuerman, "Upzoning in Williamsburg," WNYC.org, July 15, 2009, https://www.wnyc.org/story/73928-upzoning-in-williamsburg/.

25. Antonio Reynoso, "Lessons from Williamsburg and Bushwick: Mandatory Inclusionary Zoning and Affordable Housing Development," January 2016,

p. 2, http://mtprauhwprtlcouncil.nyc.gov/d34/documents/Reynoso%20-%20 Lessons%20from%20Williamsburg%20and%20Bushwick.pdf; De Paolo and Morse, p. 87.

26. *State of the City Report 2015: Focus on Gentrification* (New York: Furman Center, 2016), p. 17.

27. Daniel L. Doctoroff, letter to city council speaker Gifford Miller, "Re: Greenpoint/Williamsburg—City Council ULURP Actions," May 1, 2005. Author's collection.

28. Meredith Hoffman, "City Built Less than 2 Percent of Affordable Units Promised for Williamsburg," DNAInfo.org, May 20, 2013, https://www.dnainfo .com/new-york/20130520/williamsburg/city-built-less-than-2-percent-of -affordable-units-promised-williamsburg/.

29. For anti-harassment legislation, see City Planning Commission, "Greenpoint-Williamsburg Follow-up Zoning Text and Map Changes Summary," http://www1.nyc.gov/assets/planning/download/pdf/plans/greenpoint -williamsburg/gw_fuca_sum.pdf. For tenant action fund, see Ida Susser and Filip A. Saprowski, "Unaffordable Housing: A Case Study," *Issue Brief* (New York: Roosevelt House, Hunter College, City University of New York, 2015), p. 2, http:// www.roosevelthouse.hunter.cuny.edu/devdev/wp-content/uploads/2015/02 /Susser_Stabrowski_2-10-151.pdf.

30. See Jamie Hook, "You Bet Your BIP," GoGreenBK.org, March 1, 2018, http:// gogreenbk.org/2018/03/you-bet-your-bip/.

31. Kalima Rose, Brad Lander, and Karoleen Feng, *Increasing Housing Opportunity in New York City: The Case for Inclusionary Housing* (New York: Pratt Center for Community and Economic Development and PolicyLink, 2004), p. 18, http:// prattcenter.net/sites/default/files/inclusionary_zoning_full_report.pdf.

32. *Final Environmental Impact Statement*, pp. 3–10, 3–11.

33. *State of the City*, p. 20.

34. Lance Freeman, "Displacement or Succession? Residential Mobility in Gentrifying Neighborhoods," *Urban Affairs Review* 40, no. 4 (March 2005), pp. 479–480. Also, Freeman's definition of "gentrifying" is based on educational attainment rather than income, such that census tracts he considered gentrifying experienced an overall decrease in median income between 1990 and 2000 (p. 473).

35. Freeman, p. 480.

36. Suggesting that the same pace of gentrification continues over thirty years requires some explanation and caveats. The thirty-year time frame is what I casually suggest, based on personal observation more than statistical analysis, as the period over which a neighborhood would move from its early pioneering stage—a few middle-income interlopers among a preponderance of low-income residents—to the point where it is "stabilized"—i.e., the low-income residents who remain are rent-regulated and do not intend to move because of personal cir-

cumstances. As I show, Park Slope, Brooklyn, gentrified between the mid-1960s until the 1990s; the Mission District between the late 1980s until 2015 or 2016. Also, it is admittedly speculation to suggest that a neighborhood gentrifies at an even pace; however, Freeman's 0.5 percent annual rate was calculated by taking displacement rates over two ten-year periods (1980–1990 and 1990–2000) and dividing them by ten.

37. "Perhaps when a more direct measure of the causal mechanism behind displacement is implemented, the smoking gun will surface." Freeman, 2005, p. 481. Freeman found that low-income residents in gentrifying areas are more likely to experience displacement than their peers in non-gentrifying areas; but an article he earlier coauthored that focused only on New York City found the opposite: low-income families somehow hung onto their apartments despite the gentrification around them. One reason for the discrepancy may be that the national study focused on census tracts, which are geographically smaller than the "sub-borough areas" used in the New York City study, and therefore more likely to correspond to the small areas where gentrification pressures are most intense. Another reason may be that Freeman and coauthor Frank Braconi defined gentrifying areas based on "our familiarity with recent trends in neighborhood change" rather than statistical measures. In addition, even though the study controlled for public housing and rent-regulated apartments, only one in fifteen low-income individuals were subject to the market-rate fluctuations associated with gentrification, suggesting that the low rate of displacement may be tied to the low numbers of people who would be subject to displacement. See Freeman and Braconi, "Gentrification and Displacement: New York City in the 1990s," *Journal of the American Planning Association* 70, no. 1 (Winter 2004), pp. 39–52; Kathe Newman and Elvin K. Wyly, "The Right to Stay Put, Revisited: Gentrification and Resistance to Displacement in New York City," *Urban Studies* 43, no. 1 (January 2006), pp. 41–43. A study of Boston-area neighborhoods in the 1980s also found relatively similar levels of displacement among gentrifying and non-gentrifying neighborhoods, though that was just before the end of rent control in Massachusetts, and the areas examined may have been too large, at about 100,000 residents each, to detect displacement. See Jacob Vigdor, "Does Gentrification Harm the Poor?," Brookings-Wharton Papers on Urban Affairs, 2002, pp. 133–182.

It is also worth mentioning a prominent Federal Reserve Bank of Philadelphia study, for it similarly concludes that "vulnerable residents" are no more likely to move in gentrifying neighborhoods than in other places. The study relies on credit scores and mortgages rather than Census data; while that approach has certain advantages, there are also considerable disadvantages to it. For example, the study relies on data that do not distinguish renters from homeowners, or low-income households from high-income ones; therefore, instead of studying whether renters are more likely to move than homeowners, the study only measures whether individuals with low credit scores and without mortgages—the definition of "vulnerable residents"—are more likely to move in gentrifying environments. The answer is no; but, according to the study, 40 percent of Philadelphia homeowners have no mortgages, and many low-income residents have no or good credit scores, meaning that "vulnerable residents" fails to capture "low-income renters." These two weaknesses make it hard to draw significant conclusions from this paper. See Lei Ding et al., "Gentrification and Residential Mobility in Philadelphia," September 2016, https://www.philadelphiafed.org/-/media/community-development/publications/discussion-papers/discussion-paper_gentrification-and-residential-mobility.pdf?la=en.

38. Furman Center, *How Have Recent Rezonings Affected the City's Ability to Grow* (2009), pp. 9, 11.

39. Doctoroff, pp. 37–39.

40. Doctoroff, p. 76. Amanda Burden declined to be interviewed for this book. Email to author, March 21, 2018.

41. Furman Center, *Recent Rezonings*, p. 8.

42. Author interview with Adam Meyers, Feb. 10, 2015.

43. Author interview with Gustavo and Novita Navarro, Oct. 6, 2016.

44. Marina Cory Mundy, "Decision/Order," Index No. 60563/14, Civil Court of the City of New York, Kings County, Part B, Jan. 26, 2014, pp. 5–6.

CONCLUSION

1. Jeremy Tanner and Joe Mauceri, "Did Two Brooklyn Landlords Ruin Their Own Building Just to Evict Tenants?" Pix11.com, Jan. 14, 2014, http://pix11.com/2014/01/15/did-a-brooklyn-landlord-ruin-his-own-building-just-to-evict-tenants/; Lauren Evans, "Gentrification Sparks Surge in Landlord Sabotage," Gothamist.com, Feb. 24, 2014, http://gothamist.com/2014/02/24/landlords_rent_control.php; Mireya Navarro, "Tenants Living amid Rubble in Rent-Regulated Apartment War," *NYT*, Feb. 25, 2014, p. A20, https://www.nytimes.com/2014/02/25/nyregion/in-new-york-push-for-market-rate-housing-pits-landlords-against-tenants.html?hpw&rref=nyregion; "Housing Court Orders Brooklyn Landlord to Make Repairs to Building," newyork.cbslocal.com, Feb. 3, 2015, http://newyork.cbslocal.com/2015/02/03/housing-court-orders-brooklyn-landlord-to-make-repairs-to-greenpoint-building/; Danielle Fufaro, "Slum Dunk: Court Takes G-point Building over Sabotage Claim," *Brooklyn Paper*, Feb. 14, 2015, https://www.brooklynpaper.com/stories/38/6/dtg-300-nassau-avenue-israels-out-2015-02-06-bk_38_6.html.

2. People of the State of New York Against Joel Israel, Amron Israel, et al., Indictment No. 1753/2014, Supreme Court of the State of New York, County of Kings, Criminal Term 19, April 7, 2015.

3. People of the State of New York Against Joel Israel, Amron Israel, et al., Plea

Agreement, No. 1753/2014, Supreme Court of the State of New York, County of Kings, Criminal Term 19, Nov. 29, 2016.

4. "A.G. Schneiderman Announces Unprecedented Consent Decree with NYC Landlord Steven Croman," Press Release, Dec. 20, 2017, https://ag.ny.gov /press-release/ag-schneiderman-announces-unprecedented-consent-decree-nyc -landlord-steven-croman.

5. Office of the New York Governor, "Gov. Cuomo, A. G. Schneiderman, Mayor De Blasio Join Forces to Combat Landlord Harassment of Tenants," Press Release, Feb. 19, 2015.

6. "New Real Estate Tax Compliance Program Announced by A. G. Schneiderman, Governor Cuomo and HPD Commissioner Been Aims to Restore Thousands of NYC Apartments to Rent Regulation," Press Release, Aug. 26, 2017, http:// www1.nyc.gov/site/hpd/about/press-releases/2015/08/08–26–15.page.

7. Erica Orden, "Kushner Cos. Subpoenaed for Information Related to Housing Filings," *Wall Street Journal*, April 19, 2018, https://www.wsj.com/articles /kushner-cos-subpoenaed-over-tenant-records-1524173492; Bernard Condon, "Kushner Cos. Filed False NYC Housing Paperwork," Associated Press, March 18, 2018, https://apnews.com/002703e70347481cb993027d04f543cc.

8. "Industry Employment Data: San Francisco County, 1990–2015 (Annual Average)," State of California Employment Development Department, http:// www.labormarketinfo.ca.gov/file/indhist/sanfrhaw.xls; Ted Egan, "The Economics of San Francisco Housing" (City and County of San Francisco Office of the Comptroller, Oct. 31, 2014), p. 11.

9. City and County of San Francisco Civil Grand Jury, *The Mayor's Office of Housing: Under Pressure and Challenged to Preserve Diversity*, June 2014, p. 15.

10. "Where London Breed Stands on San Francisco's Biggest Issues," *San Francisco Chronicle*, June 13, 2018, https://www.sfgate.com/bayarea/article/London -Breed-on-San-Francisco-s-biggest-issues-12992738.php.

11. Chicago Housing Authority, *Creating Opportunity: A Progress Report* (2016), pp. 13, 16.

12. San Francisco Department of City Planning and San Francisco Redevelopment Agency, *Rapid Transit Corridor Study* (1965), p. 1. Cited in Ocean Howell, *Making the Mission: Planning and Ethnicity in San Francisco* (Chicago: University of Chicago Press, 2015), p. 253.

13. "Neighborhood Diversity: Hearings Before the Senate Committee on Banking, Housing, and Urban Affairs," US Senate, 95th Congress, 1st Session, July 7 and 8, 1977, p. 49.

14. Conrad Weiler, *NAN Handbook on Reinvestment Displacement* (Washington, DC: National Association of Neighborhoods, May 1978), p. 66.

15. Cora Moore, "Residents Need Voice in Cabrini Fate," Letter to the Editor, *Tribune*, Nov. 13, 1996, p. 20.

16. Peter D. Salins, "The Limits of Gentrification," *New York Affairs* 5, no. 4 (1979), p. 6.

17. Steven Wishnia, "Chinatown Residents Forced into Shelter Fear Landlord Won't Let Them Return," *Village Voice*, Jan. 24, 2018, https://www.villagevoice .com/2018/01/24/chinatown-tenants-forced-into-shelter-fear-landlord-wont -let-them-return/; Steven Wishnia, "Chinatown Tenants: Landlord's Mass Eviction Attempts Based on Lies," *Village Voice*, July 25, 2017, https://www.villagevoice .com/2017/07/25/chinatown-tenants-landlords-mass-eviction-attempt-based -on-lies/. Zoe Azulay, "Landlord to Pay Tenants $25,000 Each After Harassment Allegation," WNYC.org, July 12, 2018, https://www.wnyc.org/story/83-85-bowery -tenants-get-go-home/.

18. "Per Capita Carbon Emissions from Transportation and Residential Energy Use, 2005," in Marilyn A. Brown, Andrea Sarzynski, and Frank Southworth, *Shrinking the Carbon Footprint of Metropolitan America* (Washington, DC: Brookings Institution, 2008), https://www.brookings.edu/research/shrinking-the-carbon -footprint-of-metropolitan-america/.

19. Paragon Real Estate Group, "San Francisco Market Report," June 2018, https://www.paragon-re.com/trend/san-francisco-home-prices-market-trends news.

INDEX